NUCLEAR POWER IN ASIA
POST FUKUSHIMA

NUCLEAR POWER IN ASIA
POST FUKUSHIMA

ZOYA AKHTER FATHIMA

Introduction by

Air Marshal **Anil Chopra** PVSM AVSM VM VSM (Retd)

Centre for Air Power Studies
New Delhi

in association with

KNOWLEDGE WORLD
KW Publishers Pvt Ltd
New Delhi

The Centre for Air Power Studies is an independent, non-profit, academic research institution established in 2002 under a registered Trust to undertake and promote policy-related research, study and discussion on the trends and developments in defence and military issues, especially air power and the aerospace arena, for civil and military purposes. Its publications seek to expand and deepen the understanding of defence, military power, air power and aerospace issues without necessarily reflecting the views of any institution or individuals except those of the authors.

Centre for Air Power Studies
P-284, Arjan Path
Subroto Park
New Delhi 110010

Tele: (91-11) 25699131

E-mail: capsnetdroff@gmail.com
website: www.capsindia.org

ISBN 978-93-94915-35-0 Hardback
ISBN 978-93-94915-34-3 ebook

Published in India by Kalpana Shukla

KW Publishers Pvt Ltd
4676/21, First Floor, Ansari Road
Daryaganj, New Delhi 110002
Phone: +91 11 43528107
Marketing: kw@kwpub.in
Editorial: production@kwpub.in
Website: www.kwpub.in

Printed and bound in India

CENTRE FOR AIR POWER STUDIES

VISION

To be an independent centre of excellence on national security contributing informed and considered research and analyses on relevant issues.

MISSION

To encourage independent and informed research and analyses on issues of relevance to national security and to create a pool of domain experts to provide considered inputs to decision-makers. Also, to foster informed public debate and opinion on relevant issues and to engage with other think-tanks and stakeholders within India and abroad to provide an Indian perspective.

Contents

Preface

A decade ago, after the 2011 Fukushima nuclear accident, the future of nuclear power in Asia appeared to be grim. As countries around the world began to reconsider, scale down, suspend and abandon their nuclear programmes, many analysts pronounced it as the "end of the nuclear era". A decade since Asia is leading the global nuclear sector. Contributing to two-thirds of the global construction of reactors and exhibiting its technical prowess in the nuclear research and development arena, the future of nuclear power in Asia appears to be on a positive trajectory. This development is driven by a mix of urgent necessity, aided by the realisation that benefits offered by nuclear power are not just environmental in character, but also offers economic and strategic advantages. In this context, the book examines nuclear energy trends in the Asian continent and endeavours to answer the much-deliberated question of whether Asia is witnessing a nuclear renaissance again.

Interestingly, the development of civil nuclear power in the region also happens to coincide with larger trends in the field of geopolitics and international relations, where there is a significant shift in the centre of gravity moving from the West to the East. The Asian continent in this regard has emerged as the new pivot, as countries in the region have been undergoing rapid economic development and are looking for cleaner sources of energy to meet their rising demands while trying to offset the disastrous effects of climate change. In this context, the role of nuclear power in developing economies and its potential to boost sustainable development and green growth has been gaining significant attention.

To address these questions, the book explores the policy responses by Asian countries to the Fukushima disaster and studies the nuclear energy scenario in Asia from January 2011 to December 2021. It does so by examining five interesting case studies of nuclear programmes in the region. This includes the study of Japan, which used to be a leading country in nuclear power generation but is now trying to rekindle its programme while recovering from the Fukushima accident; South Korea a leader in the nuclear sector, which intends to phase out nuclear energy production in the coming years; China which is witnessing the world's biggest boost in nuclear power production and is expected to soon be a leader in the nuclear industry; India which has ambitions of leading the global nuclear power sector; Pakistan which is struggling to strengthen its countries collapsing economic defences with energy security and finally Bangladesh which stands at economic crossroads and places its bets on nuclear power to help it transition from an under developed economy to a developing one.

By closely studying the nuclear energy programmes of these countries, the book attempts to map the trajectory of nuclear power in Asia and understand the various factors that have influenced this course. In doing so, it also attempts to assess the future of nuclear power in the continent and identifies the factors that may accelerate or limit its growth.

Acknowledgements

This book is the outcome of the support I have received from the network I am very privileged to have been associated with.

I would like to thank Air Marshal Anil Chopra, Director-General, Centre for Air Power Studies (CAPS), for his constant support and words of inspiration.

This book would not have been possible without the guidance of my mentor Dr Manpreet Sethi. She has taught me more than I can give her credit for. Her professional ethics and ability to always maintain objectivity in research have inspired me and are qualities I hope to imbibe in my professional journey.

My parents, Dr Akhter and Haseena, have been my constant source of support. Thank you for your quiet sacrifices and endless love.

My Husband Jaseem's support and endless cups of coffee have pushed me through the most challenging days. Thank you for designing the book cover and everything else you do for me.

I owe thanks to K H Abdulla and Jameela, my very loving in-laws, for their endless support and love.

My sisters Taaniya and Riya, thank you for putting up with my incessant rambling on nuclear policies, a subject they care so little about but put on the pretence of being interested in anyway. I would like to thank my grandmother, Fathima, for always inspiring me.

I am grateful to those with whom I have had the pleasure to work during this project, especially Urmi, Carl and Shantanu. Discussions with them were the most helpful in forming an objective critique and have been an invaluable contribution to the book.

I am especially grateful to CAPS for providing me with a conducive environment to carry out research. The officers, research scholars and office staff have been the most helpful in this journey.

Introduction

The Fukushima nuclear accident involving the Daiichi Nuclear Power Plant in 2011 as a result of Tohoku earthquake and tsunami, was one of the most severe nuclear accidents since the Chernobyl disaster of 1986. The combination of the earthquake and the tsunami-related flooding caused the nuclear meltdown and hydrogen explosions, released radioactive contamination. Classified as level five, meant that over 150,000 had to be evacuated. While there are no concrete statistical indicators of health-related fallouts or reported deaths due to radioactivity, the evacuation had to take place and that had its adverse dynamics. Within one year after the disaster, all but two of Japan's nuclear reactors had been shut down. Interestingly, the Onagawa nuclear plant closest to the earthquake epicentre withstood the catastrophe. Yet many activists pushed for the phase-out of nuclear power in Japan, and built a case for other forms of renewable energy. The global reaction also was of deep public anxiety and dented confidence in nuclear power. The 1979 Three Mile Island accident in the United States and the 1986 Chernobyl disaster in the Soviet Union also resulted in public opposition to nuclear plants. There was a sudden slowdown in plans for new nuclear power stations. Germany decided to phase out its nuclear plants by 2022. Many other European countries like Belgium, Switzerland, Italy and France decided to go slow on nuclear energy.

Nuclear fission-generated heat is used to warm water to produce steam, which in turn is used to rotate large turbines that generate electricity. The spent fuel, though small in volume, is high-level radioactive waste, and must be separated from the environment for thousands of years. This remains an issue for environmentalists. The initial cost of a nuclear plant is high, and it takes considerable time to build one to international safety standards. The reactors also breed some plutonium-239, which can be used for nuclear weapons. This has weapon proliferation issues.

Nuclear power generation has come a long way since the first power plant came up in the 1950s. The global installed nuclear power generation capacity grew to 100 GW by the 1970s. It stands at 390 GW today from nearly 440 civilian reactors, and generates nearly 10 per cent of global electricity. Many reactors are under construction (57) or planned (102), with most in Asia. The power generation is relatively clean and is second only to hydroelectricity for the low carbon footprint. Nuclear is a power source that emits 70 times less CO_2 than coal, 40 times less than gas, four times less than solar energy, and two times less than hydroelectricity and wind energy. It also means lower contribution to air pollution and respiratory health-related issues.

The Ukraine conflict and the oil and gas energy supply chain blockage have once again brought nuclear energy back in focus, especially in petroleum-deficient countries of Europe. Germany is rethinking its plans to close down nuclear power plants. Interestingly, just 12 years after Fukushima, Japan too has adopted a new policy promoting greater use of nuclear energy amid global fuel shortages. In a major reversal, the earlier Japanese plan to phase-out nuclear energy by around 2030 has been put on hold. They plan to refurbish, restart and extend the lifespan of nuclear reactors, and build new ones. In fact, they set a target of 20-22 per cent of nuclear energy of the nation's energy mix by 2030 from the current just 7 per cent. Ten plants have already resumed operations and many others have applied to resume operations. While the government is driving policy changes and softening public opinion, and nuclear scientists evolving newer more efficient technologies, the Japanese Nuclear Regulation Authority is laying out new safety and inspection norms. The move is also driven by a plan to achieve carbon neutrality by 2050.

Asia can be divided into five sub-regions, East Asia, Asian, the Indian Sub-continent, West Asia and Central Asia. China, Japan, South

Korea and Taiwan are all large economies and energy deficient, and rely on nuclear energy in its power generation mix. Yet nuclear power accounted for just 5.02 per cent of the total electricity mix in 2021 for China. Twenty-one reactors under construction in China at the end of July 2022. In 2021, nuclear generated 28.0 per cent of South Korea's electricity. Interestingly Taiwan has six nuclear power plants. Demand for electricity is growing rapidly in the emerging ASEAN economies. Nuclear energy in most of these countries is still at the research reactor stage. The Philippines and Vietnam are a little ahead of the pack. Indonesia already has three operational research reactors. Thailand should be on-board by later this decade.

India's 22 operational nuclear reactors just 3.2 per cent of the country's electricity in 2021. Eight new reactors are already under construction. Pakistan's six operable nuclear reactors produce 10.6 per cent of the country's electricity. More are planned. Bangladesh has two plants under construction, with the first unit likely to be operational by 2023. West and Central Asia are rich in oil and gas. But these are all finite resources. Therefore many countries are looking at nuclear energy. Kazakhstan has four operational research reactors. The UAE is embarking in a big way. Between 2020 and 2022 three units of the nuclear power plant have been connected to the national electricity grid. Saudi Arabia has still to have a nuclear plant but has targets of around 17 GW of nuclear energy by around 2040. Iran has one operating nuclear power plant that took many years to construct. The second large Russian-designed unit at the Bushehris still a work in progress. A third one is planned later. Iran's nuclear program is suspected to generate uranium enrichment for weapons, and has been under international watch.

Zoya Akhter Fathima is a great scholar and a close watcher of global nuclear energy dynamics. She has written many scholarly research papers on nuclear issues. This book *Nuclear Power in Asia Post Fukushima* looks at Asia's nuclear power trajectory. She thinks that the nuclear power growth is currently on a positive trend, but such optimism can be dampened by a single nuclear accident. Improved nuclear technologies would help improve safety and stem concerns. Public trust and confidence are crucial.

Proliferation-resistant reactors are highly desirable. Clean renewable energy is a great strength of nuclear plants. Zoya's book puts together the nuclear energy dynamics of Asia in a comprehensive manner. It is a must-read for nuclear energy tracking researchers and those in the field. It will make a good reference document.

Air Marshal **Anil Chopra**
Director-General
Centre for Air Power Studies

1. Status of Global Nuclear Energy: A Survey

Introduction

The status of nuclear energy today is in a state of flux. While several countries in the West are phasing out nuclear energy, numerous countries in Asia are in the process of developing their civil nuclear programmes. As various factors are at play, such as growing energy demands in some parts of the world and a plateau in energy demands in other parts, increasing climate change awareness, public concerns about nuclear safety, etc., the debate on the future of nuclear energy is complex. In this context, this chapter attempts to analyse the global contemporary nuclear power scenario.

To do so, the chapter is divided into five sections. The first section looks at the history of nuclear power from the 1940s to 2011 and the second section analyses the effect the Fukushima accident had on the course of global nuclear power. The following section analyses the current global nuclear trend and explores the growth of nuclear energy in Asia and attempts to understand if a new nuclear renaissance is imminent. The final section is the concluding segment.

Background

Breakthroughs in science and technology impact geopolitics and international relations. The case of the advent of nuclear power amply proves this. Although the study of nuclear energy had been developing from the time the Greek philosophers first tried to understand and define atoms, it developed over the years through the cumulative efforts of various scientists around the world. However, nuclear technology for military purposes was used for the first time only during the end of the Second World War. In 1945, the United States of America dropped nuclear weapons on the Japanese cities of Hiroshima and Nagasaki. The consequence of this was not only harrowing for the residents of the two cities, but it also changed the nature of the international power dynamics. Thereupon, cognizant of the dangers of nuclear weapons, countries spearheaded by the United States tried to regulate the use and development of nuclear technology.

US President Dwight Eisenhower's speech titled "Atoms for Peace" at the United Nations General Assembly in 1953 turned out to be a watershed moment in this regard. The speech which was part of a media and public relations campaign by the US government sought to communicate to the American public the future of nuclear power. Eisenhower's speech was significant for several reasons. First, post the 1945 nuclear bombings, there was widespread fear and trepidation among people around the world about the possibility of repeated use of such weapons. Eisenhower's speech, on an issue which had been shrouded in secrecy, was helpful in pacifying the public and his call for a peaceful solution was needed to placate the citizens. Second, his speech was also meant to signal countries to give up any pugnacious plans and thus is considered to be a part of the cold war "containment" strategy. And finally, the "Atoms for Peace" programme opened up nuclear research for peaceful purposes to other countries. In the words of President Eisenhower, "this greatest of destructive forces can be developed into a great boon for the benefit of all mankind." Thus in a way, it was promoted as an incentive for countries to abstain from developing nuclear weapons.[1] The "Atoms for Peace", the programme also led to the creation of the International Atomic Energy Agency (IAEA). Thus, in the 1950s the attention was shifted towards the peaceful use of nuclear energy, focusing on generating electricity.

The US government also revised the Atomic Energy Act which enabled it to disseminate nuclear technology to other countries if they pledged to never develop nuclear weapons. Taking this ahead, the US government provided training and assistance in building research reactors to several friendly countries. They also declassified many reports on nuclear technology and signed cooperation agreements with over 20 countries such as India, Pakistan, Argentina, Brazil and Iran among others. This heralded a period of nuclear optimism. In addition, the 1973 oil crisis also added to the nuclear appeal since many countries that relied on oil to generate electricity began considering the nuclear option, to avoid facing import dependency and protect themselves from geopolitical vulnerabilities. Nuclear power also emerged as a promising option for resource-starved countries. The French, for instance, summarised their rationale to adopt nuclear power in the following words: "We have no coal, we have no oil, we have no gas, we have no choice."[2]

However, the Three Mile Island accident in the United States in 1979 created panic and uncertainty around the further development of nuclear power, although it did not result in any casualties. Anti-nuclear protests started gaining traction not only in the US but also in other countries which were developing civil nuclear programmes. In addition, in the 1980s the prices of fossil fuels dropped. The 1986 Chernobyl disaster furthered the opposition against nuclear energy. All these factors cumulatively led to some countries halting the construction of their reactors, while others contemplated phasing out nuclear power altogether.

By the late 1990s and the beginning of the new millennium, this trend started to reverse as economies of countries began to develop rapidly, which consequently led to the widening of the energy demand-supply gap. There also was a growing recognition of the serious threat posed by climate change and the search for cleaner sources of energy intensified. With the rising price of fossil fuels, recognition of the low carbon footprint of nuclear energy and the high capacity factor of nuclear reactors, the nuclear appeal increased. Thus, by the beginning of the new millennium more countries had started showing interest in going nuclear. This period known as the "nuclear renaissance", saw growing optimism about the future of nuclear power, as 15 new nuclear projects began in 2010.[3] In addition, many other countries began to seriously consider developing nuclear programmes. IAEA corroborated this sentiment in its annual report of 2010 which revealed that "60 member states have expressed interest in the introduction of a nuclear power programme".[4] In fact, the IAEA even set up an integrated nuclear infrastructure group in response to the growing interest in nuclear power by various countries.[5]

The Fukushima Accident and its Impact on the Nuclear Power Sector

The Fukushima Daiichi nuclear accident that took place on March 11, 2011, when an earthquake and a tsunami struck Japan, altered the course of global nuclear development. Technically the Fukushima accident resulted in one casualty, where a worker died of cancer due to radiation exposure, while the earthquake and tsunami led to the unfortunate death of over 18,000 people.[6] However, the Fukushima nuclear accident severely impacted people's collective memory after which there was a huge public outcry on nuclear safety, which pressurised governments to reconsider their national nuclear ambitions. Many countries that were on the verge of starting their nuclear programmes either stalled or can celled them. According to the IAEA annual report of 2015, the number of countries that had shown interest in starting nuclear programmes in 2010 had fallen by 50 per cent in 2015![7] Public acceptance of nuclear power was severely eroded once again. In 2011, polls were undertaken by *Iposos MORI*, a British market research company and *Asahi Shimbun*, a Japanese newspaper, after the Fukushima disaster revealed a significant decline in support for nuclear power technology across most countries. The poll conducted by *Ipsos Mori* showed that the nuclear industry had the lowest amount of support (38 per cent) in comparison to other forms of technology used for generating electricity. While coal technology received 48 per cent support, solar, wind and hydro power received over 90 per cent support.[8]

Immediate Country Reactions Post Fukushima

As public concerns grew, different countries responded in different ways to the Fukushima accident. The following table describes the reactions of 36 countries in the immediate aftermath of the accident. The list is compiled based on the official statements and reports made by countries that were very vocal about the accident. The Table 1 has been sequenced in the order of the severity of actions taken by countries.

Table 1: Countries Reactions Immediately Post Fukushima

Sl. No.	County	Reaction /policy change
1.	Japan	- Shut down all reactors. - All nuclear reactors undergoing two-phase stress tests. - Ongoing construction of reactors halted. - Prime minister called for reduced dependence on nuclear power.
2.	Germany	- Reviewed the safety of all German nuclear power plants. - Permanently shut down eight reactors. - Intends to shut down remaining reactors by 2022. - Has decided to completely phase out nuclear energy.
3.	Italy	- Plans to reintroduce nuclear power given up. - Declared nuclear moratorium for one year - Passed a referendum with about 94 per cent of its votes against government plans to start new nuclear power projects.
4.	Switzerland	- Banned the construction of new reactors. - Decision to gradually phase out nuclear power.
5.	Belgium	- Decision to continue with gradual phase-out which was taken before the Fukushima accident.
6.	Bulgaria	- Plans to construct the Belene national plant terminated in 2012, the decision was influenced by other financial factors too.
7.	Mexico	- Abandoned plans to build new reactors and shifted its focus to natural gas instead.
8.	Venezuela	- Ceased plans of developing nuclear power projects. - Energy Ministry ordered to look for alternate sources of renewable energy.
9.	Kuwait	- Shelved their civil nuclear project. Multiple other factors too influenced this decision.
10.	Indonesia	- Government announced a slowdown in its nuclear development.
11.	Israel	- Reconsidered nuclear project and stated that it was "unlikely" that they would develop it in the near future.

12.	The Philippines	- Was considering the revival of its nuclear project, but the Fukushima accident resulted in cancelling it yet again.
13.	Taiwan	- Suspension of plants until the completion of a safety review. - President called for reduced dependence on nuclear power.
14.	Thailand	- The Prime Minister directed the Energy Ministry to review plans for establishing nuclear power plants. - Also asked to study in detail the emergency measures in nuclear plants during crises and the potential of a nuclear power plant being a target for terrorists.
15.	Australia	- Reaffirmed its already existing position of staying non-nuclear.
16.	Luxemburg	- Reaffirmed its already existing position of staying non-nuclear.
17.	Greece	- Reaffirmed its already existing position of staying non-nuclear.
18.	Latvia	- Reaffirmed its already existing position of staying non-nuclear.
19.	China	- Suspended authorisation of construction of new reactors until a safety review was completed. - Resumed projects soon after with continued commitment to developing nuclear power with increased emphasis on safety.
20.	Canada	- Continued commitment to developing nuclear power with increased emphasis on safety.
21.	Czech Republic	- Continued plans to build 2 more units.
22.	France	- Nuclear power plants underwent stress tests. - Continued with its existing nuclear plans, stressing safety. - Hollande government in 2012 declared gradual nuclear reduction. However, other reasons influenced this decision.
23.	Finland	- Reconfirmed plans to build a nuclear power station.
24.	Hungary	- Continued commitment to developing 2 more nuclear reactors
25.	India	- Continued commitment to developing nuclear power. - However, the state government of West Bengal denied permission to construct a new facility in a town in West Bengal and the construction of two power plants in Tamilnadu was delayed.
26.	Niger	- Continued commitment to building a civil nuclear programme with increased emphasis on safety.

27.	Pakistan	- Continued commitment to developing nuclear power with increased emphasis on safety.
28.	South Korea	- Continued commitment to developing nuclear power with increased emphasis on safety.
29.	Slovakia	- Continued commitment to developing nuclear power with increased emphasis on safety.
30.	South Africa	- Continued commitment to developing nuclear power with increased emphasis on safety.
31.	Spain	- Called for a review of existing nuclear plants.
32.	Sweden	- Continued commitment to developing nuclear power with increased emphasis on safety.
33.	Turkey	- Reaffirmed their plans of continuing to build their first reactor.
34.	Ukraine	- Continued commitment to developing nuclear power with increased emphasis on safety.
35.	United Kingdom	- Continued with its existing nuclear policies and plans, with additional emphasis given to the safety aspect.
36.	United States of America	- Continued with its existing nuclear policies and plans, with additional emphasis given to the safety aspect.

Source: Author compiled from various sources.

As elucidated in the table above, countries reaction to the accident was diverse. While some countries decided to do away with nuclear power for good, the accident also instigated few others that were considering to develop their civil nuclear programmes to put their plans on hold. However, not all countries decided to do away with nuclear technology. It appears that countries that were grappling with issues of power shortages and energy deficit, the accident did not cause any major policy change. The focus was however shifted to nuclear safety, as every country with operable nuclear reactors reviewed and reassessed their systems and practices and tried to enhance their safety mechanisms.

Assessing the Current Global Nuclear Trend

As is evident from the above analysis, the effects of the 3/11 nuclear accident was not limited to just Japan but had substantial consequences on the nuclear energy industry as a whole. A decade after Fukushima, the current nuclear trend is not necessarily all downhill. Even if the total number of operational reactors may have reduced, the nuclear generation capacity of the existing reactors has not. According to the World Nuclear Association, global nuclear generation has risen consistently from 2012 to 2017 with an output of 142 TWh more than what it was in 2012.[9] In addition, with population growth expected to see a pronounced rise, the demand for energy, especially clean energy, is also expected to rise significantly. While other sources of renewable power have much higher support from civil society, they face their own share of challenges and limitations as well and are unable to meet the clean energy security goals all by themselves. Nuclear energy thus continues to pose as a worthy option towards achieving a clean energy future. In this context, let's look at the current global status of nuclear power to better understand and analyse its future trajectory.

A graphic representation presented below organises countries on various parameters to enable the understanding of the position of nuclear power in the world today. The countries marked in light green are the ones with operational nuclear reactors. Dark green represents the countries that have operational nuclear reactors and who continue to stay committed to developing their nuclear programmes. These countries are either ramping up their nuclear capabilities or are planning to do so. The countries marked in light blue are the ones which are developing their nuclear programmes and are in the process of constructing nuclear reactors. Countries marked in dark blue are the ones that have expressed interest in developing their nuclear programmes in the near future. They have either signed nuclear cooperation agreements or are in talks with other countries regarding the same. Yellow represents the countries that have at some point shown interest in developing nuclear power but have not committed to it yet. They are mostly considering the nuclear energy option at a policy discussion level. The countries in red are the ones that have phased out their nuclear power programmes. Likewise, countries marked in red with black stripes have either decided to phase out their nuclear programmes in the coming years or have already started phasing them out. The colour red with white checkers represents the countries that have decided to stay non-nuclear.

Figure 1: Current Global Status of Nuclear Energy Policies

Source: Data from IAEA, World Nuclear Association and various newspaper articles.

The True Blues of Nuclear Energy

As depicted in the figure above, there are currently 32 countries with operational nuclear reactors. The 440 nuclear reactors contribute to about 10 per cent of electricity generated globally.[10] Overall, a slightly upward trend is seen as 23 of these countries continue to remain committed to their nuclear power programmes and have robust nuclear policies. In terms of nuclear energy produced, the US tops the chart with 93 operable reactors that produce 95,523 MWe of power.[11] Owing to China's ambitious nuclear projects, it is expected to overtake the US in the coming years. In fact, nuclear energy goes beyond powering Beijing's own growth but is also a vital part of its Belt and Road Initiative, which seeks to use the platform to expand its nuclear exports portfolio for economic and strategic gains.

Another leading player in the nuclear industry is Russia. With 37 nuclear reactors and two more under construction, not only is

Moscow's domestic nuclear programme well-established but it is also emerging as a leader in the field of nuclear technology. In 2018, Russia completed the world's first floating nuclear power plant, which is now generating electricity in the remote Russian town of Pevek. In addition, Moscow is also rapidly exporting nuclear technology to other countries, having said to be working on 20 reactors in 2017 solely for exports. In the case of the United Kingdom, nuclear energy is an important component in its energy basket with about 20 per cent of its electricity generated by nuclear power. Although half of its existing nuclear capacity is anticipated to be retired by 2025, the government has begun constructing a new generation of nuclear power plants. Nuclear power has also been a major component of Canada's energy basket, with nuclear power providing 60 per cent of the country's electricity in 2016. With plans to further increase this share, a decision was taken in 2018 to further enhance its reliance on nuclear power. India likewise is planning to develop its nuclear infrastructure project substantially. With nuclear power contributing to just 3 per cent of its electricity generation (in 2016),[12] the government plans to increase this figure to 25 per cent by 2050 and hence has been focusing on increasing its installed nuclear capacity.[13] Though the pace has been slow due to a few challenges, governments support for it continues to stay strong. These countries also have dedicated institutions to promote nuclear research and development. Currently, they all have independent and collaborative programmes that are focused on the development of small modular reactors. China, India, the European Union, Japan, Russia, South Korea and the United States are also a part of nuclear fusion research and engineering mega project called the ITER, which seeks to revolutionise the energy sector.

Newcomers to the Nuclear Party

Several countries have recently kicks tarted their nuclear power projects. This includes UAE's Barakah nuclear power plant which connected its first unit to the national power grid in August 2020 and its second unit in September 2021. Likewise, Bangladesh began the construction of its first nuclear unit in 2017, and is expected to be commissioned in

2023.Countries like Belarus, Saudi Arabia and Turkey too are currently overseeing the construction of their nuclear power plants.

Prospective Entrants to the Nuclear Club

Approximately 21 countries in Europe, Asia and Africa are now in the process of signing cooperation deals or preparing the groundwork for the development of a nuclear programme by taking up tasks such as developing legal and regulatory infrastructure, conducting technical feasibility studies, considering financing options, setting up of research centres etc. Nuclear power appears to be garnering a lot of interest, especially in African countries such as Nigeria, Algeria, Tunisia, Zambia, Ghana, Kenya, Uganda, and Egypt, which are all currently under talks to develop their nuclear programmes. Russia, China and South Korea in this regard have emerged as prominent players in the nuclear exports market that are competing to win bids in these countries.

Betwixt and Between

There are about 23 other countries that too have expressed interest in starting their nuclear power programmes at some point. However, they have not made any commitments in this regard or taken any significant steps towards this end yet. The development of nuclear power is still at a policy discussion level among these countries.

The Anti-Nuclear club

While there is a substantial interest in nuclear power among many countries, anti-nuclear sentiments continue to remain strong in others. In a few countries, developing nuclear energy in itself is deemed unconstitutional. For example in Austria, the country passed a legislation in 1997 to remain anti- nuclear. 2015 onwards Austria even stopped importing nuclear-sourced electricity in its attempt to be "completely nuclear-free". Similarly, according to the Electricity Regulation Act of 1999, it is prohibited to develop nuclear energy in Ireland. A few countries have also had to scrap their nuclear programmes due to political reasons,such as in the case of Lithuania, which had to decommission two nuclear reactors as a requisite to join the European Union.

Other countries have decided to steer away from nuclear power citing safety reasons. This includes countries which are located in tectonically active zones that are prone to volcanos and earthquakes. Greece, for example, has taken a decision not to pursue nuclear energy considering the frequent occurrence of earthquakes there. Taiwan, which is situated across active fault lines, has also witnessed widespread anti-nuclear movements amidst safety concerns and other challenges. Thus, in 2019 the Taiwanese government declared that the existing nuclear power plants wouldn't be granted any life extensions, aiming to phase out nuclear energy by 2025.[14]

Similarly, strong public opposition to nuclear power has resulted in the abandonment of several other nuclear power projects. For example, countries like Germany which faced anti-nuclear protests after Fukushima decided to permanently shut eight of their reactors. This was a part of their energy transition plan called *Energywiende*, which intends to move the country towards a low-carbon economy by boosting renewable energy. However, at the same time, it also calls for the phasing out of nuclear power and intends to shut the remaining reactors by 2022.[15] Luxembourg too had to shelve its plans to build a nuclear power plant due to the growing public opposition to the idea. Another case where public opinion has managed to change the course of nuclear power is that of Italy. Post-Chernobyl, a referendum was held in Italy to decide the course of its nuclear future. With a significant anti-nuclear outcome, the nuclear plants were shutdown. In 2008, nuclear debates re-emerged in the country. However, soon after the Fukushima accident, a referendum was held again and an over whelming majority of the people decided to continue to stay clear of nuclear energy and plans to revive the nuclear programme were once again cancelled.

A recent addition to the naysayers to nuclear energy is South Korea which has a vibrant nuclear power industry. Public paranoia on safety concerns, increasing exposes to corruption in the nuclear industry and the Fukushima accident resulted in public distrust towards nuclear technology. President Moon Jae-in won the elections in 2017 with his promise to gradually phase out nuclear power. Fukushima also led to a referendum to gradually phase out nuclear power in Switzerland, where nuclear power used to contribute 40 per cent of the country's electricity.[16]

It is interesting to note that public pressure is one of the biggest factors leading countries to scrap their nuclear plans. In this regard, an effective perception management and communication strategy could go a long way in clarifying the qualms that people have and help in promoting the development of nuclear energy. This proves the importance of public diplomacy of a country with its own people to develop sustainable policies.

Asia: Nuclear Renaissance 2.0?

According to the IAEA, among the 31 countries that are operating 437 nuclear plants for electricity generation, 114 nuclear plants are in Asia.[17] This trend seems to be growing considering the fact that the World Nuclear Association stated that, as of 2018 more than two third of the reactors that were being constructed around with world were in Asia.[18] This leads to the question of whether Asia is witnessing a nuclear renaissance again.

Figure 2: Nuclear Energy Policies in Asia

Source: Author's own.

As apparent in the representation above, the nuclear energy trend in Asia gives a mixed picture, with a tilt towards a more positive trend. Asia was in fact at the forefront of the nuclear renaissance that emerged at the beginning of this century. As countries in the Asian continent were working towards rapid economic development, two important issues contributed to the nuclear appeal. First, an increase in electricity demand and second, the recognition of the problem of climate change and the need for more sustainable sources of energy. The growing interest in nuclear energy in Asian countries was evident when at the annual ASEAN summit in Singapore in 2007, South East Asian countries signed a declaration on climate change, energy and the environment. This declaration urged states to adopt more sustainable and cleaner forms of energy to tackle the issue of greenhouse gas emissions by "cooperating for the development and use of civilian nuclear power".[19] Amidst this period of nuclear optimism in Asia, the Fukushima accident in 2011 created a period of uncertainty in the development of nuclear energy. However, the region seems to be recovering from this hiatus and the nuclear energy trend seems to be on the upswing again. The economic and development climate in Asia is such right now, that many developing countries are looking for stable, independent and cleaner forms of energy that will support the pace of their development while helping them reduce GHG emissions as well. Nuclear energy in this regard ticks all the boxes.

Conclusion

The impact of the Fukushima accident evidently was not just limited to Japan. It influenced nuclear power programmes around the world. The global response to the Fukushima accident was heterogenous. With countries that were already grappling with issues of public support, the Fukushima accident prompted them to call off or reduce their nuclear power programme. However, with countries that were struggling with power shortages and were developing their civil nuclear projects, the accident did not cause any major policy change. It did, however, enable all nuclear power countries to review their safety framework. The differences in policy responses to Fukushima also to an extent reflect the level of trust people had on their governments. It is possible that it could also be linked to larger cultural attributes of countries.

There appears to be a slow decline in the nuclear energy sector in the West. This coincides with factors such as a plateau in energy demand, population growth, economic slowdown, availability of alternate sources of energy and greater expression of public concern about nuclear safety. However, a more upbeat trend is noticed in eastern European countries. The lull in Western Europe is made up of the increasing interest in nuclear energy in Asian, African, West Asian and Latin American countries. Asia especially is witnessing a positive trend in civil nuclear energy generation. This is linked to other trends in the field of geopolitics and international relations with a significant shift of the centre of gravity from the West to the East. The Asian continent has emerged as the new pivot, with many countries in the region striving for major economic development. Being the most populous continent, many countries in Asia are witnessing economic growth that has naturally increased the demand for electricity. The imperatives of economic development in Asia, necessitate a diversification of energy sources, keeping in mind long-term demand. It is here, that nuclear power gains prominence.

Nuclear power is becoming an important component in the national electricity basket to power the socio-economic growth of these countries. Furthermore, its low carbon footprint adds to its appeal as a clean and environmentally sustainable source of energy. This makes nuclear power a worthwhile solution to not just meet Asia's energy needs, but also do so without exacerbating the problem of climate change. It is also interesting to see how these countries are not limiting their nuclear capabilities to just generating electricity for themselves, but are also looking at exporting their nuclear technology. The nuclear export market which was largely dominated by the US, France and Russia is now witnessing diversification with new players such as China, South Korea and India.

Overall, the future of nuclear energy seems affirmative. The IAEA predicts nuclear power production to grow by around 46 per cent by 2040. However, over 90 per cent of this increase is expected to come from China and India.[20] With about 20 countries already developing their nuclear power projects and nearly 30 countries showing interest in going nuclear, it seems to be balancing the number of reactors that are expected to retire and phase out soon. In this regard, Asia is expected to emerge as the new leader in the civil nuclear sector.

Notes

1. Jesse Hicks, "Atoms for Peace: The Mixed Legacy of Eisenhower's Nuclear Gambit", Sciencehistory.org, July 19, 2014, at https://www.sciencehistory.org/distillations/atoms-for-peace-the-mixed-legacy-of-eisenhowers-nuclear-gambit, accessed on May 15, 2019.
2. George Dvorsky, "Is nuclear power really on the way out?", *Gizmodo,*at https://io9.gizmodo.com/is-nuclear-power-really-on-the-way-out-5917615, accessed on May 15, 2019.
3. Geert De Clercq, "Nuclear newbuild projects at decade low: report", Reuters, September 12, 2017, at https://www.reuters.com/article/us-nuclear-outlook/nuclear-newbuild-projects-at-decade-low-report-idUSKCN1BN1RM, accessed on May 20, 2019.
4. "Annual Report 2010", International Atomic Energy Agency, at https://documents.pub/document/annual-report-2010-558445e3010d3.html, accessed on May 28, 2019.
5. "Emerging nuclear energy countries", World Nuclear Association, at http://www.world-nuclear.org/information-library/country-profiles/others/emerging-nuclear-energy-countries.aspx, accessed on June 1, 2019.
6. "Japan admits that Fukushima worker died from radiation", *The Guardian,* September 5, 2018, at https://www.theguardian.com/world/2018/sep/05/japan-admits-that-fukushima-worker-died-from-radiation, accessed on July 26, 2019.
7. Manpreet Sethi, "The Asian Nuclear Power Landscape: A Contemporary Examination", *Asian Strategic Review 2017: Energy Security in Times of Uncertainty*, (New Delhi: Pentagon Press, 2018), p. 119.
8. Richard Black, "Nuclear power 'gets little public support worldwide'", BBC, November 25, 2011, at https://www.bbc.com/news/science-environment-15864806, accessed on May 18, 2019.
9. "Nuclear Power in the World Today", World Nuclear Association,at http://www.world-nuclear.org/information-library/current-and-future-generation/nuclear-power-in-the-world-today.aspx, accessed on May 17, 2019.
10. "Nuclear Power in the World Today", World Nuclear Association, at https://world-nuclear.org/information-library/current-and-future-generation/nuclear-power-in-the-world-today.aspx#:~:text=Nuclear%20energy%20now%20provides%20about,in%20about%20220%20research%20reactors, accessed on January 12, 2022.

11. "Nuclear Power in the USA", World Nuclear Association, at https://world-nuclear.org/information-library/country-profiles/countries-t-z/usa-nuclear-power.aspx, accessed June 10, 2016.
12. Aniruddh Mohan, The Future of Nuclear Energy in India, ORF Occasional papers, August 9, 2016, at https://www.orfonline.org/research/the-future-of-nuclear-energy-in-india/
13. "Nuclear Power in India," World Nuclear Association, at http://www.world-nuclear.org/info/Country-Profiles/Countries-G-N/India/, accessed June 10, 2016.
14. "Taiwan government maintains nuclear phase-out", World Nuclear News, February 1, 2019, at http://world-nuclear-news.org/Articles/Taiwan-government-maintains-nuclear-phase-out, accessed on May 20, 2019.
15. Justin Huggler, "Germany faces growing calls to delay phase-out of nuclear energy", *The Telegraph,* June 6, 2019, at https://www.telegraph.co.uk/news/2019/06/06/germany-faces-growing-calls-delay-phase-out-nuclear-energy/, accessed on June 15, 2019.
16. "Switzerland votes to phase out nuclear power", BBC, May 21, 2017, at https://www.bbc.com/news/world-europe-39994599, accessed on June 2, 2019.
17. "Atomic Power Plants in Asia", *RECAP Asia,* at http://recap.asia/climate-asia/Atomic-Power-Plants-in-Asia.html, accessed on June 12, 2019.
18. "Asia's Nuclear Energy Growth", World Nuclear Association,at http://www.world-nuclear.org/information-library/country-profiles/others/asias-nuclear-energy-growth.aspx, accessed on May 19, 2010.
19. n. 7, pp. 118-119.
20. Melissa Goh, "China and India will lead the world's nuclear power growth, experts say", CNBC, November 7, 2018, at https://www.cnbc.com/2018/11/08/china-india-will-lead-global-nuclear-power-production-growth-experts.html, accessed on June 15, 2019.

2. Understanding the Appeal of Nuclear Energy and Assessing Anti-Nuclear Debates

Introduction

In 1898 when the phenomenon of radioactivity was discovered for the first time, it was considered a scientific miracle holding the promise of a diverse range of benefits. It gained the interest not only of the scientific community but also of the public. This period witnessed what is known as the "radium craze". In fact, scientists who died because of excess radium exposure were considered martyrs of science. Similarly, when nuclear fission was discovered in 1938, there was optimism about the new "atomic utopia", which had created imageries of nuclear-fuelled aeroplanes and cities powered by unlimited electricity. However, this nuclear optimism burst when the dark side of nuclear power was exposed with the dropping of nuclear bombs on the Japanese cities of Hiroshima and Nagasaki by the United States during the Second World War. The development trajectory of nuclear power since then has fluctuant as several factors marked highs and lows in the nuclear sector. These include rising oil prices during the 1973 oil crisis, decreasing price of fossil fuel, the Three Miles Island and the Chernobyl nuclear accidents, subsequent increasing energy demands, increased awareness of climate change and most recently, the Fukushima accident. Nuclear energy has thus, gained and lost prominence in phases over the years.

Currently, the global energy deficit and climate change crisis aresuch that the nuclear industry is witnessing a resurgence after the hiatus post-

Fukushima. Projections of nuclear power development have begun to appear optimistic as it promises lower costs and higher output while assuring safety. Thus the current global scenario has once again put nuclear energy at the forefront of energy debates. However, concerns about nuclear safety still loom large and public opinion about nuclear energy continues to be clouded by scepticism.

Against this background, the chapter analyses the debates surrounding nuclear power. To do so the chapter is divided into three parts. The first section assesses the reasons why nuclear energy has gained prominence today and explores the main factors that have led countries to employ nuclear power. It also makes a comparative assessment of nuclear energy with other forms of renewable power. Next, the chapter analyses anti-nuclear debates and attempts to understand if the common arguments made against it hold any weight. The third segment is the conclusion, which sums up the pros and cons of nuclear energy, to provide an objective assessment of this energy source.

Understanding the Nuclear Appeal

Access to energy has been one of the biggest drivers of economic development globally over the last two centuries. As economies and standards of living grow, so do energy needs. However, as the irreparable damage caused to the environment by the extensive use of fossil fuels becomes increasingly apparent, the need for alternative sources of energy is gaining prominence. Nuclear energy in this regard is considered as one of the more attractive options. As discussed in the previous chapter, more countries are showing interest in developing their civil nuclear capabilities. Reasons for this are diverse ranging from economic to geopolitical to environmental. Like nuclear power, other forms of renewable energy too have certain benefits. However, an objective assessment of the most favourable form of energy could only be made by comparing the pros and cons of each of these energy sources in terms of parameters such as economic viability, sustainability, the gravity of its challenges, etc. Making this comparison is not a simple exercise, considering the number of factors that influence it. However, a modest attempt is made to assess the benefits and disadvantages of major renewable energy resources vis-à-vis nuclear power. In addition to this, the following section examines some of the reasons which have led to heightened interest among policymakers in nuclear energy.

Factors that make for Nuclear Appeal

Clean Source of Energy

The burning of fossil fuels for generating electricity is the key cause of global warming as fossil fuels release an immense amount of carbon dioxide (Co_2) in the environment. Nuclear plants, in comparison, have an extremely low carbon footprint. One may even go as far, as to say that nuclear energy has helped in preventing deaths caused due to air pollution. A study undertaken by Goddard Institute for Space Studies and Columbia University reveals that about 1.8 million deaths which would have been caused due to air pollution since 2009 were avoided by the replacement of coal plants with nuclear power plants.[1] In fact, it is estimated that the amount of Co_2 emissions that are reduced because of the use of nuclear energy for generating electricity is equivalent to removing more than 400 million cars from the road each year.[2]

In terms of environmental impact, nuclear energy is an important tool for countries that are striving to meet the decarbonising goals set up by the Paris Agreement. The key goals of the agreement are to "keep a global temperature rise this century well below 2 degrees Celsius above pre-industrial levels and to pursue efforts to limit the temperature increase even further to 1.5 degrees Celsius".[3] If these decarbonising goals have to be met, it is imperative that about 80 per cent of the electricity needs to be generated from a low-carbon source. In contrast, it is currently estimated that about 70 per cent of the world's electricity comes from the burning of fossil fuels. The importance of nuclear power to achieve sustainable development is evidenced by France, where nuclear power contributes to over 70 per cent of its power supply. France in this regard has the lowest Co_2 emissions among all developed countries in the world.[4] Currently, although nuclear power generates only about 10 per cent of the total global electricity, it makes up for almost one-third of the global low carbon electricity.[5] There is a scientific consensus that nuclear energy is required to combat the pressing challenge of climate change. It is for this reason that nuclear power has been listed in the Intergovernmental Panel on Climate Change (IPCC) pathways for decarbonisation in its "Special Report: Global Warming of 1.5°c".[6] The importance of nuclear energy to reduce carbon emissions is further corroborated by the open letter written by a group of renowned scientists in 2019, advocating that "there is no credible path to climate stabilization that does not include a substantial role for nuclear power".[7]

Modern renewable energy sources such as solar and wind power are considered to be environmentally friendly sources. They do not exude anything toxic into the atmosphere or deplete any natural resources. However, they too impact the environment negatively in other ways. For example, the Hoary Bats are speculated to go extinct due to the increasing number of bat deaths in wind farms.[8] Likewise, hydroelectric energy can cause droughts and affects the marine ecosystem as well.[9] Solar panel dumping too has proven to be hazardous. Similarly, although nuclear energy is a clean form of energy, in case of an accident it can have devastating effects. For example, in the case of the Chernobyl accident, which apart from resulting in the deaths of thousands of people, rendered an entire town inhabitable. [10] Thus, calculating the environmental impact of electricity-generating technologies is challenging.

However, one of the most effective ways to do so is through a Life Cycle Analysis (LCA). LCA is an analytical tool that enables the assessment of the environmental impact of any product from its conception to culmination. In the case of energy-generating technologies, it analyses the environmental impact at all stages including extraction, construction of a plant, transportation, operations and disposal among other stages. A project by the World Energy Council (WEC) which made a comparative LCA study of several electricity-generating technologies as a part of their

2002-2004 Studies Work Programme is notable. The results of the study reveal the following:

Figure 1: LCA of Electricity Generation Technologies

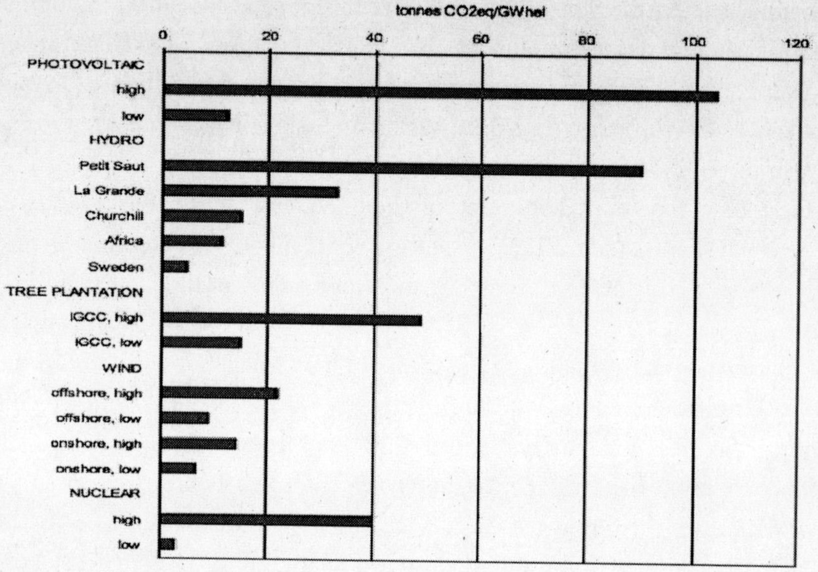

Source: World Energy Council.

Note: Figure denotes the greenhouse gas emitted from various renewable energy systems.

As indicated in the image above, nuclear energy emits the least amount of greenhouse gases in comparison to other forms of renewable energy. It is interesting to note that among renewable forms of energy, greenhouse gases are not emitted during power generation but at other stages of its life cycle such as during the extraction of unprocessed materials, transportation of items, construction of plants, etc.[11] It is for this reason that, nuclear energy would play an important role in helping nations meet their climate change commitments.

Efficiency

Technically, the efficiency or productivity of a plant is determined through the capacity factor, which is assessed by calculating the amount of energy produced by a source and then dividing it by the amount of energy the source would produce if it functioned incessantly at its highest capacity. Intermittent energy sources, such as solar energy and wind energy in this regard face challenges since the sun isn't always shining, the wind isn't always blowing and the water is not always falling through turbines in dams. Nuclear energy however has a much higher capacity factor since they do not depend on natural or environmental variables. In addition, nuclear reactors require less maintenance and need refuelling only once in two years. As nuclear technology is rapidly developing, its capacity factor is increasing as well. In the United States, from being lesser than 60 per cent in the 1980s, the average capacity factor of nuclear power plants has now increased to over 90 per cent![12] In fact, one watt of nuclear energy produces six times more energy than just one watt of solar energy.[13]

The stark contrast in the capacity factors of various renewable energy forms in comparison to nuclear energy is amply proven by the following graph which denotes the capacity factors of several renewable energy sources in the United States in 2018:

Figure 2: Capacity Factors for Various Utility Scale Generators in 2018

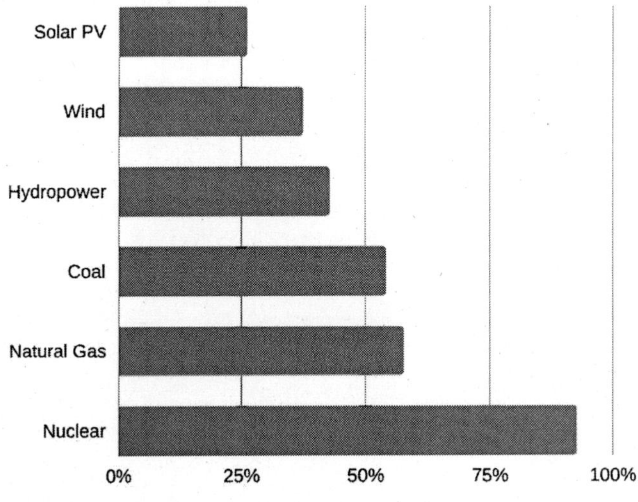

Source: US Energy Information Administration.

As evident in the graph above, nuclear energy performs at a much higher capacity than other forms of energy, at an average capacity factor of 92 per cent. Hydroelectric power performed at an average capacity factor of 38 per cent, wind energy at 34.5 per cent and solar energy at 25 per cent.[14] Geothermal energy too has a high capacity factor, of almost 70 per cent.[15] Nuclear power plants have a higher capacity factor since they are not intermittent, and once a reactor goes critical, it can perform incessantly until it needs refuelling or unless it requires to need technical servicing. They are also not constrained by the paucity of fuels, as is the case with wind or solar energy. In fact, Unit 1 of Canada's Darlington Nuclear Generating Station in 2020, set a record of functioning continuously for 963 days![16] In addition, nuclear power plants demand less amount of maintenance.[17] In the case of wind energy, the units require servicing at an average of at least once in 6 months.[18] Nuclear power plants in comparison require maintenance once in two years. Low maintenance leads to high efficiency and low operating cost too, making nuclear energy an attractive energy resource.

Even with regard to land use, nuclear energy requires much lesser land than wind or solar power. A study made by the Nuclear Energy Institute revealed that a 1000-megawatt nuclear facility requires one square mile worth of land. In comparison, wind farms require 360 times more land and solar photo voltaic facilities require 75 times the land area than a nuclear energy facility.[19]

Sustainability

Since electricity is central to economic growth, countries' desire for energy security has focused on looking out for sources of electricity generation that are long-lasting and sustainable. Coal, oil, and gas are predominant sources but these are non-renewable and are expected to run out eventually, even if their exact timeline estimates vary. Therefore even oil-rich countries are looking at alternative sources of energy. Nuclear power is believed to be a sustainable form of energy because, nuclear reactors use uranium as nuclear fuel, which is a compact or dense form of energy. Hence it requires a small amount of uranium to produce a large amount of energy. This means the energy efficiency factor is also higher than coal, gas and oil. Besides, as technology further improves, molten salt reactors and fast reactors are capable to attain up to ten times the energy from the equivalent amount of uranium fuel.[20] In addition, some have also argued that nuclear energy could be a form of renewable power. Professor Bernard Cohen from the University of Pittsburgh in this regard argues that breeder reactors can generate more fissile material than what it utilises, making it a renewable form of energy.[21] It is also believed that nuclear power could be a renewable form, if uranium is extracted from seawater, instead of being mined. Oceans are not just the biggest source of uranium but are also constantly replenished through geological processes.[22] Towards this end, for over half a century scientists have been attempting to extract uranium from seawater. Researchers at the Pacific Northwest National Laboratory and LCW Supercritical Technologies made progress in this pursuit when they used acrylic fibres to extract uranium from seawater and created five grams of yellowcake.[23] Experts argue that this won't only make nuclear energy a renewable form but would also make it more commercially viable. It is estimated that approximately 4 billion tonnes of uranium from seawater could fuel about one thousand, 1000 MW nuclear plants for 100,000 years![24] Moreover, uranium is not the only nuclear fuel that could be used in nuclear power plants. Ongoing research in thorium fuel cycles is expected to develop as a new alternative to uranium fuel cycles.

The availability of resources is another important factor that determines a country's interest in a particular energy option. In this regard, nuclear energy is a worthy option for countries that do not have ample natural resources such as in the case of countries like Japan and France. With high transportation costs and enabling import-dependency, it makes the economy of a country vulnerable. An example of this is the 1970s oil shocks which led to the power prices shooting up by 50 per cent, which created mayhem in the Japanese economy.[25] This is one of the reasons why Japan decided to develop its civil nuclear programme, despite witnessing the horrors of nuclear weapons. These events are difficult to predict as witnessed in the recent drone attacks in Saudi Arabia which led to a surge in oil prices.[26] The advantage of nuclear technology is that a small amount of fuel can generate a huge amount of electricity, hence the problem of dependency on other countries for fuel to operate reactors is minimised.[27]

Besides, factors like transportation could also create hindrances. This is witnessed, in the case of coal, where the dependency on railways for transportation causes several challenges. For example, in India, Coal India Ltd had stated that there wasn't enough rail capacity to transport coal from Coal India pithead to railhead.[28] Moreover, there is also the problem of surging coal prices. Almost 60 per cent of coal in India is transported through railways for electricity generation. On an average 85 per cent of the costs for transporting coal to the power plants is because of railways.[29] This is because the system in India is such that the freight charges are set higher to offset the lower passenger fares. Thus it results in overcharging which in turn causes the price of coal power generation to increase. Nuclear technology in this regard is unrestricted from such challenges.

Choices of energy generation technologies are also contingent on where a country is located. For example, photovoltaics would work efficiently only in countries that have enough sunlight throughout the year. Similarly, wind energy requires flat areas of land in windy places. In comparison, nuclear power does not have restrictions when it comes to physical land requirements, except in the case of a few countries that rest on tectonically fragile places, prone to earthquakes and volcanoes. However, development in nuclear technology such as the floating nuclear power plants (FNPP's) counters these challenges. FNPP's can provide electricity to energy-starved countries in remote places, such as in the newly launched project by Russia to power the arctic city of Pevek.[30]

As development in nuclear science is taking place at a rapid pace, breakthroughs such as thorium-powered nuclear reactors could provide nuclear fuel flexibility. Not only does thorium release less radioactive waste, it is also considered safer since it is not fissile on its own and thus can be easily stopped. It is also more copious in comparison to uranium and additionally prevents the production of weapons grade-plutonium which helps in minimising chances of nuclear weapons proliferation.[31] For thorium-rich countries, this also helps in reducing dependency on other countries for uranium. This technology, however, is still in the process of being commercially proven.

Issues Perceived Against Nuclear Energy

In 1998, *Nucleonics Week* remarked "nuclear needs climate change more than climate change needs nuclear".[32] Many such indictments have been made against nuclear energy, such as it is an economically unviable, dangerous form of technology. While concerns regarding nuclear power are not completely unfounded, the judgements passed on it however require a more in-depth examination. The following section in this regard analyses concerns about nuclear energy and tries to determine how much of the criticism posed against it holds true.

Perception of Nuclear Safety

No energy mishap in the world has received as much attention from the media and from people around the world as much as nuclear accidents have. Among the energy-generating technologies, nuclear energy in popular perception is considered risky. But contrary to popular belief, nuclear energy is a safer form of energy, in comparison to other electricity-producing technologies. It is interesting to note that among all energy fatalities in the world, nuclear energy accidents have resulted in the least number of casualties. The following illustration gives a well-defined picture of the fatal casualties caused because of air pollution and accidents due to energy production.

Figure 3: Death Rate from Energy Production per TWh

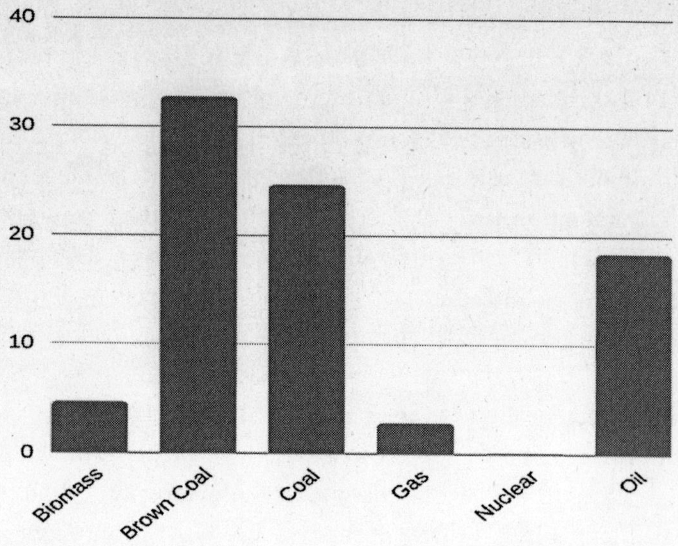

Data: Our World in Data[33]

Brown coal, coal and oil are the most prevalent and evidently also the most dangerous forms of energy production. Nuclear energy, on the other hand, is marked as a comparatively safer form of energy. The burning of fossil fuels and biomass in itself causes up to over three million deaths annually.[34] The coal industry is the most dangerous energy occupation as is evident across the many coal-related accidents in history including the explosion at Benxihu Colliery and the great smog of London among others. It is recorded to have killed more than 100,000 miners in the past century in the United States alone![35] Hydroelectric accidents have also resulted in a large number of casualties as in the case of the Banqiao dam accident in China which resulted in the death of about 230,000 people.[36] This is one of the many catastrophic energy fatalities related to hydroelectric power generation. Similarly, pipeline, oil rigs and gas explosions too have resulted in extensive loss of lives.

Another widespread concern regarding nuclear safety is the danger posed by plutonium.

Plutonium, a radioactive element is undeniably dangerous, but only if it is inhaled. In fact, the films used in solar panels are also made of dangerous elements such as Cadmium Telluride. Just like plutonium the chances of it coming in direct contact with people is very unlikely and is managed by strict regulations in both cases.

There have also been apprehensions with regard to nuclear facilities being unable to withstand natural calamities. These obvious risks are well acknowledged by authorities and several stringent systems are placed to prevent damage in case of a disaster. Radiation leakage for example was well-contained during the Fukushima accident. More recently, examples of Hurricane Harvey in Texas and Hurricane Dorian Florida demonstrate how nuclear power plants can withstand natural calamities. In fact, in the case of Hurricane Harvey, many power facilities were severely impacted, except for the nuclear facility. Considered to be the "most costly" natural disaster in America, power generation through wind and solar energy was disrupted, several refineries were closed and there was an unfortunate event of fire and explosion in a chemical plant too.[37] The nuclear power plants there, however, functioned smoothly. These nuclear power plants are designed in such a way that they can brave through storms and hurricanes. It is even said to be able to resist an aeroplane flying into it.[38]

Despite the fact that other energy disasters have had more grave and fatal outcomes, it is nuclear energy that has been perceived by the majority as a dangerous form of technology. The nuclear scare in this regard has been exaggerated. For seven decades old industry, there have been only three nuclear accidents, out of which only one resulted in casualties. This is not to downplay the graveness of the Chernobyl accident, but to point out the comparatively safer track record of the nuclear industry vis-à-vis other forms of electricity-generating technologies. it is also important to note that the Chernobyl accident is more reflective of the misadministration in Soviet Russia rather than just the dangers of nuclear energy. The RBMK reactors used in Chernobyl wouldn't be allowed to function in most other parts of the world. Neither would they have such poor safety regulations. In fact, since the 3/11 accident, almost every country with civil nuclear energy programmes has reviewed their safety framework and has enhanced regulations.[39]

High Cost of Nuclear Power Production

Nuclear energy is deemed to be an expensive form of energy production in comparison to other forms of energy. Studying the economics behind each energy source to make a comparative assessment is not an easy task since it requires factoring in many aspects such as the cost of construction, operation, installation, fuels, transportation, storage, backup and decommissioning among many others. In addition, there also exist certain variables such as subsidies which could differ from country to country. In recent times, assessments of the economics of renewable energies have also included discussions on social costs such as rehabilitation of people in case of their displacement for plant siting. It also takes in account external factors such as environmental and ecological problems. For example, concerns about birds changing their migration patterns and the death of bats due to large-scale harnessing of wind energy are difficult to assess and put a price too. In addition, there have been more recent realisations about the problem of dumping solar wastes, at the end of their life. Since solar panels are made of hazardous elements such as cadmium and lead, these pose a risk to the environment. Rainfall could result in washing cadmium out of solar components, which tends to be a major environmental problem.[40] Apart from the cost to environment, the challenges to making an economic comparison of various energy production technologies would also include the cost to health, to assess the number of people who have suffered from medical issues such as hearing troubles due to wind power generation, air pollution-related deaths due to fossil fuel industry and cancer-related deaths due to nuclear energy, among the others. This would also include the amount of money each government spends to mitigate these problems. These issues are important for a better assessment but are usually not factored in. Thus a complete economic comparison is not possible.

Mycle Shneider, Founding Board Member and Spokesperson of the International Energy Advisory Council (IEAC) with regard to the economics of nuclear power states, "Nuclear energy went from the myth of 'too cheap to meter' to 'too expensive to matter'. So the first major barrier is very unfavourable economics. It is impossible today to build a new nuclear reactor under market economy rules. The second problem is that it is very slow to implement compared to its competitors energy efficiency and renewables. The third issue is the combination of barriers one and two: new-build nuclear is too expensive and too slow to represent a tool to combat climate change. In fact, *new* PV is now competitive in India with *existing* coal, forget about new nuclear. In reality, in some countries, like the U.S., new wind or solar *plus storage* is now getting competitive with *average* nuclear operating and maintenance (O&M) costs."[41]

However, it is worth considering that high price is a small trade-off, taking into account all the benefits nuclear energy offers. In addition, as nuclear technology has been developing at a rapid pace, it is estimated to become economically viable to most countries as well. This should not be challenging considering its high fuel density and high capacity factor. Owing to advances in technology and the liberalisation of markets, the performance of the reactors to have advanced with most of the reactors operating at 90% of its capacity.[42] The extension of operating licenses to has increased, which makes it more economical. Newer technologies in the nuclear energy field, such as the case of small module reactors (SMR), make smaller-sized reactors possible, at a cheaper price.[43] This has generated a lot of interest in many countries. One other advancement in nuclear technology is the Scalable Liquid Metal-cooled small modular reactor also known as the SLIMM. SLIMM promises to be an economical option with cutting-edge safety mechanisms and advanced security features owing to low refuelling requirements and the advantage of mobility since it can be deployed on portable platforms.[44] Thus, the issue of high costs does not entirely stand up to scrutiny.

Disposal of Nuclear Waste

Safe disposal of nuclear waste is often considered to be a weak link in nuclear technology. What isn't commonly known is that nuclear energy is not the only source that discharges dangerous wastes. Many industrial wastes such as mercury and cadmium are also highly dangerous and remain hazardous for an undetermined period of time. In comparison, nuclear wastes have a finite radiotoxic lifetime and can be managed effectively. Jonathan Lesser, the president of Continental Economics consulting, describes the problem to be a political issue rather than a technical one. This is true as the safe disposal of nuclear waste has been proven to be technologically feasible. Nuclear wastes are largely classified into three types based on the level of radiation and the way they are treated and disposed of: low level wastes (LLW), intermediate-level wastes (ILW) and High-level wastes (HLW). Most nuclear wastes are of low or intermediate level. In fact, about 97 per cent of nuclear wastes are graded as LLWs and ILWs.[45] However, HLWs contribute to 95 per cent of all radioactivity from nuclear power.[46]

LLWs are mildly contaminated wastes and are comprised of items such as contaminated protective clothes and gears, cleaning materials etc which are flecked with radioactive particles. Nuclear wastes have a definite radiotoxic lifetime and are known to decay naturally. LLWs take a few decades to decay and are disposed of at near-surface repositories. Stringent regulations make sure that these items never come in contact with the external environment.[47] They are usually incarcerated before they are buried. ILWs contain more radioactive wastes than LCWs such as steel components from the reactors, reprocessing discharges etc.[48] They are usually shielded before being disposed. HLWs are highly radioactive waste materials such as uranium spent fuel. The radioactivity in HLWs degenerates from an average period ranging from one thousand to ten thousand years or more (based on the level of concentration) to the same ore state that it was originally mined from. Currently, interim storage facilities are used to contain the spent fuel before its final stage of disposal. The spent nuclear fuel is very hot and harmful and hence requires cooling and shielding, both of which is provided by water. Once the fuel is removed from the reactor underwater, it is then moved to a storage pool. After a couple of years (or indefinitely depending on the waste) it is shifted to dry ventilated concrete containers. The final stage of disposal is envisaged in deep geological repositories. This form of disposal has achieved consensus about being safe and ecologically sound.

Waste management systems can also vary from country to country. For example, countries such as India, Japan, China and France reprocess the spent fuels. Reprocessing enables the retrieval of uranium and plutonium up to almost 97 per cent (96 per cent of uranium and 1 per cent plutonium). This not only helps in avoiding wasting of such valuable resources which can be further recycled into new fuels, but it also reduces the volume of high-level wastes to just 3 per cent.[49] Finland on the other hand with the help of Sweden is building permanent geological underground repositories to bury spent fuel. As the advancement of nuclear technology is rapidly developing, newer options to manage nuclear waste are also emerging. In 2006 Bill Gates started a company called "Terrapower" that is building next-generation nuclear plants. Its travelling wave reactors (TWR) use depleted uranium as fuel, and thus at meeting success will be able to manage the problem of nuclear waste disposal effectively.[50] Future technologies in this regard are also promising better ways of handling nuclear waste.

Proliferation Concerns

Another common concern about nuclear energy is that a civil nuclear programme could also enable a nuclear weaponisation programme. At a surface level, this may seem possible since nuclear technology has dual-use applicability. However, it is not as simple. To begin with, the safeguard system placed on civil nuclear programmes by global regulatory agencies are extremely strict and thoroughly implemented and thus are not easy to violate. Several global initiatives, international institutions and treaties have been set up to prevent, limit or detect the proliferation of nuclear weapons technology and materials. The primary treaty that prevents proliferation is the Nuclear Proliferation Treaty (NPT). Signed by 189 countries (plus Taiwan), the NPT aims to achieve the eventual denuclearisation of weapons. The NPT works along with the International Atomic Energy Agency (IAEA), which was set up in 1956 to promote nuclear energy for peaceful purposes and to facilitate checks and safeguards. The IAEA conducts frequent inspections of civil nuclear facilities, verifies records and audits, examines inventories, does sampling of nuclear materials, etc., to ensure that there has been no diversion of nuclear materials from the civil nuclear programme to a nuclear weapons programme. In addition, materials required to build nuclear weapons are also strictly controlled under institutions such as the Nuclear Suppliers Group (NSG) which regulates the export of sensitive nuclear technology and The Zangger Committee, which prevents the proliferation of nuclear materials from the peaceful use of nuclear programmes to weaponisation programmes. Thus any attempt to build a weapon is unlikely to go unnoticed.

These safeguards are supported by diplomatic and economic processes in the forms of international sanctions, economic blockades, etc., which would coalesce to be a major deterrent to develop a nuclear weapons programme. This is evident from the fact that so many countries that have developed civil nuclear programmes have not built nuclear weapons as is seen in the cases of Belgium, Sweden, Canada, Japan, Spain, Netherlands, Switzerland, Bulgaria, Finland, Austria, Hungary, Poland, Romania among the many others. Nicholas L Millers work titled "*Why Nuclear Energy Programs Rarely Lead to Proliferation*" validates this argument when he states that although political obstacles may not render it to be absolutely impossible to develop a nuclear weapons programme, it certainly does make it likely to be detected.[51] In this regard, Fred McGolrick who has held high-ranking positions at the Energy and State departments and the US Mission to the IAEA, opines that most of the states that gained a nuclear weapons arsenal did so "primarily through dedicated stance from nuclear-weapon states," and not through civil nuclear energy programmes.[52]

Many innovative mechanisms have also been developing to prevent proliferation such as nuclear fuel banks which maintains reserves of low-enriched uranium (LEU). In 2017 the first low-enriched uranium bank was opened in Kazakhstan, the mandate of which is to supply low-enriched uranium to countries that are developing their civil nuclear capabilities.[53] This would not only help in lowering the costs for the recipient countries but would also minimise the risk of proliferation of nuclear weapons through their civil nuclear programmes.

Conclusion

When it comes to electricity-generating technologies there is no silver bullet that is free from imperfections. For example, natural gas may be the cleanest burning hydrocarbon, but it also faces the problem of methane leakages; Solar energy is effective, but the disposal of solar panels is a hazardous problem that is yet to be satisfactorily resolved. Similarly, nuclear energy is efficient, but also has its own shortcomings. Assessment cannot only be made by comparing one source of energy-generating technology versus others. Rather, a diverse, and mixed approach is needed. The need for energy diversity was demonstrated during the polar vortex in 2014. When coal and natural gas couldn't deliver effectively, nuclear and wind energy made up for it.[54] Thus, nuclear energy should be an important component of the policy response to the threat of global warming and a vital component of an effective mixed energy basket.

The challenges to nuclear energy is summarised aptly by Stephen W Kidd who says "Each of the main arguments used against nuclear, such as safety, waste management, risks of proliferation and economics have been rebutted as far as possible, yet, the general anti-nuclear sentiment has been very hard to shift…if the industry's case is so strong why has it not been more successful in rebutting its opponents? There are four main reasons: poor communications, the sheer number (if not quality) of arguments utilised against it, the deep emotional currents that often swamp consideration of the facts in people's minds, and finally the changes in the political process in key countries…".[55]

The energy revolution that is urgently needed, can only be possible with a realistic energy strategy and any sound strategy in this regard is not complete without nuclear energy. This is because, although other forms of renewable energy such as hydro, wind and solar energy are remarkable, their limitations do not qualify them to achieve the decarbonisation goals all on their own, just the way nuclear power isn't qualified to achieve decarbonisation goals all by itself.

Considering all factors, nuclear energy appears to be a very attractive energy source by having high fuel density and high capacity factor in addition to its attribute of producing emission-free electricity. Moreover, it does not require storage or backup like in the case of intermittent energy sources such as solar or wind energy. Plus, it ensures grid reliability. All these factors make nuclear energy capable of meaningfully contributing towards a greener and more sustainable future.

Notes

1. "Nuclear Power Has Prevented 1.84 Million Premature Deaths, Study Says", *Yale Environment 360,* May 30, 2013, at https://e360.yale.edu/digest/nuclear_power_has_prevented_184_million_premature_deaths_study_says, accessed on July 4, 2019.
2. "Nuclear Technology for Climate: Mitigation, Monitoring and Adaptation", IAEA, September 18, 2018, at https://www.iaea.org/newscenter/statements/nuclear-technology-for-climate-mitigation-monitoring-and-adaptation. Accessed on August 30, 2019.
3. "What is the Paris Agreement", UNFCCC, at https://unfccc.int/process-and-meetings/the-paris-agreement/what-is-the-paris-agreement, accessed on October 20, 2019.
4. Robert Rapier, "Russia's Floating Nuclear Power Plant Has Great Potential For Decarbonization Trends", *Forbes,* October 20, 2019, at https://www.forbes.com/sites/rrapier/2019/10/20/floating-nuclear-power-plants-could-save-numerous-lives/#3a5da4012b17, accessed on October 23, 2019.
5. n. 2.
6. Eds. Masson-Delmotte, V., P. Zhai, etal., "IPCC, 2018: Summary for Policymakers", in *Global Warming of 1.5°C. An IPCC Special Report on the impacts of global warming of 1.5°C above pre-industrial levels and related global greenhouse gas emission pathways, in the context of strengthening the global response to the threat of climate change, sustainable development, and efforts to eradicate poverty*, World Meteorological Organization, Geneva, Switzerland, p. 32.
7. "Top climate change scientists' letter to policy influencers", CNN, November 3, 2013, at https://edition.cnn.com/2013/11/03/world/nuclear-energy-climate-change-scientists-letter/index.html, accessed on September 2, 2019.
8. Michael Shellenberger, "Why Wind Turbines Threaten Endangered Species With Extinction", *Forbes.* June 26, 2019, at https://www.forbes.com/sites/

michaelshellenberger/2019/06/26/why-wind-turbines-threaten-endangered-species-with-extinction/#6791f8c064b4, accessed on October 2, 2019.

9. "Drought: Hydropower's Achilles Heel",International River.org, May 16, 2019, at https://www.internationalrivers.org/blogs/433/drought-hydropower-s-achilles-heel, accessed on October 2, 2019.

10. Christian Borys,"Will the Nuclear Ghost Town of Pripyat Ever Be Livable Again?", *Inverse*, December 6, 2016, at https://www.inverse.com/article/24784-pripyat-chernobyl-city-2016, accessed on August 2, 2019.

11. "Comparison of Energy Systems Using Life Cycle Assessment", World Energy Council, July 2004, at https://www.worldenergy.org/assets/downloads/PUB_Comparison_of_Energy_Systens_using_lifecycle_2004_WEC.pdf, accessed on September 12, 2019.

12. "Nuclear Power in the USA", World Nuclear.org, at https://www.world-nuclear.org/information-library/country-profiles/countries-t-z/usa-nuclear-power.aspx, accessed on August 19, 2019.

13. Matt Wald, "How Nuclear Punches Above Its Weight", Nuclear Energy Institute.org, June 18, 2018, at https://www.nei.org/news/2018/nuclear-punches-above-weight-uprates, accessed on August 14, 2019.

14. Richard Rhodes, "Why Nuclear Power Must Be Part of the Energy Solution", *Yale Environment 360,* July 19, 2018, at https://e360.yale.edu/features/why-nuclear-power-must-be-part-of-the-energy-solution-environmentalists-climate, accessed on August 15, 2019.

15. "Geothermal Leads in Capacity Factor For Renewables", Real Clear Energy, September 16, 2014, at https://www.realclearenergy.org/charticles/2014/09/17/geothermal_leads_in_capacity_factor_for_renewables_108020.html, accessed on October 20, 2019.

16. "Darlington Nuclear's Unit 1 sets world record for continuous operation", Ontario Power Generation, September 15, 2020, at https://www.opg.com/stories/darlington-nuclears-unit-1-sets-world-record-for-continuous-operation/, accessed on January 19, 2021.

17. "Nuclear Power is the Most Reliable Energy Source and It's Not Even Close, Office of Nuclear", Energy.gov, February 27, 2019, at https://www.energy.gov/ne/articles/nuclear-power-most-reliable-energy-source-and-its-not-even-close, accessed on August 30, 2019.

18. "Wind Turbine Lubrication and Maintenance: Protecting Investments in Renewable Energy", Power Eng.com, January 5, 2013, at https://www.power-eng.com/2013/05/01/wind-turbine-lubrication-and-maintenance-protecting-investments/, accessed on September 19, 2019.

19. "Land Needs for Wind, Solar Dwarf Nuclear Plant's Footprint", NEI.org, July 9, 2015, at https://www.nei.org/news/2015/land-needs-for-wind-solar-dwarf-nuclear-plants, accessed on September 13, 2019.

20. James Conca. "Is Nuclear Power A Renewable Or A Sustainable Energy Source?", *Forbes,* March 24, 2016, at https://www.forbes.com/sites/jamesconca/2016/03/24/

is-nuclear-power-a-renewable-or-a-sustainable-energy-source/#18b41f44656e, accessed on October 19, 2019.

21. Bernard L Cohen, "Breeder reactors: A renewable energy source", *Am. J. Phys.* 51(1), January 1983, at http://large.stanford.edu/publications/coal/references/docs/pad11983cohen.pdf, accessed on November 2, 2019.
22. n. 20.
23. "Seawater yields first grams of yellowcake", *Newswise,* June 13, 2018, at https://www.newswise.com/doescience/?article_id=696069&returnurl=aHR0cHM6Ly93d3cubmV3c3dpc2UuY29tL2 FydGljbGVzL2xpc3Q, accessed on November 2, 2019.
24. James Conca, "Uranium Seawater Extraction Makes Nuclear Power Completely Renewable", *Forbes*, July 1, 2016, at https://www.forbes.com/sites/jamesconca/2016/07/01/uranium-seawater-extraction-makes-nuclear-power-completely-renewable/#593fe566159a, accessed on November 5, 2019.
25. Sumiko Takeuchi. "Is there a future for nuclear power in Japan?", *The Japan Times,* July 16, 2019, at https://www.japantimes.co.jp/news/2019/07/16/business/future-nuclear-power-japan/, accessed on October 18, 2019.
26. Laura He, John Defterios and Anneken Tappe,"US oil prices had their biggest spike in a decade after Saudi attack disrupts global supply", *CNN Business,* September 16, 2019, at https://edition.cnn.com/2019/09/15/business/oil-prices-donald-trump-spr/index.html, accessed on October 19, 2019.
27. n. 25.
28. Mamuni Das, "Coal shortage: Railways claims it is a last mile problem",*The Hindu Business Line*, May 20, 2011, at https://www.thehindubusinessline.com/economy/logistics/Coal-shortage-Railways-claims-it-is-a-last-mile-problem/article20245341.ece, accessed on October 17, 2019.
29. Puneet Kamboj and Rahul Tongia. "Indian Railways and coal: An unsustainable interdependency", *Brookings India report,* July 17, 2018, at https://www.brookings.edu/research/indian-railways-and-coal/, accessed on October 16, 2019.
30. "World's first floating nuclear reactor arrives in Pevek after 4,700 km voyage on Northern Sea Route", *The Siberian Times,* September 9, 2019, at https://siberiantimes.com/other/others/news/worlds-first-floating-nuclear-reactor-arrives-in-pevek-after-4700-km-voyage-on-northern-sea-route/, accessed on September 12, 2019.
31. Marin Katusa. "The Thing About Thorium: Why The Better Nuclear Fuel May Not Get A Chance", *Forbes,* February 16, 2012, at https://www.forbes.com/sites/energysource/2012/02/16/the-thing-about-thorium-why-the-better-nuclear-fuel-may-not-get-a-chance/#45ff55db1d80, accessed on October 15, 2019.
32. David Elliott (ed.), "*Nuclear or Not? Does Nuclear Power Have a Place in a Sustainable Energy Future?*" (Palgrave Macmillian: England, 2007), p. 4.
33. "Death rates from energy production per TWh", *Our World in Data,* at https://ourworldindata.org/grapher/death-rates-from-energy-production-per-twh, accessed on December 2, 2019.

34. Arati Halbe and Spoorthy Raman,"Wiping off fossil fuels could save 3.6 million lives", *Research Matters,* March 26, 2019, at https://researchmatters.in/news/wiping-fossil-fuels-could-save-36-million-lives, accessed on August 18, 2019.
35. "Coal Mining Steeped in History", *ABC News,* January 5, 2006, at https://abcnews.go.com/Primetime/Mine/story?id=1475697, accessed on September 3, 2019.
36. Justin Higginbottom, "Banqiao dam accident in China which resulted in the death of about 250,000 people", *Ozy,* February 17, 2019, at https://www.ozy.com/flashback/230000-died-in-a-dam-collapse-that-china-kept-secret-for-years/91699, accessed on September 11, 2019.
37. James Conca, "Hurricane Harvey Makes The Case For Nuclear Power", *Forbes,* September 1, 2017, at https://www.forbes.com/sites/jamesconca/2017/09/01/hurricane-harvey-makes-the-case-for-nuclear-power/#1c50af43625f, accessed on October 15, 2019.
38. Ibid.
39. Stuart Diamond,"Chernobyl Causing Big Revisions in Global Nuclear Power Policies", *The New York Times*, October 27, 1986, at https://www.nytimes.com/1986/10/27/world/chernobyl-causing-big-revisions-in-global-nuclear-power-policies.html, accessed on October 1, 2019.
40. Michael Shellenberger, "If Solar Panels Are So Clean, Why Do They Produce So Much Toxic Waste?", *Forbes,* May 23, 2018, at https://www.forbes.com/sites/michaelshellenberger/2018/05/23/if-solar-panels-are-so-clean-why-do-they-produce-so-much-toxic-waste/#2862f940121c, accessed on September 20, 2019.
41. Email interview with Mycle Shneider dated October 29, 2019.
42. Ed. David Elliott, "*Nuclear or Not? Does Nuclear Power Have a Place in a Sustainable Energy Future?*" (Palgrave Macmillian: England, 2007), p. 199.
43. Jonathan Lesser, "Can Nuclear Power Be Saved?" *National Review*, August 14, 2019, at https://www.nationalreview.com/2019/08/nuclear-power-clean-reliable-energy-us-should-embrace/, accessed on September 13, 2019.
44. James Conca, "A Very Fast, Very Safe, Very SLIMM Nuclear Reactor". *Forbes,* August 31, 2019, at https://www.forbes.com/sites/jamesconca/2019/08/31/a-very-fast-very-safe-very-sllim-nuclear-reactor/#4144f3cc2c5c, accessed on October 5, 2019.
45. "Radioactive Waste—Myths and Realities", World Nuclear.Org,at https://www.world-nuclear.org/information-library/nuclear-fuel-cycle/nuclear-wastes/radioactive-wastes-myths-and-realities.aspx., accessed on September 30, 2019.
46. "What are nuclear wastes and how are they managed?" ,World Nuclear.org, at https://www.world-nuclear.org/nuclear-basics/what-are-nuclear-wastes.aspx, accessed on September 29, 2019.
47. n. 44.
48. n. 55.
49. "Processing of Used Nuclear Fuel", World Nuclear.org, at https://www.world-nuclear.org/information-library/nuclear-fuel-cycle/fuel-recycling/processing-of-used-nuclear-fuel.aspx,accessed on November 10, 2019, at https://www.world-

nuclear.org/information-library/nuclear-fuel-cycle/fuel-recycling/processing-of-used-nuclear-fuel.aspx

50. Alan Boyle, "Inside the lab where Bill Gates' TerraPower is inventing the future of nuclear energy", *Geekwire,* August 11, 2019, at https://www.geekwire.com/2019/inside-terrapower-nuclear-lab/, accessed on October 3, 2019.
51. Nicholas L. Miller. "Why Nuclear Energy Programs Rarely Lead to Proliferation". Mitpressjournals.org., at https://www.mitpressjournals.org/doi/pdf/10.1162/ISEC_a_00293, accessed on September 29, 2019.
52. Ibid.
53. Dave Kovaleski,"IAEA opens new low enriched uranium "bank" in Kazakhstan", *Homeland Preparedness News*, October 21, 2019, at https://homelandprepnews.com/stories/38258-iaea-opens-new-low-enriched-uranium-bank-in-kazakhstan/, accessed on October 22, 2019.
54. James Conca, "Polar Vortex - Nuclear Saves The Day", *Forbes*, January 12, 2014, at https://www.forbes.com/sites/jamesconca/2014/01/12/polar-vortex-nuclear-saves-the-day/#1971650f6b08, accessed on October 20, 2019.
55. David Elliott and Stephen W Kidd (eds). "Time for a Fresh Look at Nuclear", in *Nuclear or Not? Does Nuclear Power Have a Place in a Sustainable Energy Future*? (Palgrave Macmillian: England, 2007), p. 77.

3. Understanding Japan's Nuclear Power Dilemma and Assessing its Future Trajectory

---

Introduction

A striking feature of the Japanese language is the ability of simple words to convey emotional experiences and perceptions. For example, in the Japanese language, nuclear power plants are called "atomic energy power plants". They refer to the word '*Genshi*' which means atomic, instead of using the word '*Kaku*' which literally translates to mean 'nuclear'.[1] This may seem like a fairly insignificant observation, but the choice of words more often than not holds remarkable connotations. The distinction, in this case, appears to be deliberate, in order to clearly differentiate between nuclear weapons (where *kaku* is used) and nuclear power for peaceful purposes (where it is referred to as *genshi*), especially considering Japan's atrocious history with nuclear weapons.

With the Fukushima nuclear disaster in 2011, Japan once again experienced the dangers of nuclear technology. The Japanese government since then has been grappling with serious challenges with regard to its energy policies. While the current Japanese leadership wants nuclear power to continue playing an important role in the nation's energy basket, the resumption of operations of nuclear power reactors, has been exceedingly slow owing to technical challenges, lawsuits and regulatory clearances. This has led to an increase in the burning of fossil fuels to meet the demands, which affects the carbon neutrality goals that Japan hopes to achieve by 2050. Amidst this challenge, there is also widespread cynicism regarding nuclear power among the Japanese public who have been calling for a phase-out of nuclear power. However, phasing out nuclear power is not an easy decision for Japan to make either as the country's energy grid has faced immense stress since the nuclear reactors were taken offline. In January 2021 for example, Japan experienced precarious levels of power shortages because of heavy snowfall and disruption of LNG supplies. At the time, wind and solar power weren't generating enough power either, with the energy minister describing the supply as "touch-and-go."[2] In addition to these problems, there is also a huge financial strain on the Japanese economy not only with regard to the clean-up costs of the Fukushima accident but also to make up for the lost energy supply.

In this context, the chapter aims to assess the various challenges faced by Japan and tries to envisage the future trajectory of nuclear power in the country. To do so, the chapter is divided into three parts. The first part sets a background by tracing the development of nuclear power in Japan and outlines the major developments in civil nuclear energy from the 1940s to 2011. The second part focuses on the Fukushima accident in 2011 and discusses what led to the accident, its effects and the efforts taken by the government to deal with the crisis. The third part studies the effect the accident has on the future of energy policies in Japan and tries to understand if the rising civil activism can translate into policy change.

Tracing the Development of Japan's Civil Nuclear Programme: 1940s-2000

Understanding the Factors that Led Japan to Develop a Civil Nuclear Programme

It was astonishing for many when Japan a seismically active country decided to develop a civil nuclear programme within a decade of witnessing the horrors of a nuclear war. There were several compelling reasons that led Japan to do so, the primary factor being the lack of natural resources in the country. During the post-war period, Japan relied heavily on imported oil and coal making the economy vulnerable to geopolitical and price volatilities. The war also had a dire effect on the economy. It is said that the Second World War pushed back about 50 years of development in Japan.[3] To make up for this, Japan embarked upon an ambitious course to develop the economy. However, for the economy to revive, it was imperative to fulfil the soaring demand for electricity. Post-war, Japan depended on hydropower and coal to generate electricity, which did not suffice. Hydroelectric plants which generated a lot of interest among the Japanese policymakers at the time faced several challenges such as high operational costs, maintenance issues, the occurrence of regular droughts, lack of sites for dams, etc. Other forms of renewable energy too posed different challenges. Thus, there was a search for alternate energy sources which would reduce energy dependency and provide supply stability.

At the time, Prime Minister Yoshida Shigeru put forth the "Yoshida Doctrine", which stated the importance of rapid economic development fuelled by technological advancement. It was in this context that nuclear energy found prominence in Japan. In addition, in the 1940s the electrical system in Japan was in its early development stage and families were allowed only a couple of lightbulbs.[4] Thus, the parable of abundant electricity through nuclear energy which was "too cheap to meter", had a strong appeal and bought in hope that this would be the energy revolution that Japan so critically needed.

Furthermore, Japan also had the institutional capacity to develop a nuclear power industry as it was one of the countries that had embarked on projects to develop nuclear weapons during the Second World War. Further research on nuclear technology however was banned by the United States after World War Two, including research and development of nuclear technology for peaceful purposes such as for medical applications. With the end of the American occupation of Japan in 1952, the scope for the development of nuclear R&D emerged once again. However, it only developed with the 'Atoms for Peace' programme introduced by US President Dwight Eisenhower.

The Atoms for Peace Programme was first announced in 1953 in a speech at the United Nations by Eisenhower, but came into fruition in 1957 with the establishment of the International Atomic Energy Agency (IAEA). Through this programme, the US disseminated nuclear technology to friendly countries.[5] The Programme had multiple strategic objectives. Primarily, it was designed to regulate nuclear energy. It aimed to prevent the proliferation of nuclear weapons technology and apply the expertise to peaceful purposes such as electricity generation, medical applications, etc. The programme was also designed to cultivate friendships with other countries and demonstrate the material benefits of allying with the United States. In 1955, Japan signed an atomic energy cooperation agreement with the US. Apart from providing assistance to Japan to develop its civil nuclear programme, the agreement also aimed at rebranding the image of nuclear power as not just destructive but also a beneficial form of technology. But even before the agreement was signed Japan faced another unfortunate nuclear-related accident.

Japan's "Kaku Arerugi" or Nuclear Allergy

Since the nuclear war in 1945, the Japanese people had developed a social condition called *Kaku Arerugi* or Nuclear Allergy.[6] Unsurprisingly, nuclear technology remained taboo in the country. Amidst this anti-nuclear mood,an accident in 1954 called *the Daigo Fukuryū Maru* or the Lucky Dragon Number 5 accident furthered fears about nuclear power. On March 1, 1954, a fishing boat called "Lucky Dragon Number 5", with twenty-three men aboard got contaminated by nuclear fallout from the test of a thermonuclear weapon by the United States in the Bikini Atoll. All the men aboard fell ill and suffered from acute radioactive sickness, even leading to the death of one crew member. In addition, sixteen tonnes of contaminated tuna from the same boat had been sold in various markets before the vessel reached Tokyo. Fears of invisible poison alarmed the people and an atmosphere of fear and panic once again gripped Japan.[7] Newspapers both locally and internationally reported the incident extensively, triggering massive protests against nuclear weapons globally. It was at this time that the first anti-national nuclear movement was created in Japan known as *Gensuikyō*. A popular movement, its petition against nuclear weapons gained over 20 million signatures.

The situation in Japan worried the US president, Dwight Eisenhower,who sent a memorandum to the Secretary of State asking "what things can we and should we do to improve our prospects in that region?". The then-acting Secretary of State Robin Murphy replied "The Japanese are pathologically sensitive about nuclear weapons. They feel they are the chosen victims of such weapons ... in the long run, the scientific interchange is the best remedy for Japanese emotion and ignorance and we intend to push such projects ... the most important thing we can do to help is to treat Japan as a full, free-world counsel. This is essential if we are to count upon the use of Japanese bases and their cooperation in any future conflict..."[8] It was also in this context that the US offered assistance in civil nuclear technology to placate the Japanese government.

Thus, by 1955 Japan began its national nuclear program with the passing of the Atomic Energy Basic Law. This law stipulated three principles: democratic methods, independent management, and transparency as the foundation of nuclear research activities. The Atomic Energy Commission (JAEC) was setup in 1956 along with several other related organisations such as the Nuclear Safety Commission (NSC), the Science & Technology Agency, Japan Atomic Energy Research Institute (JAERI) and the Atomic Fuel Corporation.[9] Because of the limits on the export of nuclear technology by the US in the earlier days, Japan initially took the help of Great Britain who helped in the construction of the first commercial nuclear power reactor in Japan in Tokaimura in 1956.[10] The construction of the British-designed Magnox reactor began in 1961 and was completed in 1965. In 1966 Japan officially began commercialising nuclear-generated electricity.

Managing Dissent

To manage dissent and garner the support of the public the Japanese government developed several approaches. Soft control tools such as providing subsidies, incentives and creating favourable narratives of nuclear power were undertaken. Other examples included conducting annual fairs in Yokohoma where only communities that hosted nuclear power plants could sell their products. In order to address concerns about food contamination that had affected the farmers and fishermen's businesses significantly, jobs were offered to the fishermen's community for giving up their sea rights in certain areas.[11] The government also created a programme called *Dengen Sanpō* or The Three Power Source Development Laws. Under this programme, money was collected from an invisible tax on all electricity use across the country. This funded about $20 million per annum to communities that agreed to host nuclear power plants.[12] In addition, the government organised public relations campaigns in order to create a positive image of nuclear technology.

The United States also played an important role in influencing the Japanese public to change their perceptions and attitude towards nuclear power. Recently declassified documents reveal that the CIA played an important role in swaying public opinion in Japan in favour of nuclear energy.[13] They did this in cooperation with the crème de la crème of Japanese society including politicians and media moguls. Psychological operations and public perception management programmes included movies and travelling exhibitions that propagated the potential benefits of nuclear energy. Newspapers frequently featured articles that described modern societies powered by nuclear energy, featuring technological innovations such as nuclear-powered cars and electronics. The growing interest in nuclear energy even began to be reflected in popular culture. An example of this is the "*Tetsuwan Atomu*" comics, literally translating to an iron-armed atom or Astro Boy in other parts of the world. Interestingly, nuclear weapons are evidently absent in the series. Instead, the theme revolved around the peaceful use of nuclear power as the series illustrated a nuclear-powered fantasyland.[14]

Thus, serious efforts were taken to make a clear distinction between civil nuclear power and nuclear weapons. As discussed earlier, the Japanese people use two different words for nuclear energy (*Genshi*) and nuclear weapons (*Kaku*). It could be argued that this is not deliberate and is just a translation muddle as they do not make a such distinction in the English language. But, this is perhaps because this distinction is directed inwards at its domestic audience. Internationally, using "atomic" or "nuclear" in different contexts doesn't have the same effect since "atomic bomb" and "nuclear bomb" in the English language is used interchangeably. In this regard, Hiroaki Koide, assistant professor of nuclear engineering at the Kyoto University Research Reactor Institute stated in an interview with Hiroshima Peace Media Center, that "The government calls what Japan does as '*genshi ryoku kaihatsu*' (atomic energy development), but they refer to what Iran does as '*kaku kaihatsu*' (nuclear development). But in English, they both use the word 'nuclear.' The government of Japan has used different terms for the two, but 'kaku' (nuclear power) and 'genshi ryoku' (atomic energy) are the same."[15] Semantics in this regard plays an important role in creating narratives and implying emotions. This was well recognised by the Japanese leaders especially, at a time when they wanted to promote their civil nuclear programme, amidst wide scale protests. Dr. Alex Rosen, one of the two co-chairs of International Physicians for the Prevention of Nuclear War (IPPNW), Germany in this regard states "In the process of producing weapons-grade plutonium, huge amounts of energy were generated—energy which could be used to produce electricity. The worldwide promotion of 'peaceful' nuclear energy was intended to whitewash the bad image of nuclear technology and clear the way for broad public acceptance. In Japan, this idea was taken up as well–especially by politicians and companies anticipating influence, power and big profits. In Japan, politics and the economy were traditionally closely connected. In the case of nuclear power, however, the proximity between companies, politicians and comptrollers soon exceeded every acceptable limit. But first, public scepticism had to be placated. The proponents of nuclear energy knew about the importance of semantics in Japanese thinking, and therefore first modified the language: While the word "nuclear" in "nuclear bomb" had been translated with the Japanese word "*kaku*" ("core"), the word "*genshi-ryoku*" ("nuclear power") was chosen for "peaceful" nuclear energy. Only due to this linguistic differentiation was it possible to contextually separate the civil from the military nuclear industry in the heads of many Japanese, even though both industries were closely enmeshed in reality…".[16]

Development of Civil Nuclear Capabilities

Efforts at managing dissent and creating positive narratives of nuclear power proved to be considerably effective. The government's success rate at building power plants amidst the protests was considered to be around 50 percent. That is for every two attempts made by the government to construct nuclear power plants, one went through.[17] Even the public attitude towards the nuclear power programme was slowly beginning to change.

After the first reactor became operational, Japan began to rapidly develop its nuclear programme. Tokyo shifted its focus to US-designed light water reactors while developing its indigenous capabilities. Eventually, Japanese companies purchased plant designs from the US and received licenses to build similar designs with the help of Japanese companies. Soon enough they were developing their own designs and manufacturing technologies.[18] By 1973, Japan had five nuclear reactors. However, over 70 per cent of its energy continued to come from oil. Thus, when the OPEC countries imposed a global oil embargo, Japan was subjected to the oil shock. Realising the vulnerability of high oil dependency, nuclear energy started gaining greater support. This provided Japan further impetus to develop its civil nuclear program. Furthermore, nuclear power became less competitive in the 1970s and 80s, as inflation and interest rates rose due to the oil crisis.[19]

Although development in civil nuclear energy was swift, it was not free of challenges. In the 1970s and 1980s, the nuclear industry was in a state of flux. The Three Miles Island nuclear accident in 1979 and the Chernobyl nuclear accident in 1986 had once again set off concerns of nuclear safety. The Japanese government however continued its backing of civil nuclear power. To ensure that their energy policy was not affected by the crises, they underplayed the graveness of the accidents. For example, at the 12th Group of Seven Summit, which was chaired by Tokyo two days after the Chernobyl accident, Japan tried to tone down discussions about the accident. Declassified records show that references to concerns of "radiation" were deleted from the draft of the G7 summit. But, the final statement spoke about how nuclear power would be "an energy source that will be ever more widely used in the future".[20] In the 1990s several accidents took place at the nuclear facilities which were tried to be hushed up by the authorities. This again led to more protests as public trust in nuclear technology was beginning to corrode again.

However, Japan was able to deal with public mistrust as its civil nuclear programme burgeoned. By 2010 Japan had 55 operational, commercial nuclear power reactors, which produced about 1/3rd of the country's electricity. Japan also became the world's third-largest producer of nuclear power. With a successful experience in civil nuclear energy, Japan had ambitious plans for the future. However, a fateful accident at the Fukushima Daiichi nuclear power plant in 2011 not only unravelled Japan's accomplishments on the civil nuclear front but also impacted the global nuclear energy industry drastically.

The Fukushima Daiichi Nuclear Disaster

On March 11, 2011, the Tōhoku earthquake measuring a magnitude of 9.0 hit Japan's northeast coast. The impact of the earthquake was so huge that it shifted the earth on its axis. Fortunately, the eleven reactors in four different nuclear power plants that were operating in that expanse could brave the earthquake.[21] No significant damages were caused to the nuclear power plants and all the reactors automatically shut down. However, soon after, the plants at Fukushima were struck by one of the largest tsunamis to ever occur in the history of the planet. Over 19,000 people died because of the tsunami which also caused severe damage to several towns in the region.[22] It also hit the Fukushima Daiichi power plant because of the insufficient sea wall surrounding the facility. It disabled the power supply and the cooling system of three reactors in the power plant. Typically, even if the power supply does not transmit electricity, the emergency generators work as a backup to supply power. However, the tsunami knocked even the generators out.[23] This led to the melting of three cores and hydrogen explosions. Numerous aftershocks too followed. Fortunately, this did not cause any more damage to the reactors.

Impact of the Fukushima Nuclear Accident

The Fukushima accident was rated 7 on the International Nuclear Event Scale. It is the only accident to be given the high classification, apart from the 1986 Chernobyl nuclear disaster. Although it was believed that there were no casualties due to the nuclear accident, in 2018 Japan announced that one person died from radiation exposure.[24] However, several studies have pointed out that there are no cases of radiation-induced cancer due to the accident. The findings of the 2014 report by the United Nations Scientific Committee on the Effects of Atomic Radiation (UNSCEAR) and the World Health Organization also stated that there is no evident increase in cancer rates because of the Fukushima accident.[25] However, the health effects of the Fukushima nuclear disaster are disputed. Currently, there are many ongoing studies trying to determine if the accident has any veiled health effects.

Meanwhile, there is little doubt that the psychological effect of the accident on the people has been dire. Trauma from the calamities, anxiety due to the dislocation, separation from family and fear of radiation caused immense distress to the residents. Shunichi Yamashita, a Japanese medical scientist in this stated "We know from Chernobyl that the psychological consequences are enormous. The life expectancy of the evacuees dropped from 65 to 58 years—not (predominantly) because of cancer, but because of depression, alcoholism and suicide. Relocation is not easy, the stress is very big. We must not only track those problems, but also treat them. Otherwise, people will feel they are just guinea pigs in our research".[26]

The nuclear disaster also had environmental repercussions. It resulted in hydrogen-air chemical reactions which led to the release of highly radioactive material in the surrounding area.[27] However, since the radiation diffused quickly, the amount of radioactive dosage that the wildlife in the area received decreased speedily.[28] A large amount of water too was contaminated with radioactive isotopes. This contaminated water was released into the Pacific Ocean. However, considering the inherent resilience of the ecosystem and the quick diffusion of radioactive isotopes, radio-ecologists do not expect it to cause severe ecological danger or cause damage to the food chain.[29]

The economic consequence of the accident was quite harsh too. It is estimated that the direct costs of the accident will be approximately $15 billion in clean-up in the next 2 decades and more than $60 billion in refugee compensation.[30] Apprehension regarding residual radiation also posed a challenge to the mostly agriculture-based economy in the region. Worried about contaminated produce, in the ensuing months, about 54 of Japan's trading partners employed trade embargoes on Japan.[31]

Lapses That Led to the Nuclear Accident

Naoto Kan, the former Prime Minister of Japan in his book "My Nuclear Nightmare", states "...It was my understanding at the time that the accident (in Chernobyl) occurred because the reactor was old and Soviet technology was inadequate, because Japan possessed unparalleled nuclear technology and superior experts and engineers, I believed that a Chernobyl- type accident could not occur at a Japanese nuclear power plant. To my greatest consternation, I would come to learn that this was a safety myth created by Japan's "Nuclear Village" (a nuclear village refers to a vast and powerful network of individuals and institutions in Japan with vested interests in nuclear power).[32] Rightly so, he raises the question of whether the Fukushima nuclear accident was avoidable. Natural calamities have occurred in the past at places where nuclear power plants are sited without causing significant damage. For example, the tornado in 1998 that hit the expanse where the Davis-Besse nuclear power plant was situated, or the Hurricane Andrew in 1992 at the Turkey Point Plant in Florida. In both cases, the emergency generators were able to keep the equipment functioning until the personnel could fix it.[33] More recently, Hurricane Harvey in Texas and Hurricane Dorian in Florida illustrated how nuclear power plants can brave natural calamities.[34] Even, in the case of the most grave nuclear accident, the 1986 Chernobyl nuclear disaster, the incident is largely linked to the misadministration and corruption in Soviet Russia. This raises the question of whether nuclear energy is inherently dangerous, or are these accidents a result of laxity and negligence?

Indeed, major probes into the Fukushima accident revealed several lapses in the system. This could be better understood by examining the accident through the Swiss Cheese Model of Accident Causation, a template that examines how safety systems can fail. It does so by comparing human systems to numerous slices of swiss cheese that is set next to each other. The slices of cheese represent different layers of defence. These layers of defence or safety barriers could be policies, physical security systems etc. Every system however could have defects or weak points, which could lead to flaws in the functioning of the overall system. These are called latent conditions and active failures and could be in the form of bad designs, lacunae in administration or recklessness by the operators. Most often, the holes in the cheese are not aligned. Thus, even if one system fails, the probability of a hazard is mitigated by different layers of defence systems or different slices of cheese. The different defence systems thus should be able to prevent a single point of failure. However, there can be cases where all of these defence systems fail to lead to a catastrophe.[35] This applies to the Fukushima nuclear disaster as well where several lapses, cumulatively led to the unfortunate accident.

The first latent condition was the siting of the nuclear power plant. Located in the Pacific Ring of Fire, Japan is prone to earthquakes and volcanoes. Aware of this, the Japanese authorities had assured its citizens that no power plant would be constructed on top of active fault lines. However, advancements in seismological studies, over the years have unearthed more active fault lines. Researchers constantly drew attention to the high likelihood of tsunami levels stretching beyond the levels that were assumed during the time of the construction of the Fukushima nuclear power plant. Tokyo Electric Power Company (TEPCO), the operators of the nuclear power plants at Fukushima, however, disregarded these warnings.[36]

The second latent condition was the age of the Fukushima Daiichi power plant. The first unit was built in 1968 and was set to be decommissioned in 2010. However, the Japan Nuclear and Industrial Safety Agency (NISA) granted permission to extend its operation for another ten years by TEPCO. Furthermore, many laxities by TEPCO were identified as having concealed several minor safety issues from the state regulators.[37] TEPCO even confessed to having not taken stronger safety measures in the fear of drawing lawsuits.[38]

Linked to this point is another latent condition of lack of transparency and accountability. Two weeks before the natural disasters struck Japan, several organisations, such as the Fukushima Environmental Protection Organisation and the Green Fukushima Future presented petitions to TEPCO to divulge guarded information on plant safety.[39] In 2012 the official report of The Fukushima Nuclear Accident Independent Investigation Commission was released. It stated that "...the Commission concludes that there were organisational problems within TEPCO. Had there been a higher level of knowledge, training, and equipment inspection related to severe accidents, and had there been specific instructions given to the on-site workers concerning the state of emergency within the necessary time frame, a more effective accident response would have been possible..."[40] The report also stated that the measures that were in place in case of a severe accident (SA) were feeble as they only accounted for internal errors and did not consider external factors such as natural calamities, although it is a widely known fact that Japan is prone to such natural calamities.[41]

Crisis Management: Eventual Steps Taken by the Japanese Government

In the aftermath of the accident, the Japanese government took vigorous efforts to manage the crisis. A few days after the accident, the government announced a larger evacuation zone around the nuclear facility due to the radioactive contamination that was being released into the atmosphere. About 1,50,000 residents were evacuated from the surrounding areas. The clean-up programme too began soon. First, measures were taken to cool down the facility by removing heat from the reactors and dealing with the overheated spent fuel ponds.

The task to prevent the release of radioactive materials began shortly. The Japanese government even revised laws and the "Reconstruction Agency" was established in 2012. A 10-year time frame was set for reconstruction. Most of the infrastructure that was damaged by the earthquake has now been repaired.[42]

The Green Zone, where protective gears are not required, has considerably extended to cover 96 per cent of the plant site.[43] Food products such as rice that is grown in the Fukushima prefecture were tested for radioactive contamination. Since 2015, all the products have proven to have lesser than the standard amount of radioactivity. The same was proven for the marine products from the Fukushima prefecture.[44]

Another body that was set up was the "Nuclear Regulation Authority"(NRA) in 2012. NRA was set up to be independent, unlike the previous organisation that worked along with the Ministry of Economy, Trade and Industry (METI). The newly formed NRA enforced what it called "the world's most stringent requirements" for nuclear reactors to resume operations.[45] All nuclear facilities thus underwent stringent checks and adopted strict safety measures.

Impact of Fukushima on Japan's Energy Future

Immediately after Fukushima, the mood of the nation was plausibly anti-nuclear. The 2011 Energy White Paper which was approved by the Japanese Cabinet stated that there was public distrust with regard to nuclear safety because of the Fukushima accident, and called for a reduction in their dependency on nuclear power.[46] Subsequently, fifty nuclear power reactors were shut down. Eventually, the government declared that they would phase out nuclear power plants by 2040 after the plants complete their operating lifespan. The immediate policy responses to Fukushima however, evolved subsequently with changing leadership. In 2014, reversing the previous government's decision, Prime Minister Shinzo Abe's government declared that nuclear power generation would be resumed once again, after getting approval from the regulators.[47] The New Energy Plan in 2014 which was approved by the Liberal Democratic Party Cabinet stated that nuclear power was "the country's most important power source".[48] The new policy even allowed the construction of new reactors. The Japanese government's impetus to revive its nuclear energy industry could be understood by examining several important factors, which could also help us in assessing the future trajectory of nuclear energy in Japan.

Factors that Determine the Future Trajectory of Nuclear Energy in Japan

Japan's Energy Crisis

One of the major reasons that Japan developed its civil nuclear energy programme, as discussed earlier, was because of its lack of domestic energy resources. Thus, when it suspended the operations of all its reactors, it was met with the same challenges again. As Japan's domestic energy resources meet less than 15 per cent of its total primary energy use,[49] the loss of its nuclear capacity led Japan to modify its energy mix. This new energy mix places oil and natural gas at the forefront, which has further led to import dependency. Japan thus, has become the world's largest importer of LNG, second largest importer of fossil fuels and a third largest net importer of oil.[50] This has not only created import dependency, but is also proving to be uneconomical, while increasing carbon emissions.

Clean Energy Factor

Currently coal and natural gas amount to 74 per cent of Japan's energy supply.[51] This dependency on fossil fuels to meet the urgent energy requirements after the accident has led to an increase in carbon emissions which further has major health ramifications. According to a study undertaken by Matthew Neidell, Shinsuke Uchida and Marcella Veronesi, the replacement of nuclear energy with fossil fuels post-Fukushima has led to not only an increase in electricity prices but also in public mortality.[52] In some cases, the increase in energy prices led to a decrease in energy consumption which further increased death rates during extremely cold weather. Another cause of mortality stemmed from the burning of coal which causes respiratory problems. According to one study, the combined number of deaths due to these factors are higher than the number of casualties from the earthquake and tsunami in Japan in 2011.[53] David Weinstein from Columbia University in this regard states that "if Japan had decided to keep all [uneffected] nuclear reactors open in 2012 and had met its energy needs by proportionally reducing coal, oil, LNG and other energy sources, I estimate that this policy would have saved 9,493 lives based on the air pollution of that year alone."[54] Although the instinctive response of shutting down nuclear reactors after Fukushima appears to be reasonable, the effects of it however have been dire. Considering that the energy sector contributes to 80 per cent of the GHG emissions in Japan, the government intends to decarbonise its energy sector. To do so, the Strategic Energy Plan released in July 2021 envisages renewable power to contribute 36-38 per cent and nuclear power 20-22 per cent of the country's energy mix for power generation by FY 2030-31.[55] These are extremely ambitious plans and would require fervent restoration and renovation of nuclear power.

Economic Revival

The Fukushima accident had a grave bearing on the country's economy. As Japan shut down its reactors, it had to import energy resources from other countries to fill in the energy void. This led Japan to face the worst trade deficit in its history. From 2011-13 the cost of energy imports in Japan was $40 trillion and a trade deficit of $227 billion from April 2011 to March 2014.[56] In addition, the average electricity price also shot up to 25 per cent in households and to 38 per cent in industries.[57] Some studies indicate that if Japan had continued with the decision of phasing out nuclear power, as the earlier government had envisaged, it would have ravaged the economy further. According to the Japanese Institute of Energy Economics, the fossil fuel imports would have set off an outflow of national wealth equivalent to 0.6 per cent of Japan's gross domestic product.[58]

Furthermore, as there is a gradual revival of interest in nuclear power by many countries around the world, the government and the nuclear industry hopes to civil export nuclear technology and infrastructure to these foreign markets. This would also help private companies in the nuclear energy sector in Japan, which were leading nuclear technology and energy suppliers in the past. In addition, China and Russia have been rapidly making strides in this regard, by providing nuclear technologies to newer markets at lower costs and creating spheres of energy dependency. The rising dominance of China and Russia in this field has thus raised concerns among several countries. This is speculated to be one of the factors that led Japan and the US to sign a Memorandum of Understanding in 2017, to promote the global leadership roles of both countries in the civil nuclear sector. Developing nuclear power thus has once again become important to resuscitate Japan's economy.

Challenges in Reviving Japan's Nuclear Sector

While developing a sound strategy to revitalise its nuclear power sector, Japan is likely to face several challenges that it has to deal with effectively. Linked to each other, these challenges are disparate and require distinctive and well-thought strategies.

Political Factors

The current Japanese ruling party-the Liberal Democratic Party (LDP) has made it clear that it considers nuclear power to be an important component of its energy basket. The LDP's victory on October 31, 2021 in the general elections in the Lower House led to the assumption that it would allow the government to retain its energy.[59] The LDP is expected to remain in power owing to its Komeito coalition. However, Komeito has a more anti-nuclear outlook and this may impact decisions pertaining to energy policies in Japan. Likewise, the future of nuclear power in Japan will be shaped by the victors of the elections and their visions for the role of nuclear power in the country's energy basket. However, sound and effective energy policies require long-term strategies and major discrepancies in it every few years depending on electoral outcomes may impact the country's overall economic development.

In addition, despite the efforts by the government to restart the nuclear reactors, the progress has been very slow. They are delayed either because of the stringent safety regulation clearances or because of the several lawsuits that are calling to do-away with nuclear power plants. At the same time, old reactors are also being decommissioned, which is delaying the much-needed increase in nuclear output.

Restarting the nuclear reactors is a complex process. In principle, approval from the NRA should suffice to start the reactor. However, there are political nuances to it as well. These utilities require the local governments' authorisation under the Safety Agreement. This is based on trust and good faith between local governments and the utilities, and is not legally binding. In this regard, certain issues, such as evacuation is an impediment tore-start-ups. This is because evacuation plans are not a subject of NRA licensing process. Thus, there is no clarity with regard to whose dominion the appropriateness of evacuation plans lie, or even to who determines it.[60]

Challenges in the Clean-up Programme

A decade since the accident, a lot of clean- up work in the Fukushima nuclear facility and around it has been successfully carried out. Yet, a lot more remains. It appears to be a long-drawn process, as experts cite at least several decades to complete the job. Lake Barrett, senior advisor to TEPCO in this regard states, "It's of the magnitude of putting a man on the moon…Unless there's an acceleration, I would not be surprised if it takes 60 years or so."[61] Considering the complexities of the clean-up process and the scale of the project, more sophisticated and specialised technologies is required. Towards this step, TEPCO and the Japanese government is now developing next-generation robotics, to venture into parts of the facilities where humans can't go due to high levels of radiation. But several challenges subsist even in this endeavour, for example, the robots sent in earlier were damaged severely due to the high gamma radiation. In addition, there lies the problem of dealing with contaminated water. While 62 out of the 63 radioactive elements have been successfully removed, solution to remove one element called the tritium, a radioactive isotope of hydrogen, is yet to be found. The decision to release the water into the sea also involves a lot of complications. For example, it would not be taken well by the local fisherman who took years to revive their industry after the accident. In addition, South Korea has also expressed concern over the effect it would have on its seafood. There also exist other challenges such as lack of storage space for spent fuel and lack of storage of contaminated water among others that require plausible solutions.

Anti-Nuclear Sentiments

One of the biggest challenges that the policymakers in Japan are facing today is a lack of public trust in nuclear technology. Unsurprisingly and for well-founded reasons, nuclear fear has once again gripped the country. A poll that was undertaken in 2015 by Japan Atomic Energy Relations Organization reflects this fear. The results of the poll revealed that almost 50 per cent of the respondents said that nuclear energy should be abolished gradually, and another 14.8 per cent said that it should be abolished immediately. Only about 10 per cent of the respondents believe that nuclear energy use should be continued and less than 2 per cent of the respondents thought that it should increase.[62] In 2016, another survey was conducted by the Japanese newspaper *Asahi Shimbun*. The results of this survey were even more disapproving of nuclear power, where 57 per cent of the respondents were against the restarting of nuclear power plants even if they fulfilled all the safety requirements. Seventy-three per cent of the respondents supported the phasing out of nuclear power altogether. Another 14 per cent backed the immediate shutdown of the nuclear power plants.[63]

The lack of honesty by TEPCO officials which was revealed in the inquiries after Fukushima is one of the major causes of the lack of public confidence in the nuclear industry. Anti-nuclear protests drew out for a long time after the Fukushima accident. Newer, innovative initiatives also developed in this process. An example of this is the "Safecast Project", which focuses on "citizen science". This inclusive setup encourages the citizens to participate in data collection, calculation and analysis in various fields such as ecology and biodiversity. Using modern, web-based platforms they carry out research themselves. Their research findings challenge the facts and figures presented by the government and utilities such as TEPCO, the reliability of whose data collection and analysis methodology has been long disputed.[64] This stems from the lack of transparency of the power utilities and has damaged the credibility of TEPCO immensely.

Dissent in Japan, however, is a complex matter with several nuances. While the larger public mood is anti-nuclear they have not mobilised it forcefully.[65] While the protests were in full swing after the Fukushima accident, they have slackened over the years. This is perhaps because the efficacy of protests depends on the social and cultural attributes of the dissenters and the tools used by the officials. However, it could also be linked to other factors such as non-responsiveness from the government. An article in *Japan Times* by Mizuho Aoki covers various aspects of the anti- nuclear protests in Japan. One of the subjects she interviewed for the piece states "I have a sense of crisis about the current state of things. I guess people are tired of speaking up, as nobody (in the government) seems to listen to them."[66] However, interestingly, the anti- nuclear factor was also not reflected in the elections. While most polls indicate the anti-nuclear mood in Japan, when it came to elections, citizens voted for Shinzo Abe as their new Prime Minister in 2012, despite his popular pro-nuclear stance. This raises questions such as if the election represented a choice that the Japanese people had to make between immediate economic recovery over long-term safety concerns. It could however also be reflective of other factors such as leadership, management capabilities, etc.

Post-Fukushima Japan faced a huge dilemma of whether to do away with nuclear or not. They had no easy choices and were faced with complex trade-off's. While the public sentiment was anti-nuclear, doing away with nuclear energy completely would pose severe challenges to their economy and energy policies. The Japanese government eventually decided to continue to employ nuclear power in their energy basket, despite the anti- nuclear sentiments among the public. This, however, does not mean that public opinion was not considered by the Japanese authorities. The fact that all reactors are temporarily shut down since the Fukushima accident, and are being resumed only after clearing extremely stringent safety checks and regulations, demonstrates that the Japanese government has acknowledged the concerns of its citizens well while taking pragmatic steps to protect their economy.

Lessons from Fukushima

As unfortunate as the Fukushima accident was, it did however provide adequate lessons to the world. It brought in the realisation that there is no space for even minor carelessness and laxity. It reset the safety norms followed by other countries. Immediately after Fukushima, all the countries with civil nuclear capabilities reviewed their safety systems and re-examined their emergency preparedness plans. Some even halted their operations until their safety checks were tested and verified. In addition, it brought to light the importance of transparency by authorities to maintain credibility, and thus by extension to garner public support. The Fukushima accident also revealed important realisations to both sides of the nuclear debate. To the ones supporting nuclear power, it exposed the dangers of nuclear technology and made clear that the slightest recklessness could lead to a big catastrophe on the other hand, it also invalidated the claims of anti-nuclear proponents, who exaggerated the effects of nuclear accident.

Conclusion

The Japanese people are known to have a strong and indomitable spirit which they have demonstrated numerous times in the past. Within two decades of being attacked by nuclear bombs, they were able to use the same technology to generate power and fuel their development. The Japanese government's decision to start the torch in Fukushima for the 2020 Olympics only goes to show the continuity of this spirit. It attempts to illustrate how the country has bounced right back within a decade of the unfortunate Fukushima accident. The Japanese government also deserves credit for acknowledging the mistakes and dealing with them transparently. The efforts taken by the government after the Fukushima accident to increase safety measures have been commendable and beneficial to the nuclear industry worldwide.

The future of nuclear energy in Japan currently appears to be uncertain. New construction of reactors in the future will depend on how Japan effectively Japan manages to deal with its energy and economic challenges. In this regard, Tsuyoshi Yamaguchi, the Environment Minister of Japan stated" We are still not at a stage where we can discuss building new nuclear power plants".[67] However in the short-run, it appears that nuclear reactors will continue to run, at least until they meet their operational life-times.

Considering the absence of an alternate indigenous source of energy for Japan and the importance of nuclear energy for economic and environmental reasons, it would be difficult for Japan to do away with nuclear energy completely. In addition, completely phasing out nuclear energy is not a practical solution. This would not only lead to drastic increase in electricity prices, increasing the burden on households by $10 billion ($115 per household), but would also lead to a loss of jobs. The Institute of Energy Economics Japan (IEEJ) estimates that this would set an annual $11 billion decline in corporate tax revenue.[68]

However, other factors could impact the nuclear discourse that Japan has embarked on. Political uncertainty and leadership are one such important factors that could determine the future of nuclear energy in Japan. In addition, Japan is mired in several complex challenges that need to be addressed effectively. Garnering public support for one requires increased communication with the citizens. Nuclear issues are shrouded in confidentiality, thus the inscrutability and secrecy of the unknown tend to fuel fear. More transparency and information dissemination could go a long way in quelling the fears of the public and garnering support. It would do Japan well to revisit the principles of democratic methods, independent management and transparency upon which the Atomic Energy Basic Law was premised on.

While the future of nuclear power in Japan appears to be uncertain, it would however be sardonic, if the country that hosted the naissance of the world's first climate pact to reduce greenhouse gas emissions, the Kyoto Protocol, scales back on its most important source of achieving its green commitments.

Notes

1. Scott Wilson, "Haruki Murakami's Solution to Nuclear Power Debate: Just Call It 'Nuclear Power'", *Japan Today*, April 10, 2015, at https://japantoday.com/category/national/haruki-murakamis-solution-to-nuclear-power-debate-just-call-it-nuclear-power, accessed on December 24, 2019.
2. "Nuclear Power in Japan", World-nuclear.org, at http://www.world-nuclear.org/information-library/country-profiles/countries-g-n/japan-nuclear-power.aspx, accessed on January 26, 2022.
3. Craig Nelson, "The Energy of a Bright Tomorrow': The Rise of Nuclear Power in Japan", *Origins,* vol. 4, issue 9, June 2011, at https://origins.osu.edu/article/energy-bright-tomorrow-rise-nuclear-power-japan, accessed on February 2, 2020.
4. Olga Belogolova and National Journal, "Why Japan Can't Quit Nuclear Power", *The Atlantic,* February 14, 2020, at https://www.theatlantic.com/politics/archive/2013/02/why-japan-cant-quit-nuclear-power/437028/,accessed on February 22, 2020.
5. Medhurst, M.J. "Atoms for Peace and Nuclear Hegemony: The Rhetorical Structure of a Cold War Campaign", *Armed Forces And Society,* 23(1), pp. 571–593, accessed on January 20, 2020.
6. Daniel P. Aldrich , "Post-Crisis Japanese Nuclear Policy: From Top-Down Directives to Bottom-Up Activism", *East West Center,* n. 103, January 2012, at https://www.Eastwestcenter.Org/Sites/Default/Files/Private/Api103.Pdf, accessed on January 22, 2020.
7. n. 3.
8. Ibid.
9. n. 2.
10. Kennedy Maize, "A Short History of Nuclear Power in Japan", *powermag.com,* March 14, 2011, at https://www.powermag.com/blog/a-short-history-of-nuclear-power-in-japan/,accessed on March 30, 2020.
11. Daniel P. Aldrich, "With a Mighty Hand", *News Republic,* March 19, 2011, at https://newrepublic.com/article/85463/japan-nuclear-power-regulation, accessed on February 3, 2020.
12. Ibid.
13. Richard Krooth, Morris Edelson, Hiroshi Fukurai, "Nuclear Tsunami: The Japanese Government and America's Role in the Fukushima Disaster" (Lexington Books: United States, 2015), p. xv.
14. n. 3.

15. Yumi Kanazaki and Yoko Yamamoto, "Fukushima and Hiroshima: Impact on the A-bombed city, Part 3", *Hiroshima Peace Media Center*, July 25, 2011, at http://www.hiroshimapeacemedia.jp/?p=28547, accessed on March 2, 2020.
16. Dr. Alex Rosen, "Yin and Yang – why Japan accepted nuclear energy despite Hiroshima and Nagasaki, *IPPNW*, at https://www.ippnw.eu/print/en/abolition-of-nuclear-weapons/artikel/aa4d551dedbd49773584c5a89842cbee/yin-and-yang-why-japan-accepted.html, accessed on May 1, 2020.
17. n. 11.
18. n. 2.
19. "Responses After Chernobyl and Fukushima Comparative Analysis of Germany and The Netherlands as Amplified Examples", Laka.org, March 5, 2012, at https://www.laka.org/info/publicaties/2012-chernobyl-fukushima.pdf,accessed on February 5, 2020.
20. "Japan downplayed Chernobyl concerns at G-7 for energy policy's sake, documents show", *The Japan Times,* December 20, 2017, at https://www.japantimes.co.jp/news/2017/12/20/national/history/japan-downplayed-chernobyl-concerns-g-7-energy-policys-sake-declassified-documents/, accessed on January 28, 2020.
21. "2011 Japan earthquake and tsunami: Facts, FAQs, and how to help",World Vision.org, at https://www.worldvision.org/disaster-relief-news-stories/2011-japan-earthquake-and-tsunami-facts. Accessed on December 26, 2020.
22. "Fukushima Daiichi Accident", World-Nuclear.org, at https://www.world-nuclear.org/information-library/safety-and-security/safety-of-plants/fukushima-daiichi-accident.aspx, accessed on February 10, 2020.
23. Naoto Kan, "My Nuclear Nightmare: Leading Japan through the Fukushima Disaster to a Nuclear-Free Future" (Cornell University Press: New York, 2017), p. 4.
24. "Japan confirms first Fukushima worker death from radiation", BBC, September 5, 2018, at https://www.bbc.com/news/world-asia-45423575, accessed on January 26, 2022.
25. "Increase in Cancer Unlikely following Fukushima Exposure—says UN Report", Unisvienna.org, April 2, 2014, at http://www.unis.unvienna.org/unis/en/pressrels/2014/unisous237.html, accessed on February 18, 2020.
26. "Studying the Fukushima Aftermath 'People Are Suffering from Radiophobia'", *Spiegel International,* August 18, 2011, at https://www.spiegel.de/international/world/studying-the-fukushima-aftermath-people-are-suffering-from-radiophobia-a-780810.html, accessed on February 20, 2020.
27. Dylan Sarkisian, "Effect of Fukushima Nuclear Disaster on Japanese Ecosystems", large.stanfdord.edu, February 20, 2017, at http://large.stanford.edu/courses/2017/ph241/sarkisian1/, accessed o February 18, 2020.
28. Ibid.
29. n. 27.
30. James Conca, "Shutting Down All of Japan's Nuclear Plants After Fukushima Was A Bad Idea", *Forbes,* October 31, 2019, at https://www.forbes.com/sites/

jamesconca/2019/10/31/shutting-down-japans-nuclear-plants-after-fukushima-was-a-bad-idea/#456d88f919a4, accessed on January 29, 2020.

31. Elliot Waldman , "The Unlearned Lessons of Japan's Fukushima Nuclear Disaster", *World Politics Review,* March 20, 2019, at https://www.worldpoliticsreview.com/insights/27673/the-unlearned-lessons-of-japan-s-fukushima-nuclear-disaster, accessed on February 20, 2020.
32. n. 23, p. 2.
33. John Sullivan, "Can U.S. Nuclear Plants Handle a Major Natural Disaster?", *Pro Republica,* March 13, 2011, at https://www.propublica.org/article/can-u.s.-nuclear-plants-handle-a-major-natural-disaster
34. James Conca, "Hurricane Harvey Makes The Case For Nuclear Power,*Forbes,* September 1, 2017, at https://www.forbes.com/sites/jamesconca/2017/09/01/hurricane-harvey-makes-the-case-for-nuclear-power/#1c50af43625f, accessed on October 15, 2019.
35. "Identifying error Swiss cheese model", YouTube, January 16, 2019, at https://www.youtube.com/watch?v=JRCMxfBULB4, accessed on February 21, 2020.
36. "The official report of The Fukushima Nuclear Accident Independent Investigation Commission", *The National Diet of Japan Fukushima Nuclear Accident Independent Investigation Commission,* 2012, p. 27, at https://www.nirs.org/wp-content/uploads/fukushima/naiic_report.pdfp, accessed on February 24, 2020.
37. Georgui Kastchiev, Ed Lyman, Mycle Schneider, et al., "An Account of Events in Nuclear Power Plants Since the Chernobyl Accident in 1986", large.stanford.edu, May 2007, p. 26.
38. Martin Fackler, "Japan Power Company Admits Failings on Plant Precautions", *New York Times,* October 12, 2012, at https://www.nytimes.com/2012/10/13/world/asia/tepco-admits-failure-in-acknowledging-risks-at-nuclear-plant.html, accessed on January 22, 2020.
39. n. 13, p. xvi.
40. n. 36.
41. n. 36.
42. "Efforts for Reconstruction of Tohoku", *reconstruction.go.jp,* https://www.reconstruction.go.jp/english/, at accessed on January 23, 2020.
43. Turner Jackson, "3Q: The future of nuclear energy in Japan", *energy.mit.edu,* May 29, 2019, at http://energy.mit.edu/news/3q-the-future-of-nuclear-energy-in-japan/, accessed on February 20, 2020.
44. n. 42.
45. "Japan Commercial Guide", *International Trade Administration,* at https://www.export.gov/article?id=Japan-Nuclear-Decommissioning, accessed on January 24, 2020.
46. Tsuyoshi Inajima and Yuji Okada, "Nuclear Promotion Dropped in Japan Energy Policy After Fukushima", *Bloomberg.com,* October 28, 2011, at https://www.bloomberg.com/news/articles/2011-10-28/nuclear-promotion-dropped-in-japan-energy-policy-after-fukushima, accessed on February 27, 2020.

47. "Three years after Fukushima, Japan forges ahead with nuclear energy", *DW.com,* April 11, 2014, at https://www.dw.com/en/three-years-after-fukushima-japan-forges-ahead-with-nuclear-energy/a-17560046, accessed on January 27, 2020.
48. "Japan reverses its withdrawal from nuclear power", *DW.com*, April 13, 2014, at https://www.dw.com/en/japan-reverses-its-withdrawal-from-nuclear-power/a-17563405,accessed on January 27, 2020.
49. "Japan is the second largest net importer of fossil fuels in the world", *US Energy Information Administration,* November 7, 2013, at https://www.eia.gov/todayinenergy/detail.php?id=13711, accessed on January 29, 2020.
50. Ibid., n.4.
51. "Japan plans carbon emission cuts, more nuclear energy", *The Asahi Shimbun,* June 10, 2019, at http://www.asahi.com/ajw/articles/AJ201906100044.html, accessed on January 30, 2020.
52. n. 30.
53. Ibid.
54. n. 30.
55. "Japan's election gives reprieve for nuclear: Correction", argusmedia.com,November 2, 2021, at https://www.argusmedia.com/en/news/2269158-japans-election-gives-reprieve-for-nuclear-correction, accessed on January 26, 2022.
56. "Manual Herrera, "Nuclear energy challenges in Japan", *Global Risks Insight,* July 5, 2019, at https://globalriskinsights.com/2019/07/japan-nuclear-energy/, accessed on March 3, 2020.
57. "Japans Energy 2018, 10 Questions to understand the current energy scenario", *Ministry of Economy, Trade and Industry Agency for Natural Resources and Energy,* June, 2019, accessed on January 31, 2020.
58. n. 4.
59. n. 55.
60. Tatsujiro Suzuki, "Nuclear Energy Policy after the Fukushima Nuclear Accident: An Analysis of 'Polarized Debate' in Japan", intechopen.com, February 6, 2019, at https://www.intechopen.com/online-first/nuclear-energy-policy-after-the-fukushima-nuclear-accident-an-analysis-of-polarized-debate-in-japan, accessed on January 31, 2020.
61. James Martin, "A rare look at the meltdown inside Fukushima Daiichi Nuclear Power Plant", Cnet.com, March 4, 2019, at https://www.cnet.com/news/inside-fukushima-daiichi-nuclear-power-station-nuclear-reactor-meltdown/, accessed on December 13, 2019.
62. Anne C. Cunningham (ed.), *Revisiting Nuclear Power* (Greenhaven Publishing LLC: 2017), p. 21.
63. n. 62, p. 22.
64. Daniel P. Aldrich , "Post-Crisis Japanese Nuclear Policy: From Top-Down Directives to Bottom-Up Activism", *East West Center,*n.103, January 2012., pp. 7-8, at https://Www.Eastwestcenter.Org/Sites/Default/Files/Private/Api103.Pdf,, accessed on January 22, 2020.

65. Mizuho Aoki, "Down but not out: Japan's anti-nuclear movement fights to regain momentum", *The Japan Times,* March 11, 2016, at https://www.japantimes.co.jp/news/2016/03/11/national/not-japans-anti-nuclear-movement-fights-regain-momentum/, accessed on February 2, 2020.
66. Ibid.
67. "Japan's clean energy strategy to push nuclear technologies", *The Asahi Shimbun,* January 19, 2021, at https://www.asahi.com/ajw/articles/14525409, accessed on January 26, 2022.
68. n. 4.

4. Understanding the Development and Future of Nuclear Energy in China

Introduction

The Fukushima accident in 2011 altered the course of global nuclear development. After the accident, there was a huge public outcry on nuclear safety, which compelled governments to reconsider their national nuclear ambitions. However, while many countries either stopped, stalled or re-examined their civil nuclear aspirations, China ramped up its nuclear capabilities. According to the International Energy Agency, China has had the biggest installed power capacity since 2012. In fact, its growth trajectory since then contributes to almost a quarter of the global nuclear capacity, having reached 2011 GWe in 2019.[1] For a country whose civil nuclear programme only advanced in the previous decade, China has come a long way in a short span of time and has more ambitious plans in the offing. In 2000, China had only three commercial nuclear reactors. Today, it has 45 reactors with 12 more under construction.[2] China's nuclear ambitions go beyond just powering its own development and also focus on exporting nuclear power technology to other countries through its Belt and Road Initiative (BRI).

This rapid pace of development, however, has raised concerns regarding China's nuclear safety and security, not only within its country but also in other countries which have signed nuclear cooperation deals with China. In this context, the paper aims to study the growth of China's civil nuclear programme, while trying to foresee its future trajectory and assess the possible challenges in this course. It also aims to understand the implications of its civil nuclear projects on its foreign policy and tries to examine the consequences of it, especially in the context of the Belt and Road Initiative. The paper is divided into three parts. The first part will examine the history and development of the civil nuclear programme in China. It will assess the rationale behind China's decision to develop its civil nuclear programme and the factors that are motivating it to press on. The second part analyses the effect Fukushima had on China's civil nuclear industry and the policy responses to it. The third part examines China's ambitions with regard to its nuclear energy programme and tries to assess its future trajectory, while also addressing the challenges that China faces in this regard.

I: History and Development of China's Civil Nuclear Programme

The market systems reform in China in the late 1970s was a key factor in transforming the country. Ending centuries of isolation, the economy opened up to pave the way for economic development. However as economic growth is contingent on ample access to electricity, the focus was to establish reliable power sources. This was a pressing need for China as in the 1980s, electricity demand increased at a monthly rate of 15 percent.[3] To meet these demands, China built thermal power plants which provided electricity at low cost. However, thermal power generation in China was met with several challenges. First, there emerged a problem of import dependency as the domestic coal reserves fell short to keep up with the rising energy demands. It also led to increasing Co_2 emissions, which not only impacted public health but also had serious economic repercussions. Considering the graveness of these challenges, in the 1990s China shifted its focus to explore cleaner and more reliable sources of energy. Thus, nuclear energy gained prominence along with other renewable forms of energy such as wind and solar power.

While nuclear energy in China developed only by the end of the last century, plans to develop nuclear power for electricity generation date back to the 1950s. A reference to it can be found in the First Five-Year Plan of 1953. But, this did not gain momentum until the Chinese city of Shanghai witnessed a severe power supply crisis in the 1970s, which brought nuclear power back to the discussion table. However, it remained there owing to bureaucratic scuffles between different agencies. It was only in 1978 that China officially declared its plan to develop a civil nuclear programme.

As the country embarked on a civil nuclear programme, it was decided to begin by developing Pressurized Water Reactors through both foreign collaboration as well as the development of indigenous ones.[4] The first reactor came into commercial operation in 1994, after which plans were devised to build four more nuclear power plants with the plan for 'moderate development of nuclear power' so that they could maintain technical expertise while limiting capital requirements. China built four plants with designs adopted from the USA, Canada, Russia and France, which helped them to test different designs and avert any common design problems.[5]

At the beginning of the new millennium, growing awareness of climate change led to elevating the importance of clear energy sources in China's energy policies. In this regard, the 11th national Five-Year Plan (2006-2010) of China acknowledged the importance of clean energy generation by not only mandating the shutting down of old coal-fired power plants but also shifting its focus on cleaner forms of energy with lower carbon footprints.[6] Having virtually no carbon footprint, nuclear energy began to grow in prominence. This trend was reflected in China's *Medium to Long Term Plan for Nuclear Energy Development 2005-2020*, which envisioned to achieve 45 GW in operation by the year 2020. China has been able to come very close to achieving this goal, currently having a capacity of 42.8 GW (as of March 2019).[7] This goal, however, has seen modifications over the years, most recently having envisioned 58 GWe capacity by 2020, in addition to having 30 GWe under construction. This was outlined in the *Energy Development Strategy Action Plan 2014-2020*.[8] In the last two decades, China has been able to develop its civil nuclear programme at an expeditious pace.

Today, China has 53 operable nuclear power reactors and 18 more under construction, with several more in the pipeline.[9] China has also developed its own indigenous design for a Pressurised Water Reactor and has achieved full fuel cycle capability.[10]

Rationale for Developing a Civil Nuclear Programme (1970s-present)
Several reasons led Beijing to develop its civil nuclear programme and focus on advancing it over the years:

To Mitigate Environmental and Public Health Concerns
China's rapid industrialisation led to high demand for power. To fuel its development, China's dependence on fossil fuels grew significantly. By 1990, the total energy consumption rate of coal in China grew to 76.25 per cent as it becomes one of the world's largest producers and consumers of coal.[11] Initially, as the focus was solely on industrialisation and economic development, China did not pay much heed to environmental concerns. Instead, it viewed international concerns about its Co_2 emissions as a ploy by developed countries to hinder the progress of developing countries. However, by the beginning of the century, the effects of climate change had become apparent in China, and impacted public health immensely. Having the largest carbon footprint amongst other sources of power, coal inevitably results in large death prints as well.[12] The excessive use of fossil fuels contributes momentously to air pollution. A study undertaken by physicists at the University of California, Berkeley, revealed that around 1.6 million people die annually (which amounts to roughly 4,000 people every day) in China due to the deleterious impact of air pollution. The study attributes this problem to the extensive burning of coal.[13] This has economic repercussions as well, as it leads to loss of productivity and a high amount of healthcare cost among others. In fact, the World Bank estimates that the economic loss to China caused by air pollution is about 6.5 per cent of its GDP.[14] Currently, China is the largest emitter of greenhouse gases in the world. Thus, as the problem of air pollution worsened, it became a strong impetus for the development of nuclear

power. Having one of the smallest carbon footprints of just 15g of CO_2 emitted per kWhr, in comparison to coal, which releases 900g of CO_2 per kWhr, nuclear energy has appealed to Chinese technocrats and policymakers.[15] In addition, it is an important source to achieve the goals set by the Paris Agreement, which is an environmental accord that was adopted by 197 countries, to collectively combat global warming. The Paris Agreement set a target to ensure that global temperature rise should be controlled below 2 degrees Celsius until the end of the century, while limiting the increase to lesser than 1.5 degrees Celsius. Numerous specialists around the world have explored ways to achieve this target. An important study which assessed the role of nuclear power in achieving this target in China, based on simulations, carbon emission funds and other factors revealed that major changes would be required in China's energy policies and existing trends. In pursuit to make these changes to energy policies, the study states that nuclear power has high-level expectations.[16]

To Fuel Economic Development

Since the opening up of its economy, China evolved from an agrarian economy to a global economic superpower in a matter of few decades. Along with the rise of its annual per capita GDP, its energy consumption rate has also increased proportionally. For example, China's rise of annual per capita GDP was about $100 in 1980 and increased to a whopping $7000 in 2017. Correspondingly, the per capita energy consumption rate in the same time period also increased from 600 kg to 2,000 kg(of oil equivalent).[17] By extension, this has had a proportional increase in the electricity sector as well. For example, in 1990 China's electric power consumption rate was just about 1/5th of that of the United States'. By 2013, China became the world's largest consumer of electricity, with its energy use growing by 8.4 per cent in 2007 in comparison to the overall global demand growth of 2.4 per cent.[18] This burgeoning energy demand is only expected to grow with the International Atomic Agency (IAEA) predicting that Chinese households will use almost twice the amount of energy by 2040.[19] One of the key factors that drive China's energy consumption is production expansion.[20] As it is crucial for the country's development, China is not willing to reduce its production at the cost of its economic growth. As coal has proven to be detrimental in so many ways, nuclear power has emerged as a viable, alternate option to support its development. These factors have elevated nuclear energy to play an important role in China's energy strategy.

In addition, recognising the need for cleaner sources, China has boosted its renewable energy capabilities. However, these renewable sources of energy, although very effective, have their own limitations. They are intermittent sources of energy, making them erratic and thus insufficient to meet all the energy demands by themselves. In addition, the dearth of high-voltage transmission infrastructure has led to a substantial percentage of energy from solar and wind power to go unused in China's remote provinces.[21] Nuclear energy in this regard is free of these challenges and offers several advantages. For example, in industrial parts of China that require a high amount of energy, nuclear power projects are developed to make up for the insufficient supply of energy.[22] It also has a much higher capacity factor, since nuclear reactors require less maintenance, need refuelling only once in two years and does not depend on natural or environmental variables. In addition, they can be built close to areas of demand. Recognising this and understanding the problem of uneven distribution of energy resources in China, the government has been boosting nuclear energy projects along with renewable power projects.

To Further its Geo-Economic Strategy

With the rapid development of its nuclear technology and nuclear programme, China has been using clean energy technology, specifically nuclear power for strategic leverage. In the context of a speech delivered by Liu Baohua, the Nuclear Energy Director of the China Atomic Energy Authority (CAEA), a Chinese media platform stated that nuclear energy is "an important cornerstone of strategic power, a vehicle for civilian-military integration, and a 'China card' to play in the country's international cooperation diplomacy."[23] In this regard, China's nuclear industry is now developing to be a part of the country's dirigiste business model. China is doing this by exporting civil nuclear technology and equipment to other countries through its Belt and Road Initiative. Increasing nuclear cooperation with other countries is not only expected to bring in more money to China but also to create energy dependency, achieve influence in these countries and increase its say in issues of global nuclear governance. This appears to be China's version of the United States'"Atoms for Peace"programme of the 1950s. The Atoms for Peace programme was so influential that vendors of the American nuclear industry sold reactors to more than 50 countries globally.[24] This not only boosted US ties with other countries but also paved way for it to become a global leader in nuclear technology, which allowed the United States to influence the formation of global norms in the nuclear power sector.

China has signed several agreements (or is in the process of signing MoUs) with countries such as Argentina, Egypt, Kenya, Pakistan, Romania, Sudan, South Africa and Turkey among others. In a meeting of China's political advisory body, a senior nuclear industry official stated that China could build at least 30 overseas nuclear reactors through its BRI project by 2030.[25] China's nuclear export sector operates in a systemised manner, enabling Chinese vendors to set up supply chains and establish new projects in other countries with relatively more ease than other countries. This is in distinct contrast to the US and European firms which once held prominence in nuclear exports but are now facing problems of financial challenges and technological stagnation.[26]

In addition, China is currently in the process of constructing its first floating nuclear power plant and has 30more in pipeline.[27] It plans to deploy it in the South China Sea, where it could not only support its offshore oil and gas exploration projects but also provide power to its artificial, militarised islands and gain a strategic advantage in the contested area.

Evidently, nuclear energy plays a very important role for China, offering not just economic, but also military and strategic benefits. Acknowledging these benefits, China decided by 2010 to "actively promote nuclear power"[28] and since then the country's nuclear sector has witnessed unabated growth. In 2011 China amounted to approximately 40 per cent of the reactor constructions globally[29] and had about 100 more projects lined up in the coming decades. However, as the unfortunate Fukushima accident impacted nuclear programmes around the world, it also threw a wrench at China's ambitious plans.

II: The Accident at Fukushima and its Impact on China's Nuclear Energy Programme

The Fukushima nuclear accident, in one of the world's most technologically advanced and experienced nuclear power generating countries, raised apprehensions among other countries with nuclear power capabilities, if they too were vulnerable to such catastrophes. While several countries such as Belgium, Germany and Switzerland decided to do away with nuclear power altogether after the 3/11 accident, China's reaction however was more balanced and calculated.

Policy Responses by China Post Fukushima

Temporary Suspension of Nuclear Power

Immediately after the accident, the State Council in China temporarily suspended the approval of new nuclear power projects in order to warrant higher safety standards. It also mandated a thorough and scrupulous inspection of its existing nuclear facilities to make sure they met with the necessary safety requirements.

Increased Emphasis on Safety

The Fukushima accident alarmed the Chinese authorities who had significantly accelerated their nuclear power development.

The national policy on nuclear energy thus shifted from "moderate development" of nuclear power to "steady development with safety".[30] Just five days after the accident, China's State Council declared that "…We will temporarily suspend approval for nuclear power projects, including those that have already begun preliminary work, before nuclear safety regulations are approved … Safety is our top priority in developing nuclear power plants…".[31] Since then, the Chinese authorities made several promises to ensure safety and presented several new measures to take this ahead. In May 2012, a new safety plan for nuclear power was introduced and in October 2012, the government released a White Paper on energy policies. This document paid excessive emphasis on the high safety standards of nuclear power reactors. Among the many initiatives, two important decisions were taken. The first was to restrict the construction of reactors in inland areas. This was done for safety reasons since reactors in inland areas would not have enough access to water supply in case of a serious accident. The other important decision was to adopt "third generation" designs for new reactor constructions. This was significant because third-generation power designs although has enhanced safety standards, it also costs more and take more time to be constructed.[32] In addition, new safety regulations were passed. This included the 2020 Vision for Nuclear Safety and Radioactive Pollution Prevention, which placed increased safety standards and stricter inspections. The Nuclear Safety Act was also passed which would ensure higher levels of nuclear safety. The Environmental Protection Department of China also issued new protocols that specified restrictions on site conditions for new power plants. These new regulations took into consideration factors such as geology and earthquakes while choosing potential sites for new power plants. New bodies were instituted to ensure high safety standards such as the National Nuclear Safety Administration and China Earthquake Administration among others. A report by the IAEA revealed that all Chinese nuclear plants were even presented with new power supplies and water pumps, as a precautionary step against flooding and loss of power, as a lesson from Fukushima. Along with this, new emergency response procedures were also created.

Impact of Fukushima on China's Nuclear Energy Programme

Slowing down of Nuclear Growth

The Fukushima accident slowed the pace of China's development in the civil nuclear sector. In 2011, China was said to have been considering almost 100 new nuclear projects that would be lined up in the coming two decades. However, the safety inspections and assessments delayed the timeline set up for the projects significantly. As approvals were held for new projects, it resulted in a slow-down of their nuclear programme. Although the government allowed the construction of coastal plants towards the end of 2012, it also revised its previously set target to achieve 80 GWe by 2020 down to 58 GWe.[33]

Continued Support for Nuclear Power

Although the Fukushima accident slowed the pace of the development of nuclear energy in the country, Chinese officials made it abundantly clear that the accident would not alter the course of their nuclear energy strategy.[34] Tian Shujia, the director of two nuclear safety centres of the Ministry of Environmental Protection in this regard stated "There is a guarantee for the safety of China's nuclear power facilities and (China) will not abandon (its nuclear power plants) for fear of slight risks".[35] China reiterated its ambitious plans in the nuclear sector by announcing at the end of 2011 itself, that China would make nuclear energy the base of its power-generation system in the next "10 to 20 years", having planned to add almost 300 GWe of nuclear capacity in that time period.[36] China's continued support of civil nuclear power was also evidenced in the White Paper on Energy Policy, released in October 2012, which reiterated the role of nuclear energy in China's plans to boost greener sources of power in its primary energy mix. The White Paper even made references to "invest more in nuclear power technological innovations, promote the application of advanced technology, improve the equipment level, and attach great importance to personnel training."[37]

Erosion of Public Trust

One of the biggest outcomes of the Fukushima accident was the corroding of public trust in nuclear technology. Concerns of nuclear safety created paranoia among Chinese citizens. It was reported that in the immediate aftermath of the Fukushima accident, panicked citizens hoarded bags of iodized salt in the erroneous belief that it would protect them from radiation.[38]

Public support for nuclear power also declined significantly after the accident. This is evident from comparing the results of polls taken before and after the accident of people living near the Tianwan nuclear power plant in Lianyungang. The first poll was conducted in August 2008 and the second in March-April 2011. Response to the statement "Nuclear power should be used in our country", got 68 per cent agreement in the first round of polls and declined to 32 per cent in the second one. Similarly, concurrence to the idea "We should quickly increase the number of nuclear power stations in China" saw a steady decline from 40 per cent to 17 percent! The number of people who opposed nuclear power increased from 13 per cent to 54 per cent.[39] These anti-nuclear sentiments were translated into widespread protests across the country. In fact, the following year, China's plans to build a uranium processing plant in Guandong province was also called off due to protests.

III: Assessing the Future Trajectory of Nuclear Energy in China

The future of nuclear energy in China, just like in other nations, is determined by several domestic as well as international factors. This section analyses these factors and attempts to envisage the future trajectory of nuclear energy in China, while discussing the challenges that it faces in this course.

Assessing the Current Trends in China's Civil Nuclear Programme

Optimistic Nuclear Future

Considering the strides China has been making in the field of civil nuclear energy in the past two decades, China's future in this regard appears to be optimistic. Not only has it achieved a reasonable amount of experience in civil nuclear power generation, but has also made headway in indigenous nuclear technology and designs. In addition, considering the urgency to tackle the challenging problem of climate change, China appears to stay committed to nuclear power to deal with the crisis. Projections made by official agencies also appear to be sanguine. The National Development and Reform Commission of China aspires to achieve the target of 200 GWe of nuclear-generating capacity by 2035.[40] In order to achieve these targets, several educational establishments to have been instituted which would help in setting a basis for the training of nuclear specialists. The Chinese government has also announced plans to develop nuclear power industrial parks which would not only provide training but also enable the development of its nuclear supply chain.

In fact, China has also gone on a uranium buying spree to support its domestic as well as international nuclear ambitions. It has been buying a huge amount of uranium from countries such as Australia, Kazakhstan and Namibia and is also exploring the markets of Canada, Mongolia and Niger. This is because its domestic production of uranium has ceased to meet its ambitious course of development. It is estimated that China may require as much as 12,300-16,200 metric tonnes of uranium in 2030.[41] China plans to procure uranium from the following sources to meet its increasing demands: From its domestic reserves, overseas resources from its foreign investments, etc., and purchases from open markets.[42] In expectation of its future uranium requirements, China has already begun hoarding uranium from these sources. In fact, in 2015 China's inventory had 85,000 metric tonnes of uranium, which is equivalent to 140 per cent of the total annual global uranium demand. This amounts to imply that

China is buying almost a quarter of the available uranium in the global market.[43]

The Chinese government is also encouraging innovation and technology development. This is evidenced by a number of floating nuclear power plants that China is building to safeguard its interests and provide energy to remote areas. In addition, China is also looking to export this technology to other countries such as Bangladesh which has a small territory with a large and dense population. China is also making strides in the development of indigenous nuclear reactor designs. The Hualong One being a key example of this, having earned the nickname "China's business card", considering its efficiency.[44]

Slow Domestic Growth Rate

As discussed earlier, China has reduced the goal it had set to achieve by 2020 significantly. From the initial goal set in 2009 to achieve 70 gigawatts of energy by 2020, it was reduced to just 58 gigawatts by 2020 in 2016. The decline in this target is speculated to be for several reasons. First, the Chinese authorities have mandated more stringent safety clearance's after the Fukushima accident which takes more time in setting up new reactors. Anti-nuclear protests too have led to the stalling of several projects.

Analysts such as M.V. Ramana and Amy King also argue that China has been entering into a phase "of new normal". This phase is marked by a lower domestic growth rate in the nuclear energy sector. They maintain that China is transforming into a comparatively low-growth economy, shifting from heavy industries to a service-providing one, which sees a relegation in energy demands. They contend that the electricity demand has reduced even in the past when the Chinese economy had undergone some structural changes.[45] Other analysts like Jiang Lin, Gang He and Alexandia Yuan, caution against the need to keep up with the changing trends in China's energy sector. These trends that they refer to are based on their study on GDP and electricity consumption for20years, which suggested that there is going to be a quiescent period in energy demands, specifically in richer provinces.[46] Numbers have also been indicating a decline in electricity demand in China. For example Thermal power plants in China operated for about 400 hours lesser in 2015 than they did in 2014. Similarly, there was a reduction of about 100 hours of nuclear power plants supply of electricity into the grid. There has thus been an electrical supply surplus in China. [47] However, it is not clear if this is a short-term or a long-term trend. Thus, a plateau or a reduction in electricity demands may continue in China, which may result in a slower pace of nuclear development in the country. This however does not necessarily suggest that the nuclear growth trajectory in China is pessimistic. Some experts perceive this as a "maturing" of the Chinese nuclear industry.[48]

In addition, Considering that China is the world's largest emitter of greenhouse gases, its environmental policies have a significant impact on the global fight against climate change. Lately, analysts have been observing a slackening in Beijing's renewable energy growth and an increase in its use of fossil fuels. Carbon dioxide emissions by China has increased by approximately 4 per cent in the first half of 2019. Coal consumption has increased, taking it back to the levels China had in 2013.[49] In this regard, it is important for China to keep the momentum of its green energy drive on.

Challenges to China's Nuclear Power Ambitions

While China's nuclear future appears to be optimistic, it is, however, mired in several challenges.

Safety Concerns

China's nuclear industry holds a safe record, with official documents and statistics suggesting that no serious accidents have taken place in their facilities. The few minor incidents that have taken place have been graded at a low degree of Levels 1 and 2 on the International Nuclear and Radiological Event Scale. The IAEA which leads teams of Integrated Regulatory Review Service (IRRS) experts to assess the safety of nuclear regulatory infrastructures of countries too stated in 2016 that China's nuclear safety regulatory framework for nuclear and radiation safety is effective. However, considering the rate of growth of nuclear power in China the experts stated the need for more efforts to ensure safety.[50]

However, these aspects when taken into account with other factors such as China's poor industrial safety history raises safety concerns. China Labour Bulletin, a Hong Kong-based organisation on workers' rights in this regard states that while China's safety record has improved over the years "...accident rates, death tolls and the incidence of occupational disease are all still comparatively high..."[51] Official figures estimate that there were on average about 81 deaths every day in the year 2019 from work-related accidents.[52] In addition, considering the poor working conditions and safety culture in China, there are concerns about how profits are given priority over safety. Mark Hibbs, author and analyst at the Carnegie Endowment for International Peace, in this regard says "China faces numerous challenges from its historically weak industrial safety culture and the strain on the regulatory capacity that has been exacerbated by nuclear growth."[53] A study undertaken by Jacqueline CK Lam, Lawrence YL Cheung, Y. Han, and SS Wang addressed the question of if China's response to nuclear safety after Fukushima was genuine or just rhetoric. The paper studied the promises made by the Chinese government and followed up the actions it took to enhance safety mechanisms. One of their research findings in this regard revealed that "... China's safety governance has been continuously challenged by institutional fragmentation, inadequate transparency, inadequate safety professionals, weak safety culture, and ambition to increase nuclear capacity by three-fold by 2050..."[54] In addition, the government of China has admitted to 16 safety failures in operating nuclear power plants in 2016. These safety failures were caused due to personnel errors and included reasons such as breaching operation guidelines and "pressing the wrong buttons".[55] The National Nuclear Safety Administration too in this regard has discovered a series of flaws and inadequacies in China's nuclear industry ranging from designs to materials. Although these may appear to be small gaffes and oversights, if there is anything that

Fukushima has taught regulators is that small negligence's cumulatively adds up to cause big disasters.

Concerns of nuclear safety in China are not just limited to their own facilities but also to the nuclear goods and services that they offer to other countries through their nuclear exports. This is even more alarming considering that China has been offering nuclear technology know-how to countries with lenient nuclear regulatory bodies. This holds larger implications a nuclear accident in any country impacts the global nuclear industry as a whole. Thus, China needs to focus on minimising oversights, increasing transparency, setting up institutional reforms, increasing quality controls and promoting a safe working environment.

Public Opinion and Anti- Nuclear Sentiments

Decisions regarding nuclear issues in China have historically been made without taking public opinion into consideration. In fact, when China first embarked on constructing nuclear power plants in the 1980s and 1990s, the petitions signed against constructing nuclear reactors were ignored and protestors were arrested.[56] Only recently has the government and nuclear regulators been trying to engage with the public. This is timely, considering the anti-nuclear sentiments that is brewing amidst the Chinese public. A survey undertaken by the Chinese Academy of Engineering in 2017 revealed that only 40 per cent of the Chinese public supports the development of nuclear power in the country.[57] As the dissension has been getting more vocal, it has also been impacting China's nuclear power programme. For example, in 2013 and 2016, plans to build nuclear fuel cycle installations were cancelled due to public objections. Protests also led to the cancellation of plans to build a nuclear waste processing plant in Jiangsu.[58]

However, questions about how effective the protests will be in the future remain. As dissent is carefully monitored in China, protests and demonstrations may be curbed if it gains more momentum, especially since the government considers nuclear power to be of national strategic interest. Xi Jinping has reiterated several times that social stability is a principle priority for him, having stated that "winning or losing public support is an issue that concerns the CPC's survival or extinction".[59] In this regard, the Chinese leadership has recognised the need to communicate with the public and has taken several measures to garner public support. This includes initiatives such as the Nuclear Safety Law. This makes several important provisions, for example, it lays emphasis on increased public engagement. Plant operators are required to hold public meetings with the citizens who live within 30 km of a plant site. These meetings also help the authorities to communicate the benefits of nuclear power projects such as with regard to providing jobs and public services. It also enables the National Nuclear Safety Administration and nuclear facility operators to provide information related to nuclear safety to the public, if requested.[60] Since 2014, the National Nuclear Safety Administration issued several notices and measures to augment the information available for the public. Their website too now includes more information on their nuclear programme. China General Nuclear Power Group, the largest nuclear operator in China also hosts visitors and works with schools to familiarise nuclear science to the public. They have been devising innovative ways to gain support and promote nuclear power by holding events such as "Most beautiful wedding photos taken at a nuclear power plant etc."[61] However, China's reputation with regard to its low level of transparency and high level of government control has resulted in the questioning of the credibility of the statements and figures that it puts out in public.

BRI: Mistrust and Concerns of Civil Nuclear Trap

As discussed earlier, China intends to use its civil nuclear capabilities through its BRI projects to push for strategic gains. This has raised serious concerns in other countries for several reasons. Primarily, this is because China has been signing cooperation agreements with countries which do not necessarily have the regulatory requirements to handle a civil nuclear programme. Several countries with whom China has been discussing cooperation agreements with are feared to have weak and lax regulatory environments. For example, Sudan recently signed a nuclear cooperation agreement with China to get its first nuclear power reactor. However, Sudan ranked 194 in a study undertaken by the Institute for Science and International Security which rated countries based on their capabilities to limit nuclear trafficking.[62]

In addition, there have been concerns of how China may take advantage of a country that it has engaged in nuclear cooperation with. It may give them strategic leverage and they may use this to coerce decisions in their favour in case of discord or tension with partnering countries. For example China could implicitly threaten to disrupt their nuclear power supply. The most recent example of this is the brewing tensions between UK and China. The relationship between the two countries are currently strained due to several reasons. First, China introduced a new security law for Hong Kong on June 30, 2020, which reduces Hong Kong's autonomy and increases China's power to punish protestors and dissenters. In response to this, Britain offered help to up to 3 million Hong Kong citizens who sought to flee Hong Kong, by making provisions for them to live and work in the UK. This was not taken well by China, who threatened that if the UK does so, it would have to "bear all consequences".[63] In addition, the Chinese company Huawei which was given permission to increase 35 per cent of the 5G network in the UK, has witnessed a rescinding of this deal. The recent meeting of Britain's National Security Council decided on new plans that would build western alternatives to Huawei. In this regard, the nuclear power deal between the two countries are speculated to be the next flash point, as China has threatened Britain to withdraw its support for their new 20 billion pounds Hinkley Point C power station. China General Nuclear Power Group (CGN) holds a 30 per cent minority stake in this project, in partnership with EDF.[64] China is well aware of the importance of this nuclear power project for Britain to achieve its decarbonizing energy goals, and thus has the leverage of coercing negotiations in its favour. In this regard, Anthony Glees, the director of the Centre for Security and Intelligence Studies at The University of Buckingham considers the Chinese involvement in Britain's civil nuclear power industry as a "ticking time bomb."[65]

China's nuclear export industry too has been facing several challenges. Foremost among them being the suspicion and scepticism of other countries. State-owned energy corporations like the China General Nuclear Corporation (CGN) for example has been speculated to be an agency for espionage. The United States has accused CGN of spying and attempting to steal the military secrets of the US. Correspondingly, CGN was featured in a list put out by the Pentagon, of companies that have connections to the Chinese military.[66] Recently, the Romanian government asked *Nuclearelectrica,* the state-owned energy company in Romania to terminate its partnership with CGN. Although the deal was signed 5 years ago to build two new reactors in Romania, it was scrapped after the Romanian Ministry of Economy and Energy, which is a majority shareholder of the energy company, asked to end the cooperation agreement due to concerns of Chinese investments and reliability of Chinese expertise.[67] As more countries are getting sceptical of engaging in nuclear cooperation with China, Beijing will have to craft an extensive rebranding strategy to develop its credibility to take its nuclear business further.

Conclusion

Owing to the numerous advantages of nuclear power ranging from strategic, economic, diplomatic and environmental benefits, nuclear power has emerged to be of strategic importance to China. The future of nuclear power in the country, thus appears to be positive as it is backed by strong policy and financial support from the Chinese government. The ongoing covid19 crisis has also gone to prove the efficiency of China's nuclear power industry. No immediate setbacks are expected because of the current pandemic. In this regard, Tang Bo, director of the nuclear safety inspection department at the Ministry of Ecology and Environment (MEE), stated that the operational reactors have not been affected by the pandemic as any of them had to be suspended and the construction work of new reactor units too have resumed construction work.[68]

Beijing's focus on nuclear power is also likely to remain in the foreseeable future. The annual parliamentary meeting in Beijing that took place in 2020 in this regard illustrated China's continued interest in nuclear development. Delegates during this meeting suggested that China should begin with the construction of 6 to 8 nuclear reactors each year, as it won't only help in curbing the problem of climate change but would also help in creating more jobs, as lack of employment has been emerging as a pressing challenge for the country.[69]

The global warming crisis has also become an important impetus for China to develop nuclear power, especially considering that it contributes to 27 per cent of the global greenhouse gases (excluding Land use, land-use change, and forestry) making it the largest emitter of GHG in the world.[70] While China claims to achieve its 2020 carbon emission goals three years ahead of its target,[71] it is important to note that its Nationally Determined Contribution to achieve the 2030 Paris Agreement goals are graded by the Climate Change Tracker as "highly insufficient".[72] In this regard, there is a need to accelerate its green growth policies, in which nuclear power can play an important role.

China is also likely to dominate the global nuclear industry. This will not only have domestic implications but will also have a wide range of impacts, from altering the global nuclear architecture to international trade and climate change mitigation. China's growth in nuclear power could also give rise to a new dimension to world power politics among countries such as the US, China and Russia. For example, former US president Donald Trump called for efforts in revitalizing the US nuclear industry in order to prevent China and Russia from creating spheres of energy dependencies around the world.

Although the future of nuclear power appears to be going on a successful trajectory, there are several challenges that require more attention from Chinese authorities. How China manages these risks and challenges, would go a long way in determining its future not just in China but in other nuclear power-pursuing countries. First, this positive trajectory could slow considering the increasing contradictions in China's green energy policies and the ebbing of energy demands as discussed earlier. In addition, matters of nuclear safety remain to be a critical challenge. Although China has ramped up efforts to enhance nuclear safety in the wake of Fukushima, it still requires more scrutiny. China's nuclear export strategy too, if not handled with utmost levels of precaution and safeguards could lead to disastrous effects in other countries.

These are important factors, which have the potential to change the trajectory of the development of nuclear power in China. In addition, other factors such as breakthroughs in alternate power generation and storage technologies could also impact this growth trajectory. All in all, the way China manages these risks and makes constant, systematic changes to manage them will go a long way in determining China's future in civil nuclear power development.

Notes

1. "Nuclear Power in China", World Nuclear.org, at https://www.world-nuclear.org/information-library/country-profiles/countries-a-f/china-nuclear-power.aspx, accessed on May 3, 2020.
2. George David Banks, "The Rise Of China's Civil Nuclear Program and Its Impact on U.S. National Interests", *ACCF Center for Policy Research*, January 2017, at http://accf.org/wp-content/uploads/2017/03/ACCF_China_paper_03.pdf, accessed on May 7, 2020.
3. Manpreet Sethi, "China's nuclear energy Scenario: three years after Fukushima", *Defence and Diplomacy Journal*, Vol. 3 no. 4, 2014 (July-September), at http://capsindia.org/files/documents/Defence-Diplomacy-Jul-Sep-2014-inside.pdf, p. 77.
4. Philip Andrews-Speed, Sufang Zhang, *China as a Global Clean Energy Champion: Lifting the Veil* (Springer, January 2019), p. 111.
5. Philip Andrews-Speed, "The Governance of Nuclear Power in China", *The Journal of World Energy Law & Business*, v. 13, i. 1, March 2020, pp. 23-46, at https://doi.org/10.1093/jwelb/jwaa004, accessed on May 15, 2020.
6. n. 3 p. 77.
7. "World Nuclear Power Reactors & Uranium Requirements", *World Nuclear Organisation,* May 2020, at https://www.world-nuclear.org/information-library/facts-and-figures/world-nuclear-power-reactors-and-uranium-requireme.aspx, accessed on May 10, 2020.
8. n. 1.
9. Ibid.

10. n. 3, p. 86.
11. "China Coal Consumption Cap Plan and Research Report: Recommendations for the 13th Five-Year Plan, *China Coal Cap Project,* October 2015, at https://d2ouvy59p0dg6k.cloudfront.net/downloads/china_coal_consumption_cap_plan_and_research_report__recommendations_for_the_13fyp.pdf, accessed on June 10, 2020.
12. Deathprints refers to the number of deaths caused by a certain kind of energy technology.
13. "Air pollution in China is killing 4,000 people every day, a new study finds", *The Guardian,* August 14, 2015, at https://www.theguardian.com/world/2015/aug/14/air-pollution-in-china-is-killing-4000-people-every-day-a-new-study-finds, accessed on May 21, 220.
14. Costs of Selected Policies to Address Air Pollution in China", Rand Corporation,at https://www.rand.org/content/dam/rand/pubs/research_reports/RR800/RR861/RAND_RR861.pdf , p. ix, accessed on June 12, 2020.
15. James Conca, "How Deadly Is Your Kilowatt? We Rank The Killer Energy Sources", *Forbes,* June 10, 2012, at https://www.forbes.com/sites/jamesconca/2012/06/10/energys-deathprint-a-price-always-paid/#33ab4771709b, accessed on June 3, 2020.
16. Xin-JianXiao, Ke-JunJiang, "China's nuclear power under the global 1.5 °C target: Preliminary feasibility study and prospects", *Advances in Climate Change Research,* v. 9, i. 2, June 2018, p. 138.
17. Mark Hibbs, "Other Issues Critical to Chinese Decision-making", *The Future of Nuclear Power in China,* Carnegie Endowment for International Peace, May 14, 2018, at https://carnegieendowment.org/2018/05/14/other-issues-critical-to-chinese-decisionmaking-pub-76316, accessed on June 2, 2020.
18. "Renewable Energy in China: A Necessity, Not an Alternative", *Wharton University of Pennsylvania,* April 20, 2009, at https://knowledge.wharton.upenn.edu/article/renewable-energy-in-china-a-necessity-not-an-alternative/, accessed on June 2, 2020.
19. James Griffiths, "China's gambling on a nuclear future, but is it destined to lose?", CNN Business, September 14, 2019, at https://edition.cnn.com/2019/09/13/business/china-nuclear-climate-intl-hnk/index.html, accessed on May 29, 2020.
20. Feng Wang, Haitao Yin, Shoude Li, "China's Renewable Energy Policy: Commitments And Challenges" , *Energy Policy* 38 (2010), at https://www.ourenergypolicy.org/wp-content/uploads/2014/07/China.pdf, accessed on May 19, 2020.
21. Michael Standaert, "Why China's Renewable Energy Transition Is Losing Momentum", *Yale Environment 360,* September 26, 2019, at https://e360.yale.edu/features/why-chinas-renewable-energy-transition-is-losing-momentum, accessed on June 4, 2020.
22. Zhou Ping, "Nuclear Power Development in China", *Special Reports, IAEA Bulletin,* 1987, at https://www.iaea.org/sites/default/files/29204784346.pdf, accessed on May 3, 2020.

23. n. 17.
24. n. 17.
25. "China could build 30 'Belt and Road' nuclear reactors by 2030: official", Reuters, June 20, 2019, at https://www.reuters.com/article/us-china-nuclearpower/china-could-build-30-belt-and-road-nuclear-reactors-by-2030-official-idUSKCN1TL0HZ, accessed on June 6, 2020.
26. Manpreet Sethi, "The Asian Nuclear Power Landscape: A Contemporary Examination", in *Security in Times of Uncertainty*. Asian Strategic Review 2017 (Pentagon Press, New Delhi: 2018), at https://idsa.in/system/files/book/book_ASR2017.pdf
27. Viet Phuong Nguyen, "China's Planned Floating Nuclear Power Facilities in South China Sea: Technical and Political Challenges", *Belfercenter.org*, November 21, 2018, at https://www.belfercenter.org/publication/chinas-planned-floating-nuclear-power-facilities-south-china-sea-technical-and, accessed on June 10, 2020.
28. n. 26, p. 134.
29. Jane Nakano, "The United States and China: Making Nuclear Energy Safer", *Brookings.edu*, June 2013, at https://www.brookings.edu/wp-content/uploads/2014/01/USChina-Making-Nuclear-Energy-Safer_JNakano.pdf, accessed on June 20, 2020.
30. n. 26, p. 121.
31. M.V. Ramana and Amy King, "A New Normal? The Changing Future Of Nuclear Energy In China", from *Learning from Fukushima: Nuclear power in East Asia* (ANU Press: Canberra, 2017), at https://press-files.anu.edu.au/downloads/press/n3873/pdf/ch04.pdf, accessed on June 13, 2020.
32. Ibid.
33. n. 31.
34. Hooman Peimani, "Nuclear Energy in Asia: A Post-Fukushima Perspective", *Journal Of Energy Security*, May 31, 2011, at http://sites.asiasociety.org/asia21summit/wp-content/uploads/2010/11/Nuclear-Energy-in-Asia.pdf, accessed on June 15, 2020.
35. Ibid.
36. Lt. Gen. Prakash Katosh, "Nuclear Energy—The Politics Of It" , *Indian Defense Review*, April 13, 2015, at http://www.indiandefencereview.com/news/nuclear-energy-the-politics-of-it/, accessed on June 2, 2020.
37. Ming Yang, Xin Yu, Energy Efficiency: Benefits for Environment and Society (Springer, 2015), p. 152.
38. n. 19.
39. n. 31.
40. "China's nuclear power output jumps 18% year on year", *World Nuclear News*, February 24, 2020, at https://www.world-nuclear-news.org/Articles/Chinas-nuclear-generating-capacity-continued-to-gr, accessed on May 17, 2020.
41. n. 17.
42. Ibid.
43. n. 17.

44. Sam Reynolds, "Why the Civil Nuclear Trap Is Part and Parcel of the Belt and Road Strategy", *The Diplomat,* July 5, 2018, at https://thediplomat.com/2018/07/why-the-civil-nuclear-trap-is-part-and-parcel-of-the-belt-and-road-strategy/, accessed on June 2, 2020.
45. n. 31.
46. Ibid.
47. Ibid.
48. Ibid.
49. n. 21.
50. "IAEA Mission Says China's Nuclear Regulator Effective; Should Continue to Enhance Safety Programme", *International Atomic Energy Agency,* September 8, 2016, at https://www.iaea.org/newscenter/pressreleases/iaea-mission-says-chinas-nuclear-regulator-effective-should-continue-to-enhance-safety-programme, accessed on September 10, 2020.
51. n. 19.
52. "Work Safety, *China Labour bulletin,* March 20, 2020, at https://clb.org.hk/content/work-safety, accessed on May 25, 2020.
53. n. 19.
54. Jacqueline CK Lam, Lawrence YL Cheung, Y. Han, and SS Wang, "China's Response to Nuclear Safety Post- Fukushima: Genuine or Rhetoric?", *Energy Policy Research Group, University of Cambridge,*at https://www.eprg.group.cam.ac.uk/wp-content/uploads/2018/11/1834-Text.pdf. Accessed on May 18, 2020.
55. n. 4., p. 114.
56. n. 17.
57. Ibid.
58. Peter Fairley, "China's losing its taste for nuclear power. That's bad news", *Technology Review.com,* December 12, 2018, at https://www.technologyreview.com/2018/12/12/138271/chinas-losing-its-taste-for-nuclear-power-thats-bad-news/, accessed on May 26, 2020.
59. "China Protest Forcing Nuclear Retreat Shows People Power", *Bloomberg News,* July 15, 2013, at https://www.bloomberg.com/news/articles/2013-07-14/china-protest-forcing-nuclear-retreat-shows-people-power, accessed on July 16, 2020.
60. n. 5, pp. 23-46.
61. "CGN wins honor for innovative social communication", *CGN,* November 25, 2017, at http://en.cgnpc.com.cn/encgn/c100035/2017-11/25content_58c264d74cc5492fa6c1bf33550a0d3a.shtml#:~:text=The%20%E2%80%9CMost%20beautiful%20wedding%20photos,%2C%20in%20Shenzhen%2C%20Guangdong%20province, accessed on August 10, 2020.
62. n. 43.
63. Lily Kuo and Patrick Vintour, "Hong Kong: China threatens retaliation against UK for offer to Hongkongers", *The Guardian,* July 2, 2020, at https://www.theguardian.com/world/2020/jul/02/china-could-prevent-hongkongers-moving-to-uk-says-dominic-raab, accessed on July 16, 2020.

64. Catherine Kennedy, "Risk to UK nuclear plants as China threatens to remove support", *New Civil Engineer,* June 9, 2020, at https://www.newcivilengineer.com/latest/risk-to-uk-nuclear-plants-as-china-threatens-to-remove-support-09-06-2020/, accessed on July 17, 2020.
65. James Cooke, "Chinese involvement in nuclear power is a 'ticking time bomb,' expert warns", *The Telegraph,* July 7, 2020, at https://www.telegraph.co.uk/technology/2020/07/07/chinese-involvement-nuclear-power-ticking-time-bomb-expert-warns/, accessed on July 17, 2020.
66. Tony Capaccio and Jenny Leonard, "Pentagon names 20 'Communist Chinese military companies' operating in US, sanctions likely", *The Print,* June 25, 2020, at https://theprint.in/world/pentagon-names-20-communist-chinese-military-companies-operating-in-us-sanctions-likely/448281/, accessed on July 16, 2020.
67. Ella Kietlinska and Gina Sturdza, "Romania Cancels Deal With Chinese Nuclear Power Company After Raising Concerns In January", *Epoch Times,* June 2, 2020, at https://www.Theepochtimes.Com/Romania-Cancels-Deal-With-Chinese-Nuclear-Power-Company-After-Raising-Concerns-In-January_3373821.Html, accessed on June 5, 2020.
68. "China says virus outbreak will not impact nuclear power plant construction", Reuters, April 15, 2020, at https://www.reuters.com/article/us-china-energy-nuclear/china-says-virus-outbreak-will-not-impact-nuclear-power-plant-construction-idUSKCN21X0B4, accessed on June 18, 2020.
69. "China to dominate nuclear power as Beijing bets on homegrown reactors", *The Japan Times,* June 2, 2020, at https://www.japantimes.co.jp/news/2020/06/02/business/china-nuclear-power-homegrown-reactors/, accessed on July 20, 2020.
70. "China, Country Summary", *Climate Action Tracker,* at https://climateactiontracker.org/countries/china/, accessed on September 10, 2020.
71. "China Meets 2020 Carbon Target Three Years Ahead of Schedule", *United Nations Climate Change,* March 28, 2018, at https://unfccc.int/news/china-meets-2020-carbon-target-three-years-ahead-of-schedule, accessed on September 10, 2020.
72. n. 71.

5. Assessing the Development and Future of Nuclear Energy in South Korea

Introduction

At the beginning of the millennium, the Republic of Korea emerged as a prominent player in the civil nuclear sector. With a highly developed nuclear industry, nuclear energy contributed to about 1/3rd of the country's electricity generation, with efforts underway to increase the share to 59 per cent by the year 2030.[1] South Korea's nuclear power industry had proven to be economically successful too, as it was the only country where the cost of nuclear power construction declined over time.[2] With a burgeoning nuclear export profile and a rapidly developing nuclear research and development industry, South Korea was on its way to becoming a model of economic development powered by green growth.

However, in the last few years, there has been a strong realignment in Seoul's energy policies, which seeks to diminish the role of nuclear power in the country's energy basket. This decision to phase out nuclear power was taken by President Moon Jae-in when he was elected to power in 2017. The public opinion on this matter is divided, with a section of civil society supporting this decision, at the backdrop of a series of corruption scams in the nuclear industry that was exposed at the beginning of this decade. These scams prompted a crisis of confidence in the country's nuclear industry. On the other hand, there is also a call by other members of civil society who implore the need for nuclear power generation for sustainable green growth through a cost-effective source of electricity. With this backdrop, the chapter analyses what these recent developments mean for South Korea's nuclear future. In trying to do so, the chapter is divided into three parts: The first part traces the history and development of nuclear power in South Korea. The second part analyses the effect Fukushima had on South Korea's nuclear policies and other factors that led to the decline of nuclear power in the country. The third part assesses the future trajectory of nuclear power in Korea by assessing the impact of the new energy transition policy. The final segment is the conclusion.

I: History and Development of South Korea's Civil Nuclear Industry

In less than four decades, South Korea transformed from a country that depended entirely on foreign technology and assistance to develop its nuclear programme, to one of the emerging exporters of nuclear power technology. Its success as one of the most lucrative nuclear industries in the world could be attributed to several factors that enabled its rapid development.

Factors that Led to the Development of Nuclear Power in South Korea

Lack of Domestic Energy Resources

The primary reason for developing nuclear power in South Korea was the lack of indigenous energy resources. With scarce domestic sources of coal, oil and natural gas and limited potential for hydroelectric power, Korea depended on foreign imports to fulfil its energy needs. Thus, to avoid import dependency and reduce external vulnerabilities, the government decided to develop a civil nuclear programme. Initiated in the 1960s, the programme developed at a slow but steady pace. In 1973, the energy imports of South Korea (as per cent of total energy use) stood at 68.65 per cent.[3] Thus, as the oil supply crisis of the 1970s intensified, South Korea's efforts to develop its civil nuclear programme, to avoid volatile energy externalities accelerated.

To Power its Economic Growth

The 1950 Korean War ravaged South Korea's economy. The GDP of South Korea in the 1960s was akin to poor African and Asian countries, and the country took aid and assistance from institutions such as the International Development Association and the Asian Development Bank.[4] To develop the economic situation and bolster growth, Park Chung-hee, the then president of South Korea, took strong measures to develop the economy with a focus on industrial development. However, the paucity of natural resources posed a major challenge towards this end. The development of a civil nuclear program promised self-reliance in electricity generation which was crucial to fuel development. This became an important factor in South Korea's transformation from a developing to a "developed" country, which is commonly referred to as "The Miracle on the Han River". In the 1970s, when it launched its civil nuclear programme, the size of South Korea's economy was just 7.5 per cent of that of Japan. Currently, South Korea is the 11th largest economy in the world reaching a GDP of $31,362 per capita, in comparison to Japan which has a GDP per capita of $39,286.[5] One of the many factors that enabled South Korea's economic success was the economic liberalisation of the early 1980s which boosted industrial growth. Nuclear power in this regard gained traction as it helped in providing a sustained energy supply. Since then South Korea's economy has developed significantly becoming one of the most high-tech and industrialised economies in the world.[6] In this regard, nuclear energy is one of the factors that is attributed to South Korea's economic development and is considered to be a part of the 'virtuous' development cycle. This virtuous development cycle refers to the situation where nuclear power enabled a steady electricity supply which helped in the development of the economy. This in turn produced more capital to build more nuclear power plants.[7] By the year 2000, nuclear power contributed to around 30 per cent of South Korea's electricity generation and was able to keep electricity prices lower in comparison to other countries.[8] An IAEA report that was released in 2006 revealed that the electricity price in South Korea was 5 cents/kWh, in comparison to the 8-16 cents/kWh range in other countries. This gave the South Korean economy leverage in price competitiveness for its exports.[9] This cost-effective feature, coupled with South Korea's vast experience in nuclear technology and lower construction costs[10] has also helped Seoul to emerge as one of the most promising players in the nuclear export market.

To Reduce Greenhouse Gases and Curb the Disastrous Effects of Climate Change

As South Korea sprang into major economic development under the leadership of Park Chung-hee, the industry and manufacturing sectors witnessed a major boost. This period of rapid industrialisation was marked not only by economic success but also by increased air pollution due to the burning of coal. At that time the priority was solely on development and little attention was paid to matters of the environment.[11] However, as South Korea became the 7th largest Co_2 emitter in the world, the appeal for nuclear power further increased owing to its small carbon footprint. Thus over time, nuclear energy became a key component in Korea's green growth development strategy. In fact, nuclear power was one of the ten key green growth policy objectives that were put forth by former President Lee Myung-Bak in 2008.[12] As many countries in the world are trying to find a balance between green growth and economic development, South Korea has been trying to establish itself as a model for green growth globally.

Political Setting

An important factor that enabled the rapid development of nuclear power in South Korea was the support of political leadership. At the time of the commencement of Korea's civil nuclear programme, the political system was highly centralised, under strong authoritarian leadership. Thus, there was little space for public debates or protests on the decision to develop a civil nuclear program.[13] The media too was largely state-controlled. Hence, any decision taken by the leaders were easy to implement, without any interference from the public. This helped in the promotion of nuclear power in the country. There also were close links between the government, its utilities, and privately-owned conglomerates called the "Chaebols". Having come to be known as the "nuclear mafia", this network of key actors facilitated the promotion of the country's nuclear industry, and was very similar to Japan's "Nuclear Village".[14]

Along with the favourable political scenario within the country, interestingly, another political dimension that became helpful for South Korea's civil nuclear programme was the prevalent speculation in the 1970s that the top leadership in South Korea was devising plans to develop nuclear weapons by 1977.[15] A special report for Secretary of State Henry Kissinger stated that if South Korea was successful in developing nuclear weapons it could "have a deeply unsettling impact on regional stability" and on US non-proliferation strategy. Thus foiling South Korea's weaponisation plans would require "early cooperation" with allied nuclear suppliers and some use of US "political leverage."[16] Thus, the United States worked with France and Canada, to discourage the South Korean government from doing so by offering technical agreements in exchange, which helped to boost its civil nuclear programme.[17] Close nuclear energy cooperation with South Korea thus enabled the US to monitor and influence South Korea's actions.

Popular Support and Public Acceptance

The authoritarian regime in South Korea in the 1960s left little space for public debates on issues of governance. When the South Korean government began to develop its civil nuclear programme, the priority then was to ensure the quality and safety requirements of reactors and making sure the project fell well within the designated timeline. Issues such as public opinion thus were not given much importance. Civil activism was also only beginning to develop in South Korea and thus dissent was shot down by the government. However, the Three Miles Island accident of 1979 and the Chernobyl nuclear disaster of 1986 began to create concerns of nuclear safety among the citizens. In the 1980s, rising activism and the process of democratisation began to develop in the country. The first presidential election of 1987 transformed the highly centralised and authoritarian regime into a more open political system, with increased diffusion of power to local governments. This provided space for increasing public discussions and debates. Several citizens' groups and activist organisations began to demand public involvement in matters of governance. In addition, the ICT revolution in the 1990s enabled more diffusion of information and enabled larger discussions. The digital revolution gave voice to the citizens, which pressurised the government to engage with the public.

While there was a significant number of anti-nuclear protests and petitions, there was also a larger understanding among the citizens of the importance of nuclear power in ensuring energy security and fostering economic development. In fact, surveys conducted in the late 1980s and early 1990s reveal that public support for nuclear energy ranged from 63-72 per cent[18] Another survey commissioned by the IAEA in 2005 revealed that among the 18 countries that were included in the study, only South Korea had majority support for building new reactors.[19] Even among several activist organisations, the attention began to shift from calls to do away with nuclear reactors to the need for more safety measures in nuclear power plants. The government thus in response began to engage more with the public and took up several public diplomacy initiatives to communicate with them regarding nuclear safety. Thus when the 1990s witnessed a lot of nuclear power programmes being shelved in other countries, a surge in nuclear power projects was witnessed in South Korea. Public support thus played a major role in developing the country's nuclear programme.

Tracing the Development of Nuclear Power in South Korea

The development of nuclear power in South Korea can be understood by tracing its growth in four stages:

Stage 1: Conception and Planning (1950s–1960s)

South Korea's interest in nuclear energy began in the 1950s when the government set up the Atomic Energy Department in the year 1956. It was also one of the first few members of the IAEA when it joined the organisation in 1957. By 1959, the Atomic Energy Commission was set up and the Korean Atomic Energy Research Institute was established. With the support of the *chaebols* backing the development of nuclear power, the 1960s witnessed a national effort in nuclear research and development. To develop an industrial force, the South Korean government merged three utilities which coalesced into the Korea Electric Company (which was later renamed as the Korea Electric Power Corporation or the KEPCO). South Korea's close ties with the United States were an important factor that helped in bolstering its civil nuclear programme. In 1962 The TRIGA-MK II research reactor was imported from the United States. This marked the beginning of plans to develop commercial nuclear power in the country as the government set up committees to prepare for it. With that, feasibility studies began to be undertaken and necessary steps to boost the country's civil nuclear program commenced. South Korea also reached an agreement with the United States for the training of Korean scientists, engineers and other executives in the US.

Stage 2: Commercial Generation of Nuclear Power (1970s -1980s)

It was in the 1970s, amidst the country's major industrialisation efforts, that South Korea's push into nuclear power took place. In 1978 its first commercial nuclear reactor came into operation. In its early years, due to its inadequate industrial capabilities and lack of technical know-how, Seoul took a great deal of assistance from other countries. In fact, the first generation of Korean nuclear reactors were almost all built by US contractors. Foreign utilities such as Westinghouse not only helped in constructing their first nuclear reactor but also operated it in the initial phase.[20] With the reactors being imported, its domestic nuclear industry had little prospect of participating in the designing or construction of the reactors. The successful operation of its first nuclear power plant, coupled with other factors such as the 1970s oil crisis, encouraged the South Korean government to focus on the construction of more nuclear reactors. The government even set up an ambitious target of getting 46 new nuclear power plants by the year 2000.[21] Although this target was not met, South Korea did witness impressive progress in its nuclear power programme. The nuclear power capacity for example increased from 2.86 GWe in 1980 to 14 GWe by 2000.[22]

Stage 3: Indigenisation and Self-Reliance (1980s onwards)

Within a decade, the involvement of Korean firms and utilities in the construction and management of nuclear reactors expanded. Although the later reactors were built on designs by foreign firms, they involved greater participation by local firms. In an effort to achieve more self-reliance in the nuclear industry and to develop a Korean model, by the mid-1980s the Korean utilities began to develop a standard design of reactors. Towards this effort, a technology transfer agreement was signed with Combustion Engineering, a US firm, which assisted South Korea to develop a Korean version of the OPR-1000 reactor. By the beginning of the 1990s, the focus was solely on achieving self-sufficiency. South Korea was successful in meeting this objective, when it introduced its first domestic nuclear power plant in 1998. In fact, by the end of the 90s, most of the power plants being constructed were based on models that were almost completely Korean-designed.

Stage 4: Exploring the Nuclear Exports Market Advancing Nuclear R&D

By the beginning of the millennium, South Korea had one of the most successful civil nuclear programmes in the world, with nuclear power contributing to almost 45 per cent of the total electricity generation in the country.[23] Seoul's success in the field of nuclear energy can also be gauged by its capability to make nuclear power cost competitive. This has enabled South Korea to emerge as an important player in the nuclear exports market, which is largely dominated by the US, French, Chinese, Japanese and Russian firms. For example, building South

Korea's APR1400 reactors costs $2300 per kilowatt, in comparison to Areva's EPR which costs $2900 to be built.[24] Beating experienced players such as France's Areva and Russia's Rosatom, KEPCO won an $18.6 billion contract to build four nuclear power reactors in the United Arab Emirates in 2009. As more countries are exploring the civil nuclear option, due to the dual benefit of green growth and energy security promised by nuclear power, the nuclear energy market has been expanding. In this regard, South Korea has been trying to tap into this market and is currently in talks with countries such as India, China, Indonesia, Turkey and several other countries in South East Asia, West Asia, Africa and Latin American to export its nuclear technology.

After creating a standard Korean model and achieving reasonable success in the field of nuclear power generation, the South Korean nuclear industry began to focus on developing safety features and upgrading its technology. Towards this end, the focus shifted to nuclear research and development. The new APR-1400 reactor for example has been designed and engineered in a way that it meets all the international regulatory conditions to ensure high levels of safety. This includes features such as aircraft impact resistance. They are also working on new and more advanced designs which is expected to have better safety ratings than the APR-140. In addition, several new projects are in the pipeline. This includes the KSTAR, System-integrated Modular Advanced Reactors, Sodium Fast Reactor (SFR), Fuel Cycle-Korea Advanced Liquid Metal Reactor and advanced fuel cycle technologies including pyro processing among others. The role of nuclear energy in South Korea's long-term energy strategy was also evident with initiatives such as the establishment of the Kori Nuclear Power Education Institute and KEPCO's International Nuclear Graduate School. These institutions conduct highly specialised training in nuclear technology, thus creating a pool of nuclear experts and leaders in the nuclear industry. It also admits foreign students, along with its own, which helps in creating a global cooperation network in the field of nuclear research and development.[25]

Thus in a matter of few decades, South Korea transformed from a resource-poor country, which depended on importing nuclear reactors to emerging as one of the most prominent suppliers of nuclear power technology, now competing with the same countries that helped it develop its civil nuclear programme.

II: Fukushima and its Effect on South Korea's Nuclear Aspirations

With a promising future in the nuclear industry, South Korea had more ambitious plans in the offing, having set bold targets set for the coming years. However, since the beginning of the last decade, a new stage in South Korea's nuclear energy trajectory has been witnessed—the most bleak in its history so far. This decline in nuclear power was fuelled by several factors, both by internal causes as well as exogenous shocks.

Strike One: The Fukushima Accident

As discussed earlier, the 2011 Fukushima accident, had a tremendous impact on the nuclear power policies of countries around the world. While many countries either shelved or slowed down their nuclear programmes, South Korea was not one of them. It was, in fact, one of the few countries whose nuclear aspirations were not deterred by the nuclear disaster. However, a nuclear accident in one of the world's most technologically advanced countries, and that too in Korea's neighbourhood created a sense of panic among some sections of the Korean civil society. The Fukushima accident incited pre-existing anti-nuclear movements and also led to the rise of new ones. Initiatives such as the South Korean Women's Group, for example, appealed to do away with nuclear power altogether, claiming that they felt an "enormous sense of crisis" after the Fukushima and that the accident "'collapsed the 'safety myth'".[26] However, the mood of the country was not anti-nuclear altogether. The mixed and indeterminate reaction could be understood by looking at the example of the coastal town of Samcheok, where new power plants were scheduled to be built. In a survey conducted in 2011, before the Fukushima accident 75 per cent of the residents polled, were in favour of the new plant being constructed in their town. However, a poll conducted there after the 3/11 accident, revealed that the support fell to 50 per cent. The citizens who were still pro-nuclear cited reasons such as the importance of economic development in their town.[27] Thus, the public support on the matter was divided.

Strike Two: The Nuclear Corruption Scandals

While the authorities were trying to manage the mushrooming dissent against nuclear power, a series of corruption scandals in Korea's nuclear industry were exposed, which created an uproar in the country. In May 2012, about a year after the Fukushima accident, severe mismanagement and failure of safety protocols were revealed at the Kori 1 nuclear power plant. Several staff members including the manager and engineers at the plant were indicted for covering up a power failure incident at the Kori 1 nuclear reactor which could have potentially been very dangerous. Not only did the accused staff delete the records, in spite of their legal obligations to inform the Nuclear Safety and Security Commission,[28] but it was also revealed that many parts of several reactors at the plant were also falsely certified. Seven local, as well as one US company, was said to have forged many quality control certificates for numerous components. A few months later in November 2012, two other reactors too were discovered to have been granted fake certificates.

Alarming laxities in the management of the nuclear power facilities and more corruption in the South Korean nuclear industry continued to get exposed. Notably, in 2013, another scandal was unveiled where counterfeit parts were used in nuclear power plants. Several staff members including the chief executive of Korea Hydro and Nuclear Power and vice-president of KEPCO were charged for authorising fake quality assurance and safety documents. As the investigation progressed, more corruption cases were unearthed. This series of scandals revealed the graveness of endemic corruption in South Korea. If undetected, these corrupt practises could potentially have had catastrophic consequences. In response, several reactors were shut down for inspections. Since nuclear energy contributed to nearly 30 per cent of the country's electricity at that time, its impact was felt clearly. According to a parliamentary audit of 2014, the temporary holdup of nuclear power operations amounted to a loss of 10 trillion won (US$ 8.9 billion).[29]

In the aftermath of the expose, a series of reforms were undertaken at different levels from legal to institutional. The only possible positive outcome of the Fukushima accident and the corruption scandals was that the regulators became alarmed and took additional measures to ensure safety. The Korea Institution of Nuclear Safety states that more than 7,500 reactor parts were replaced soon after and a thorough inspection was undertaken.[30] A new chief executive officer for KHNP, Cho Seok took office in September 2013 and introduced new plans to change the existing work culture in the company with a priority on the safety of reactors and weeding out corruption. He introduced the "Three Reformation Movement" which laid emphasis on transparent communication with the public, focus on public service and a new working culture that rejected nepotism and "behind the scenes" deals. He engaged with the employees and conducted polls to study the "unhealthy practises" that were present in the company. KHNP also chose "role model" companies that were known for their safety culture and effective operations.[31] Although these measures were notable, the corruption scandals created a huge dent in public trust, which would require a lot more efforts to set right.

Strike Three: The Earthquake

Post-Fukushima and the nuclear corruption expose, fears of nuclear safety loomed large among the public. These fears were intensified when an earthquake struck the southern city of Gyeongju in 2016, situated close to the Wolsong nuclear power plant. It was the most powerful earthquake to be recorded in the history of the modern Korean Peninsula. However, having measured to be of 5.8 magnitudes on the Richter scale it did not cause any severe damage.[32] The 400 aftershocks that were recorded, however continued to create panic among the citizens.[33]

The 2016 earthquakes brought in the realisation that traditional studies and identification of earthquakes could be outdated and wrong.[34] In addition, having the most number of reactors per square mile, South

Korea has the highest density of nuclear reactors in the world. Each site has multiple units, which ensures lower costs and more effectual maintenance. This raised concerns among the people of the impact an earthquake could have if the safety systems fail in any of the plants. It was debated that the magnitude of such an accident could be much bigger than what was witnessed in Fukushima. It did not help that the people had little faith in the safety systems, after the recently exposed corruption scandals. All these factors, together created an impending sense of doom among the people.

Perhaps the biggest impact of these incidents was felt on public attitudes towards nuclear power. It created severe distrust towards the nuclear industry. It did not help when a 2014 parliamentary audit revealed that the officials who were fired due to the corruption scandals were rehired.[35] Anti-nuclear movements continued to gain large public support. Up until the Fukushima accident, these movements were largely supported by environmental groups and people who lived near nuclear waste disposal sites. However, post the nuclear scandal, the movement diversified and included more groups ranging from consumers to even religious groups.[36] One of the most popular movements in this regard is "One Less Nuclear Power Plant". This was an energy policy launched after the Fukushima accident. This movement became so popular that it even received the UN Public Service Award under the category of fostering participation in public policy decision-making through innovative mechanisms.

Strikeout: The Decline of Nuclear Power in South Korea

The Problem of Nuclear Waste Management

Amidst the rising anti-nuclear sentiments in the country, other pertinent issues such as the problem of managing spent nuclear fuel gained more attention. While South Korea focused on rapidly boosting its civil nuclear programme in the last couple of decades, it is however yet to find a permanent solution for radioactive waste management. With increasing nuclear power generation, came nuclear waste which does not have sufficient storage space or facilities in the country. By the year 2013, the on site storage facilities for spent nuclear fuel rods were filled up to over 70 per cent of its capacity,[37] and other on site storage facilities were predicted to reach their saturation point in the coming few years. This issue gained attention since the Fukushima accident taught a lesson on the importance of handling spent fuel storage pools and the dire challenges it can pose if unmanaged. However, gaining public support to construct more storage facilities continued to be a challenge. While the authorities implemented several storage solutions over the years such as dry-casket storage methods, etc., the limitations of these technologies called for a permanent solution to managing nuclear waste. The Korean Atomic Energy Research Institute (KAERI), the nodal organisation responsible for the research and development in the field of nuclear energy in South Korea, in this regard, has been pushing for pyroprocessing. Pyroprocessing of spent nuclear waste is a technological process in which the uranium is separated from plutonium and other transuranic elements. This separated uranium can be further reused for electricity generation.[38] Advocates of pyroprocessing argue that with this technology, less spent fuel wastes would need to be buried. KAERI stated that pyroprocessing could reduce nuclear waste by 95 per cent in comparison to the 20-50 per cent range of the existing reprocessing technologies. [39] However, The 123 Agreement that South Korea signed with the United States in 1974, bans South Korea from reprocessing nuclear fuels. As the deal was set to expire in 2014 pyroprocessing became an important factor in the negotiations for the renewal of the agreement. South Korean officials appealed for rights to reprocess spent fuel as the US had granted to Japan in 1988. However, one of the most pertinent challenges linked to pyroprocessing among several others, is the serious proliferation concerns it raises, as several experts say that this technology could help in developing nuclear weapons. Thus, although the US denied allowing Seoul to pursue pyroprocessing, the new agreement between the two countries which came into being on November 2015, however, let KAERI undertake further research on the subject. It was decided that depending on the results of the joint study and by gaining assurance that there won't be any proliferation risks, the agreement could be revised in the future.[40] However, public opposition to this proposition too arose. In fact, an electroreduction experiment in this study was delayed due to the increasing protests locally.[41] Although the government announced a new national plan for spent fuel management, the problem of nuclear waste management continues to be mired in several complexities, strengthening the anti-nuclear sentiments in the country.

Popular Culture and its Impact on Public Opinion

Cinema is one of the most accessible and impactful mediums of art and has significant power to influence topical social issues. In the case of South Korea, a movie called "Pandora" was released in December 2016, after the Gyeongju earthquake. The movie's plot which revolved around a fictional nuclear accident in the country created a heightened sense of fear among the public, especially in the backdrop of the Fukushima accident, the nuclear industry scandals and the 2016 Gyeongju earthquake. The audience found the movie relatable as the leaders in the movies were depicted as corrupt and conniving. The then president Park Geun-hye was also impeached around the same time amidst charges of corruption. With increasing anti-corruption movements rising, the movie resonated with the public mood. An article published by the Korean Times during the release of the movie, titled "Disaster movie 'Pandora' rings true more than ever", states "...The film 'Pandora,' the first local film dealing with a nuclear disaster here, is striking in that it bears much on what is happening in Korea now... At the end, the film reminds the audience that Korea is the first country in the world to have its population living near nuclear power plants but even at that, the nation is heading in the wrong direction because it is going against the global trend in nuclear energy. Other nations are closing down nuclear power plants but Korea plans to build more. The movie is meaningful in that it raises alarms by describing the danger of disaster in great detail. It also shows that even those who live within 100 km from the disaster-hit area will be affected once a nuclear disaster strikes. After the film, the questions and bitterness linger why an ordinary person such as Jae-hyuk should sacrifice himself for the privileged 1 per cent of the people who started all of this to begin with…"[42] It is also noteworthy that the movie was premiered just before the country's presidential elections. It is said that over five million Koreans, who made up almost 1/5th of the country's voting population saw the movie. Considered to be an influential movie, it is assumed that it had some impact on the voters.

Nuclear energy transpired to be an important electoral issue and in 2017 Moon Jae-in, who incidentally expressed his admiration for the movie and who is known for his anti-nuclear stance, was voted as the 27th President of South Korea.[43]

III: Assessing the Future Trajectory of Nuclear Energy in South Korea

Soon after taking office, President Moon Jae-In announced major overhauls in the country's energy policies. True to the promises he made in his election campaigns, within months of taking office, Moon Jae-in declared phasing out of nuclear energy. The key policy changes also included the decision to phase out coal-powered plants and boost other renewable sources of energy. In accordance with his new energy policies, by mid-June 2017, Kori 1, the first nuclear reactor in the country ceased operations. He also temporarily discontinued the construction of reactors in the Shin-Gori Nuclear Power Complex and set up a "citizens' jury" to decide the fate of these nuclear units. It was decided that the new reactors which were close to completion will be allowed to finish construction but will be the last ones to be built. As the existing plants are planned to close after the end of their 40 years life, they are expected to be substituted with other forms of electricity generating technologies.[44] In addition, President Moon also rejected applications for the extension of the lifespans of old reactors.[45]

Emphasis was paid on boosting renewable sources of energy, with a focus on natural gas. Moon Jae-In proposed increasing the share of natural gas in the country's electricity production from 19 to 27 per cent by the year 2030.[46] To take this ahead, he revived discussions to build a natural gas pipeline that would run through North Korea from Russia.

In addition, the Green New Deal also plans to establish low-carbon energy sectors. Some of the proposed initiatives in this regard include the "smart grids", which will allow power utilities to communicate directly with the consumers and instalment of smart meters in the homes of the consumers, enabling them to monitor and reduce their electricity consumption. As the South Korean government has begun to implement these policy changes, the question of what does this overhaul in energy strategy mean for the country's future remains.

Assessing the Plausible Downsides of Phasing Out Nuclear Power in South Korea

Several experts have voiced their concerns over the dire effects the decision of phasing out nuclear power could have on the country. While the new energy transition policy appears to be impressive on paper, this transition however may not be as easy to implement. In this regard, the following section analyses the possible pitfalls of phasing out nuclear power in South Korea.

Economic Consequences

Considering that nuclear energy is one of the cheapest forms of electricity in South Korea, a sharp increase in electricity prices is anticipated.[47] This could also have a significant impact on the manufacturing base and the energy-intensive industries which is the backbone of the South Korean economy. Cheap electricity prices is a key factor in the country's successful export industry. In this regard, one of the policy advisors to the President stated that if the phasing out of nuclear energy is fully implemented by 2030, it could decrease profits by 30 per cent if there is an even 10 per cent increase in energy prices.[48] The ongoing pandemic has already affected the country's economy, with its export industry seeing a 24 per cent dip in May 2020.[49] In addition, replacing nuclear power with other renewable sources of energy too is a very expensive task. A researcher from the Korea Energy Economics Institute, in this regard, states that the wholesale cost of power from other sources of energy in Korea is estimated to cost six times more than nuclear power.[50] In addition, a report titled "The High Cost of Fear" by *Environmental Progress*, collated data from public sources and scientific research papers to calculate the cost of phasing out nuclear power in South Korea. Its findings reveal that the cost of replacing nuclear power plants with natural gas would cost about $10 billion in natural gas purchases alone.[51]

The phasing out of nuclear power is also expected to impact South Korea's burgeoning nuclear exports market. After its success with UAE, Seoul has ambitious plans to promote itself as a leading provider of nuclear technology. This ambition was not limited to the earlier leaders alone but is also shared by Moon Jae-in's government. President Moon in this regard, emphasised the merits and benefits of Korean nuclear reactors, during his visit to the Czech Republic in 2018 where he urged Czech Prime Minister Andrej Babis to back South Korea's bid to build a nuclear power plant in the country. However, domestically phasing out nuclear power, is unsurprisingly proving to be a challenging factor in marketing South Korea's nuclear reactors. In this regard, Michael Schellenberger, an environmental policy writer says "Let's think this way. If the government says Hyundai cars are not safe, no one would buy Hyundai cars. If it fears and gives up nuclear reactors, no one would buy nuclear reactors from South Korea. Giving up nuclear reactors means giving up huge economic profits..."[52] Losing out on the nuclear exports market can prove to be disadvantageous for several reasons. First, the value of this market is extensive as many countries around the world have been considering to develop civil nuclear programmes. In addition, it is a high-value market. Song Young-gil, a democratic member of the National Assembly in South Korea,in this regard, stated that the price of exporting a nuclear reactor is about $5 billion which is equivalent to exporting 2,50,000 mid-size cars or 5 million smartphones![53] Besides, with major nuclear exporters such as Areva and Westinghouse, facing financial crises, KEPCO has a good chance of being a key player in the market. The primary players currently are Russia and China, both known for using the export market to control and manipulate their trading partners. South Korea in the context can prove to be a more reliable partner.

The ongoing COVID-19 pandemic is having a grave effect on the Korean economy. The *Korean New Deal National Strategy for a Great Transformation,* Korea's new national development strategy designed to support the country's recovery from the pandemic in this regard states "…in the face of the COVID-19 pandemic, the Korean economy has encountered two major challenges: aiding recovery from a severe economic recession while addressing the structural transformation. The unforeseen shock of the pandemic has resulted in the worst economic downturn that the world has seen since the Great Depression."[54] In this context, the phasing out of nuclear power may only aggravate the ongoing economic crisis. Access to such assessments may influence the opinions of the young South Koreans who currently form a huge pool of job-seekers, 80 per cent of whom in a poll admitted to having skipping meals for budgetary reasons.[55]

Unsound Energy Strategy

The new energy strategy lays focus on boosting the LNG and renewable sector to replace nuclear power. However, this course of action is not without challenges. Considering that energy dependency was the primary reason for developing nuclear power in Korea, phasing it out is likely create this problem once again. This does not only include the problem of energy dependency but also external vulnerabilities such as price volatility and energy supply disruption by exporters for political or economic leverage. Furthermore, LNG In addition to natural gas, the new plan calls on replacing the share of nuclear power with other sources of renewable power. While renewable sources of energy are undisputedly effective and clean sources of power, the development of this sector is still at a nascent stage in South Korea. The following pie chart in this regard illustrates the share of different sources contributing to the generation of electricity in South Korea in 2018.

Figure 1: Total Share of Electricity Generation in South Korea

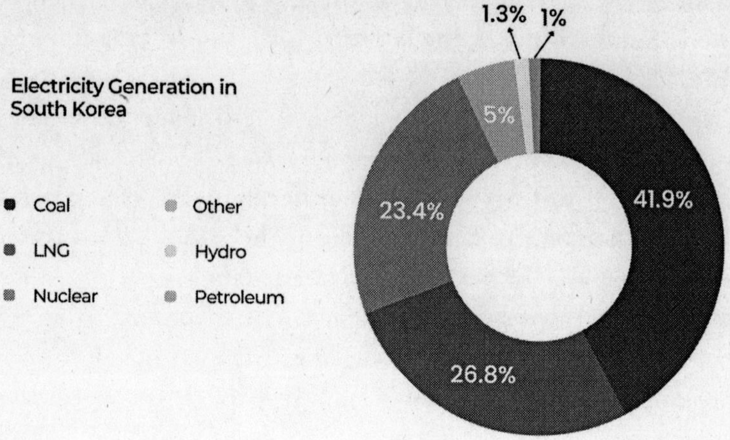

Source: Statista

As shown in the above figure, coal contributed to almost 42 per cent and nuclear power to 23.4 per cent of the total share of electricity generation in the country. Replacing two big sources of electricity, which amount to almost 65 per cent of the total electricity generating capacity would be an extremely challenging task, not only because it would require a multi-fold increase in the contribution of other renewable forms of energy but also because the intermittent nature of the renewable sources make it difficult to do so. According to the International Energy Agency (IEA), the characteristics of South Korea's geography and its weather type present challenges for the development of renewable energy in comparison to other IEA countries.[56] For example, the lack of wind blowing resulted in a mere 13 per cent operating ratio of wind power in 2018.[57] Similarly, there is an unavailability of land, for a major boost in solar and wind power generation. One of the estimates by Kylie Feger, an EP Fellow, claims that for solar power alone to replace the nuclear power plants, it would require the construction of over 4,000 solar farms, which would in total cover land area five times larger than Seoul! Wind energy, similarly would require area 15 times larger than Seoul.[58] One of the reasons for this is that nuclear fuels have more energy density than wind or solar energy. There also is the price aspect that needs to be factored in. In 2016, the cost of generating wind power was 22 per cent higher than nuclear power. Similarly, the generation cost of photovoltaic was196 per cent higher.[59]

In addition to this, several scientists and climate change activists have voiced their concerns over the subsequent environmental impact of phasing out nuclear power. Although, LNG generates 45 per cent less Co_2 than coal,[60] it is not entirely a clean source. Significantly boosting the LNG sector, in this regard may not help the already existing problem of air pollution in Korea but it may also hinder Seoul's pursuit of achieving net-zero carbon emissions by the year 2050.[61] Alternatively, nuclear power could play a significant role in realistically achieving this goal.

Taiwan poses as a relatable example to understand the potential challenges in phasing out nuclear power. Taiwan faces the problem of high import dependency and geographical constraints, just as South Korea does. Since the policy of nuclear energy phase-out was carried under the leadership of Sui-bian from 2000 to 2008, Taiwan has had to deal with challenges ranging from enormous power blackouts, and susceptibility to foreign supplies to significant increase in coal consumption which lead to the intensification of air pollution.[62] In this regard, Taiwan can be an important case study in understanding the challenges that emerge from phasing out nuclear power and could help Seoul in avoiding the same.

Conclusion

While the decision to phase out nuclear energy was a bold and decisive one, it also appears to have a lot of complexities involved. As discussed in the above section, there are several pertinent challenges such as the economic and environmental impact of phasing out nuclear power, managing the demand and supply of electricity and increasing self-reliance in power generation among others. As these challenges continue to come to light, the decision to phase out nuclear power may yet be reconsidered once again.

The future of nuclear power in South Korea, despite looking bleak depends on several factors. For example, scepticism over the nuclear phase-out strategy was expressed during the 2018 heatwave in South Korea which left 42 people dead. At the time the electricity demand increased significantly, which eventually led the South Korean government to announce plans to increase the operations of five more nuclear power plants to meet the demands.[63] This led to the popular opinion tilting towards nuclear power as concerns of energy security and the rising cost of electricity were raised.[64] More recently, in January 2020, Na Kyung-won, a South Korean politician stated that "The ruling party has finally begun to notice the problem with the nuclear phaseout. The policy destroys Korea's power plant ecosystem and future profit generator."[65] In addition, the future of South Korea's nuclear energy, could also be determined by the outcome of the upcoming 2022 presidential elections considering that in a democracy nothing is definitive. Political parties like the People Power Party, Korea Liberty Party and Bareun Party, have been pressuring the ruling party to maintain nuclear power and is even amassing signatures to petition against the nuclear phaseout policy. If any of these parties win the mandate in the next elections, the decision of phasing out nuclear energy may be reversed. However, matters of energy security require foresight, long-term commitment and planning, and understanding of the economic and market situations. Frequent shifts in policies with every change of administration could prove to be detrimental to the country's economy.

There also appears to be an increasing wave of opposition among the public against the phasing out of nuclear power. In July 2017, several international scientists and imminent personalities wrote an open letter to the President requesting him to reconsider the nuclear phase-out policy, urging that "If South Korea withdraws from nuclear, the world risks losing a valuable supplier of cheap and abundant energy needed to lift humankind out of poverty and solve the climate crisis."[66] Since then, in the last few years, this appeal has been extended by university professors and research scholars as well, who have asked the government to take a more researched stance on the matter, with the involvement of experts in decision-making.[67]

Democratic processes in this regard, also have the capacity to overturn the current decision of phasing out nuclear power. This was evidenced when President Moon accepted the verdict of the Citizens' Jury to allow the construction of two nuclear reactors to finish completion. President Moon's deepening of public engagement in this regard is commendable and sets precedence for more public involvement in matters of public policy. Interestingly, this development appears to be taking place at a time when there is a significant shift in political and cultural elements of Korean society, where it appears to be moving towards a more open and participatory democratic system. The candlelight demonstration, the overthrowing of the former President, and the increased involvement in matters of politics seem to indicate that the future of South Korea's nuclear industry will be located in public support. An important tool in this process would be increased communication with the public. More information could help in shaping public attitudes and opinions regarding important issues. Thus, the consequences of the nuclear phase-out policy on the economy and environment, the increasing awareness of the benefits of nuclear power, the role of public opinion and the uncertainties in future politics indicate that the future of nuclear power in South Korea is uncertain.

However, regardless of the decision to promote or phase out nuclear power, safety needs to be given the utmost priority. Fukushima set a harrowing example of how even minor laxities and oversight could cumulatively add up to cause huge catastrophes. The 3/11 accident and corruption exposed in the nuclear industry thus would hopefully make the authorities more accountable and place more stringent safety systems in place. In this regard, considering the benefits offered by nuclear energy and the downsides to phasing it, South Korea may find it more pragmatic to focus on making the nuclear industry safer and increasing transparency to boost credibility. In this regard, South Korea will be required to make some difficult choices in the coming years.

Notes

1. Jill Kosch O'Donnell, "Nuclear Power in South Korea's Green Growth Strategy", *Council on Foreign Relations,* June 28, 2013, at https://www.cfr.org/report/nuclear-power-south-koreas-green-growth-strategy, accessed on September 20, 2020.
2. "Chosun Biz Interview with Michael Shellenberger", *Environmentalprogress.org,* July 12, 2017, at https://environmentalprogress.org/big-news/2017/7/12/chosun-biz-interview-with-michael-shellenberger, accessed on September 18, 2020.
3. "Energy imports—Country rankings", *The Global Economy,* at https://www.theglobaleconomy.com/rankings/Energy_imports/, accessed on September 25, 2020.
4. Shrey Jain, Amrit Dasgupta, "South Korea's Economy after the Korean War", *International Journal of Advance Research and Development,* v. 3. I.1.
5. Jung H. Pak and Ethan Jewell, "South Korea and Japan have more in common than they think", *Brookings.edu,* at https://www.brookings.edu/blog/order-from-chaos/2019/09/05/south-korea-and-japan-have-more-in-common-than-they-think/, September 5, 2019, accessed on October 2, 2020.
6. Armstrong, Margaret and D'Arrigo, Rafael and Petter, Carlos and Galli, Alain G, "How Resource-Poor Countries in Asia are Securing Stable Long-Term Reserves: Comparing Japan's and South Korea's Approaches (January 15, 2016)", *Resources Policy,* v. 47, n. 1, 2016, p. 26, at https://ssrn.com/abstract=2796117, accessed on October 2, 2020.
7. Xu Yi-chong (ed.), *Nuclear Energy Development in Asia: Problems and Prospects* (Palgrave Macmillian: UK, 2011), p. 150.
8. Philip Andrews-Speed, "South Korea's nuclear power industry: recovering from scandal", *The Journal of World Energy Law & Business,* v. 13, i.1, March 2020, at https://doi.org/10.1093/jwelb/jwaa010, accessed on October 18, 2020.
9. X. Yi-chong, Nuclear Energy Development in South Korea, "Nuclear Energy Development in Asia: Problems and Prospects" (Springer: New York, 2011), p. 150.
10. n. 1.
11. Brett Smith, "How Clean is Your Country?", *Azo Clean Tech,* July 9, 2015, at https://www.azocleantech.com/article.aspx?ArticleID=552, accessed on September 29, 2020.
12. n. 1.
13. Se Young Jang, "The Development of South Korea's Nuclear Energy Industry in a Resource-and Capital-Scarce Environment", in Economic Development and Environmental History in The Anthropocene, *Carnegie Endowment for International Peace,* October 19, 2017, at https://carnegieendowment.org/2017/10/19/development-of-south-korea-s-nuclear-energy-industry-in-resource-and-capital-scarce-environment-pub-73509, accessed on October 2, 2020.
14. n. 8, pp. 47-57.
15. "Stopping Korea from Going Nuclear, Part I", *National Security Archive,* March 22, 2017, at https://nsarchive.gwu.edu/briefing-book/henry-kissinger-nuclear-vault/2017-03-22/stopping-korea-going-nuclear-part-i, accessed on October 18, 2020.

16. Ibid.
17. n. 15.
18. Viet Phuong Nguyen, "An Analysis of Moon Jae-in's Nuclear Phase-out Policy: The Past, Present, and Future of Nuclear Energy in South Korea", *Georgetown Journal of Asian Affairs*, Winter 2019, p. 2.
19. Jim Green, "Is South Korea's nuclear industry a model for others to follow?", *Nuclear Monitor*, No. 844, May 25, 2017, at https://www.nirs.org/wp-content/uploads/2017/12/NM844.pdf, accessed on October 18, 2020.
20. n. 7, p. 141.
21. n. 8, pp. 47-57.
22. Ibid.
23. n. 18, p. 2.
24. "South Korea targets $400 billion nuclear plant orders", *Tehran Times*, January 14, 2010, at https://www.tehrantimes.com/news/212161/South-Korea-targets-400-billion-nuclear-plant-orders, accessed on October 12, 2020.
25. Will Davis, "South Korea nuclear power: Are the dark times over?", ANS.org, February 6, 2014, at https://www.ans.org/news/article-1510/south-korea-nuclear-power-are-the-dark-times-over/, accessed on September 19, 2020.
26. "South Korea: We want a nuclear-free peaceful world" say south korea's women", *Peacewomen.org*, January 18, 2012, at http://peacewomen.org/content/south-korea-we-want-nuclear-free-peaceful-world-say-south-koreas-women, accessed on September 12, 2020.
27. n. 1.
28. "South Korea: Nuclear scandal widens", *Friends of the Earth*, Australia, at https://www.foe.org.au/south-korea-nuclear-scandal-widens, accessed on October 22, 2020.
29. n. 19.
30. Ibid.
31. Will Davis, "South Korea nuclear power: Are the dark times over?", *ANS.org*, February 6, 2014, at https://www.ans.org/news/article-1510/south-korea-nuclear-power-are-the-dark-times-over/, accessed on September 19, 2020.
32. Records of earthquakes however only began in 1978.
33. Chang May Choon, "S. Koreans shaken by their largest recorded earthquake", *The Strait Times,* September 22, 2016, at https://www.straitstimes.com/asia/east-asia/s-koreans-shaken-by-their-largest-recorded-earthquake, accessed on October 2, 2020.
34. Hyun-Tae Choi, Tae-Ryong Kim, "Necessity of management for minor earthquake to improve public acceptance of nuclear energy in South Korea", *Nuclear Engineering and Technology*. v. 50, I.3, April 2018, pp. 494-503.
35. n. 19.
36. Ibid.
37. Youkyung Lee, "Nuclear waste a growing headache for S. Korea, *Stars and Stripes,* March 26, 2013, at https://www.stripes.com/news/pacific/nuclear-waste-a-growing-headache-for-s-korea-1.213595, accessed on January 7, 2020.

38. Juangmin Kang, "South Korea in focus: The politics of spent fuel storage and disposal", *Bulletin of the Atomic Scientists,* October 13, 2016, at https://journals.sagepub.com/doi/full/10.1177/0096340211407146#articleCitationDownloadContainer, accessed on January 9, 2020.
39. "Nuclear waste a growing headache for South Korea", NDTV,March 23, 2013, at https://www.ndtv.com/world-news/nuclear-waste-a-growing-headache-for-south-korea-517345, accessed on January 9, 2020.
40. Eunjung Lim, "South Korea's Nuclear Dilemmas", *Journal for Peace and Nuclear Disarmament*, v. 2, 2019, I.1.
41. Ibid.
42. Park Jin-hai, "Disaster movie 'Pandora' rings true more than ever", *The Korea Times,* December 4, 2016, at https://www.koreatimes.co.kr/www/news/culture/2016/12/141_219461.html, accessed on November 1, 2020.
43. Michael Shellenberger, "Greenpeace's Dirty War on Clean Energy, Part I: South Korean Version", *Environmental Progress,* July 25, 2017, at https://environmentalprogress.org/big-news/2017/7/25/greenpeaces-dirty-war-on-clean-energy-part-i-south-korean-version, accessed on November 2, 2020.
44. "Korea's nuclear phase-out policy takes shape, *World Nuclear News,* June 19, 2017, at https://www.world-nuclear-news.org/NP-Koreas-nuclear-phase-out-policy-takes-shape-1906174.html, accessed on October 30, 2020.
45. n. 18, p. 4.
46. Rod Adams, "Moon Jae-in Making Friends By Importing More Gas", *Forbes,* July 12, 2017, at https://www.forbes.com/sites/rodadams/2017/07/12/geopolitical-advantages-of-moon-jae-in-plan-to-increase-south-koreas-natural-gas-consumption/?sh=15d6fa6614df, accessed on October 3, 2020.
47. Sotaro Suzuki, "Moon's bold reforms weigh heavily on Korea Inc.," *Nikkei Asian Review*, August 19, 2017.
48. Ibid.
49. Sung-Young Kim, Elizabeth Thurbon et al, "South Korea's Green New Deal shows the world what a smart economic recovery looks like", *The Conversation*, September 9, 2020, at https://theconversation.com/south-koreas-green-new-deal-shows-the-world-what-a-smart-economic-recovery-looks-like-145032, accessed on October 29, 2020.
50. n. 1.
51. Michael Shellenberger, Mark Nelson, et al, "The High Cost of Fear", *Environmental Progress,* August 22, 2018, at https://environmentalprogress.org/big-news/2017/8/22/the-high-cost-of-fear, accessed on November 2, 2020.
52. n. 2.
53. By Kim Bo-gyung, "Resistance grows to Moon's nuclear phase-out", *The Korea Herald,* January 15, 2020, at http://www.koreaherald.com/view.php?ud=20190115000538, accessed on October 29, 2020.
54. "National Strategy for a Great Transformation. Korean New Deal", *Government of the Republic of Korea*, July 2020.

55. n. 43.
56. n. 1.
57. n. 53.
58. David Dalton, "Scientists and Environmentalists Urge South Korea To Reconsider Nuclear Phaseout", *Nucnet.org*, July 7, 2017, at https://www.nucnet.org/news/scientists-and-environmentalists-urge-south-korea-to-reconsider-nuclear-phaseout, accessed on October 18, 2020.
59. Sanghyun Hong and Barry W Brook, "A nuclear- to-gas transition in South Korea: Is it environmentally friendly or economically viable?", *Energy Policy*, January 2018.
60. "LNG: An Energy of the Future", *Elengy*, at https://www.elengy.com/en/lng/lng-an-energy-of-the-future.html, accessed on October 20, 2020.
61. Tim Ha, "In East Asian first, South Korea announces ambitions to reach net zero by 2050", *Eco-Business,* March 17, 2020, accessed on December 14, 2020.
62. n. 18, p. 5.
63. "South Korea's nuclear phaseout plans to face headwinds", *Asian-Power.com,* July 31, 2020, at https://asian-power.com/power-utility/news/south-koreas-nuclear-phaseout-plans-face-headwinds, accessed on November 1, 2020.
64. Ibid.
65. n. 65.
66. "Moon urged to halt South Korean nuclear exit", *World Nuclear News,* July 5, 2017, at https://www.world-nuclear-news.org/NP-Moon-urged-to-halt-South-Korean-nuclear-exit-0507174.html, accessed on October 18, 2020.
67. "Nuclear Power in South Korea", world-nuclear.org, at https://www.world-nuclear.org/information-library/country-profiles/countries-o-s/south-korea.aspx, accessed on October 30, 2020.

6. Assessing the Development of Nuclear Power in South Asian Countries: A Case Study of Pakistan and Bangladesh

Introduction

Countries in South Asia have witnessed rapid industrialisation, robust economic development, and advancement in the fields of healthcare and education in the past decade. According to the World Bank, the growth rate in South Asian countries[1] increased from 6.2 per cent to 7.5 per cent between the years 2013 and 2016.[2] While the growth projection for South Asia has been uncertain since the COVID-19 pandemic, it is expected to recover as it has been the world's fastest-growing sub-region for several years since 2014.[3] This course of economic development is marked with high energy demands. However, South Asia is mired with deep-rooted challenges of energy deficiencies which is posing as a serious challenge to the development of countries in the region. The fact that South Asia is home to 24 per cent of the total world's population today only exacerbates the energy challenge. As some countries in South Asia have been trying to find a solution to meet the rising energy demands while trying to combat the serious problem of climate change, nuclear power has emerged as a promising option. Countries like Pakistan and Bangladesh in this regard have emerged as interesting case studies analyse the role played by nuclear power in emerging economies.

The chapter in this regard studies the civil nuclear programmes of Pakistan and Bangladesh. To do so the chapter is divided into two parts. The first part will assess the civil nuclear programme of Pakistan, which seeks to significantly scale up its nuclear power capacity over six-fold in the coming decade.[4] Pakistan's intensifying nuclear drive, however, has raised several pertinent concerns regarding the safety of its reactors and the chances of nuclear weapons proliferation, despite the civilian nature of its projects. The first part will thus assess the development of the civil nuclear programme in Pakistan and its emerging challenges and assess if the safety concerns hold any merit.

Part B analyses the development of nuclear power in Bangladesh which signed a nuclear cooperation agreement with Russia in 2009 to build two 1200 MWe nuclear reactors.[5] Referred to as "A Dream Comes True" in a project brochure for the Rooppur nuclear plant in 2017,[6] the Bangladeshi government has been ardently pursuing a civil nuclear programme since the 1960s. As the two-unit nuclear power plant is scheduled to finish completion by 2024, this section assesses the development of Bangladesh's nuclear power programme and the challenges that it might face in this course.

I: Assessing the Emergence and Development of Civil Nuclear Programme in Pakistan

Drivers for the Development of a Civil Nuclear Programme

Limited Availability of Electricity Sources

In the 1950s when Pakistan developed its civil nuclear programme, it was a newly formed country with an impoverished economy, marked by a growing population and major energy scarcity. Energy deficit since then has been an endemic issue that the country has been facing till date, with the average shortage in the energy sector having been estimated at 7000 MW in 2017.[7] It is assessed that over 50 million Pakistanis do not have access to electricity, with another 90 million citizens suffering from the unreliable power supply.[8] As an uninterrupted electricity supply is imperative for economic development, the escalating energy crisis has led Pakistan to explore and promote sustainable energy sources.

Currently, Pakistan's energy mix is comprised of diverse energy sources with an installed electricity generation capacity of 35,972 megawatts (as of April 2020).[9]

Figure 1: Pakistan's Energy Mix

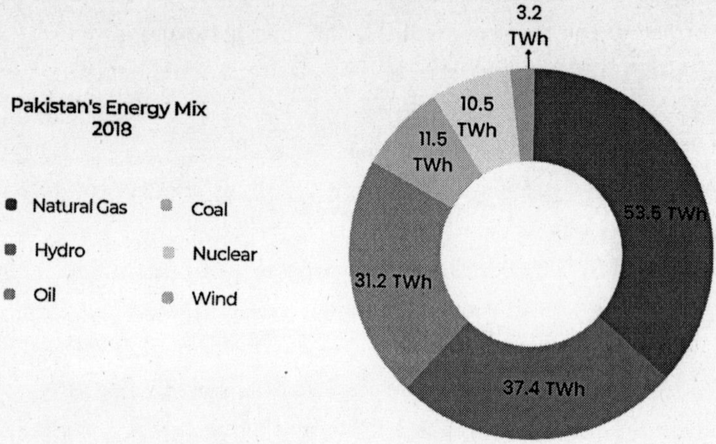

Source: world-nuclear.org

As depicted in the pie chart above, a major portion of Pakistan's energy mix is made up of fossil fuels, specifically natural gas. The development of natural gas however faces several complex political challenges. For example, the major gas fields in Pakistan are located in Baluchistan, where the local Baloch's have voiced their objections against the tapping of these resources to power big cities and industries, while the province remains underdeveloped.[10] The Baloch's claim to be discriminated against unfairly by the Centre and have expressed their grievances over the lack of access to their own resources, underdevelopment and lack of job opportunities. The region has witnessed over 5 insurgencies since 1948 has continued to be in discord with the Centre. Their resentment has resulted in them carrying out attacks on critical infrastructure such as gas facilities, oil pipelines, electricity transmission towers, etc with one of these attacks causing a nationwide blackout in 2015.[11] Apart from these problems, the domestic reserves are also ceasing to suffice due to the increasing demand for gas owing to lower costs and the expansion of the CNG vehicle industry.[12] This has led to the problem of high import dependency. In 2018, Pakistan imported about 7.7 million tonnes of oil equivalent LNG gas.[13]

The other major source of electricity in Pakistan is hydroelectric power. Pakistan's Water and Power Development Authority (WAPDA), estimated that there exists 60,000 MW worth of hydropower potential in the country. However, only 7,320 MW worth of power has been developed.[14] Although the last few years have witnessed increasing development in this sector, with the commissioning of new plants and installation of micro hydropower projects, further development of hydro power has been limited by several challenges. First, there has been push back by local communities who have been displaced by the construction of dams and claim that they have not yet been adequately compensated.[15] Thus many residents in the North-West Frontier Province have been opposing the construction of dams in the region. In western Punjab, plans to build the Kalabagh dam have not been short of problems either. Disputes between the local resident and the government have been ongoing for over three decades, as residents have been claiming that the dam would limit downstream water access and by extension affect the livelihood of the people living there.[16] In addition, the last several years have witnessed a decline in the share of hydropower in electricity generation, as the total percent share in the fiscal year 2017-18 dropped to 7.7 per cent from 13.1 per cent in 1998.[17]

Oil is another major source of electricity in Pakistan. However, since the domestic reserves of oil are limited, Pakistan has been importing a large quantity of oil from countries like Saudi Arabia. The consumption of oil however has significantly decreased over the last few years due to factors such as an increase in global prices.

Pakistan has significant potential to develop renewable sources of power. Considering the geographical location of Pakistan, with the sun shining for almost 300 days annually in the country, the World

Bank estimates that utilising only 0.071 per cent of the country's area for solar photovoltaic power generation would be enough to meet the current electricity demand in Pakistan.[18] Towards this end, Pakistan is in the process of developing the world's largest solar farm, under the umbrella of China-Pakistan Economic Corridor (CPEC).[19] Similarly, there is immense potential to develop wind power with some estimates suggesting that wind power alone can produce 340 GW of power in Pakistan.[20] Tapping on this potential, Pakistan signed an agreement with Siemens Gamesa, a renewable energy industry to install 205 units of turbines for eight wind power projects which is projected to have 410 MW worth of combined capacity.[21] Pakistan also has abundant indigenous geothermal and biomass resources. However, these resources haven't yet been explored sufficiently.[22] One of the reasons for this is the fragile security condition in Pakistan. Geological surveys indicate that several untapped resources exist in Pakistan, but the security scenario has been limiting the scope of foreign investments and other developmental activities.[23] Thus, while Pakistan has major potential to develop its renewable power sector, the development of it has been limited by factors such as a dearth of financing, lack of skilled manpower, etc. As evident in Figure 1, the contribution of renewable power in electricity generation has been miniscule.

The utilisation of coal in Pakistan for electricity generation is very low. However, coal consumption may increase as new coal power plants are slated to be constructed under the CPEC project. Currently, 9 out of the 21 energy projects under the China-Pakistan Economic Corridor are coal power plants.[24] While Pakistan's contribution to global Co_2 emissions is less than 1 per cent, the development of coal power however will lead to an increase in Co_2 emissions by the country. Pakistan is already at risk of a climate change crisis as it has been ranked as the fifth most vulnerable nation in the world to climate change. The Global Climate Risk Index estimated that over 10,000 people died due to climate inducted disasters, and faced losses worth $4 billion between 1998 to 2018.[25] The increase in coal power generation is thus only expected to worsen the impact of the ongoing climate change on Pakistan.

Considering the limitations of these energy sources ranging from intermittency to import dependency, increasing the share of nuclear power in its energy basket would thus help Pakistan in ensuring energy security. Reports on Pakistan's power sector has consistently pointed out the challenges in generating electricity which include a deficit of power generation, inapt policies, transmission losses and the lack of long-term planning. In addition, problems in transmission and distribution (T&D) also persist. Thus, while the installed generation capacity in Pakistan has increased significantly in the last few years, the challenges in T&D have been limiting the supply of electricity. However, even though the installed generation capacity has increased, a spike in electricity demand is expected.[26] As the increase in power consumption is likely to increase as the electricity demand has been increasing in Pakistan at a rate of 6-8 per cent per year,[27] nuclear energy in this regard has emerged as an important source to meet any rising demands in a sustainable, clean and cost-effective manner.

Development of Pakistan's Economy

While the installed generation capacity in Pakistan has increased significantly over the years, the energy crisis persists due to bottlenecks in the energy sector which limits the transmission and distribution of power. The resulting energy shortfall has been exacerbating Pakistan's ongoing economic crisis. The dependency on energy imports has been adding pressure on the country's budgets and reserves. In addition, the lack of capacity in Pakistan's electrical grid resulted in the loss of an average of $9.38 million per year in economic production through the years 2012-17.[28] The energy deficit also has a direct impact on the GDP of the country as several industries have plummeted due to a shortage of electricity. For example, over 50 per cent of the textile industry in Pakistan has reportedly been shifted to China and Bangladesh due to the energy crisis.[29] In fact, in 2015 it was estimated that Pakistan's GDP faced a loss of about 7 per cent due to a lack of electricity.[30] This further leads to problems of unemployment and a rise in prices. Considering these challenges, the advantageous features of nuclear energy such as its high capacity factor and low carbon footprints haveled it to emerge as a promising option towards achieving sustainable electricity supply in Pakistan.

History and Development of Pakistan's Civil Nuclear Programme

Inception and Preparation (1950s-1960s)

Pakistan's nuclear power programme began in the year 1954, inspired by Eisenhower's "Atoms for Peace" programme. In 1955, the government announced its decision to set up an Atomic Energy Institute. Towards this end, the Atomic Energy Committee (PAEC) was established under the leadership of Dr Nazir Ahmad, who was given the responsibility to look at all matters regarding nuclear power, with the objective to develop an atomic energy programme. In the following years, the focus was on nuclear research, promoting nuclear power in the country and training the next generation of nuclear scientists and technicians. The PAEC however faced several challenges such as a lack of trained personnel, a shortage of funds and lack of political support in its pursuit to acquire a research reactor.[31]

In 1959, with a change in leadership, I.H. Usmani a physicist, replaced Dr Nazir Ahmad. Under his headship, Pakistan was able to acquire its first 5 megawatt light water research reactor- the PARR-1 from the US in 1962. Usmani is also credited for developing Pakistan's orientation towards the peaceful use of nuclear power.[32] He focused on the development of nuclear research in the country and successfully set up a training programme through which bright, young Pakistani students were selected and sent abroad for technical training. In the 1960s around 600 students were selected to study abroad, out of which 106 of them were said to have returned with doctorate degrees.[33] With the objective of developing research and training in the field of nuclear power, the *Pakistan Institute of Nuclear Sciences and Technology (PINSTECH)* too was established in 1965.

As institutions were being set up and manpower being trained, Pakistan also gained considerable help from other countries in developing its civil nuclear programme too. For example in 1965 Pakistan acquired the Karachi Nuclear Power Plant (KANUPP) from Canada's Canadian General Electric (CGE) which attained commercial operation in November 1972. Similarly, Pakistan also gained support from countries such as the US, France and the UK.

Withdrawal of International Support (1970s and 1980s)

The 1970s marked a period of increased hostility between India and Pakistan. Although Pakistan claimed that its interest in nuclear power was solely for peaceful purposes, Pakistani interest in developing nuclear weapons is also known. For example, Zulfiqar Ali Bhutto, as Foreign Minister in General Ayub Khan's cabinet had pressed for a nuclear weapons programme. However, he was unable to convince Ayub Khan for the same. He voiced his interest in nuclear weapons vocally again after Pakistan's defeat in the 1965 war against India, when he famously stated "If India builds the bomb, we will eat grass or leaves, even go hungry, but we will get one of our own".[34] His intentions to develop a weapons programme could also be traced back to the 1950s where he states in his book titled *If I am Assasinated*, "...I have been actively associated with the nuclear programme of Pakistan from October 1958 to July 1977, a span of nineteen years. I was concerned directly with the subject as Foreign Minister, as Minister for Fuel, Power and Natural Resources and as Minister in Charge of Atomic Energy...Assiduously and with granite determination, I put my entire vitality behind the task of acquiring nuclear capability for my country..."[35] After Pakistan's defeat once again in the 1971 war against India, its aspirations to develop nuclear weapons were furthered. In 1972, Zulfikar Ali Bhutto, directed top nuclear scientists of the country to build a nuclear bomb.[36]

In 1974 India conducted a peaceful nuclear explosion after which there was a withdrawal of international support and the placement of stricter controls to prevent the proliferation of nuclear weapons technology. Consequently, with rising concerns regarding Pakistan's interest in developing nuclear weapons, countries such as Canada and

France withdrew their support from Pakistan. It was decided that nuclear cooperation would only be extended to signatories of the Nuclear Non-Proliferation Treaty (NPT) or to the countries that complied to full-scope safeguards.[37] Since Pakistan did not agree to either of these conditions, vendor support to Pakistan from other countries was stopped. As Pakistan relied heavily on foreign assistance until then, several challenges in its nuclear programme emerged. For example, they had no replacement parts or fresh fuel assembly supplies. Operation of KANUPP also significantly declined with the performance level of the reactor not exceeding over 48 per cent.[38]

Period of Self-Reliance

Having no choice this eventually led Pakistan to become more self-reliant in matters of its nuclear programme. PAEC began to get better and more efficient at maintenance and operations of the plant, in manufacturing of spare parts and in the development of indigenous fuels. While Pakistan approached other countries to engage in nuclear commerce within the IAEA safeguards these plans did not take off. It however began to receive limited external support from other organisations such as the CANDU Owners Group (COG) and the World Association of Nuclear Operators (WANO). The decision to engage with Pakistan was taken after the unfortunate 1979 Three Mile Island accident, as concerns of nuclear safety grew. PAEC also began receiving technical assistance from the IAEA. This helped the PAEC in improving the performance levels of the KANUPP reactor which had dropped after the withdrawal of foreign assistance.

The part-II reactor which was commissioned in 1974 was built completely under the expertise of PAEC scientists. By 1980, PAEC was also able to achieve domestic proficiency in CANDU fuel assemblies. Since the United States also called off its projects with the PAEC, Pakistani scientists were forced to continue to work without any Western help and were able to complete the plutonium nuclear reprocessing plant—*The New Labs* and *Khushab Nuclear Complex*—a plutonium reactor all by themselves.

The Beginning of the China-Pakistan Nuclear Cooperation

The only country that agreed to help Pakistan was China and the two countries began to engage in nuclear cooperation in the 1970s. The late 1980s witnessed serious energy shortages in Pakistan with frequent power cuts that lasted for long hours during the scorching summers. This added pressure on authorities to bring in more power capacity online.[39] Towards this end, in 1986 China and Pakistan signed an agreement for the transfer of civil nuclear technology. Within this agreement, China agreed to provide Pakistan with nuclear reactors and other products and services related to nuclear technology. In 1993 China began the construction of Chashma Nuclear Power Plant-1 (CHASNUPP-1 or C-1). This 325 MWe reactor came under the IAEA safeguards and was based on the Chinese plant design the Qinshan-1 power plant. The reactor went critical in 2000. This agreement marked the first case of South-South technology transfer in the field of nuclear power.

This period also saw the establishment of several institutions for the development of nuclear studies and technical services in Pakistan such as the Karachi Institute of Nuclear Power Engineering (established in 1993), CHASNUPP Centre of Nuclear Training (1996) and Pakistan Institute of Engineering and Applied Sciences (1997) among others.

After witnessing the successful operations of CHASNUPP-1, the Nuclear Regulatory Authority permitted PAEC to sign an agreement with China National Nuclear Corporation (CNNC) for the construction of another reactor- the CHASNUPP-II. The construction of this unit began in December 2005 and was completed in 2011.[40] As energy demands rose, the Pakistani government instructed the PAEC to set up more nuclear power plants with a target to produce 8800 MW of electricity by 2030.[41] In 2015, during the historic visit of Chinese President Xi Jinping to Pakistan, Beijing pledged $46 billion for energy and infrastructure projects in Pakistan.[42] It is also expected to add 16,400 MW to Pakistan's generation capacity.[43] For Pakistan, these generous investments could potentially solve its energy crisis and help in the recovery of its crippling economy. In fact, Pakistan's National Transmission and Despatch Company (NDTC) and K-Electric Limited (KEL) claimed in 2018 that in the next three years Pakistan was expecting a power surplus.[44] While both China and Pakistan claim these projects through the China-Pakistan Economic Corridor (CPEC) as the cornerstone of friendship between the two countries, their alliance, however, seems to be driven more out of economic and geostrategic factors.

One of the main motives for China is to ensure stability in Pakistan, so that it would on extension provide stability in its neighbouring Xinjiang province. In the words of a Chinese scholar "China believes economic development can strengthen Pakistan's internal stability, thus reinvigorating the latter's economy through investment in infrastructure projects as well as the construction of oil and gas pipelines. China hopes that this will create a certain level of stability within Pakistan and in turn stabilise China's western periphery, particularly the province of Xinjiang".[45] Xinjiang is an important part of China's BRI strategy since China intends to build an oil storage facility and a refinery at Gwadar port to enable the transportation of oil through roads and pipelines, into mainland China through the Xinjiang province.[46]

In addition, hefty aid and generous investments are analogous to Beijing's strategy that creates long-term financial and energy dependency on China. China in fact has been signing energy cooperation agreements with numerous countries in the world, in a move that is largely perceived to be an attempt at creating spheres of energy dependencies. China's interest in Pakistan is also speculated to cultivate a strategic partner in the region, as a part of its larger balance of power approach in South Asia vis-à-vis India. For Pakistan, with its current economic situation and diminishing foreign aid and US investments, Chinese support is of immense help, at least for the short-term. In addition, with regard to nuclear commerce, it is the only country willing to help Pakistan. A common enemy in India also appears to be a motivating factor for the two countries. Interestingly, a list prepared as a part of a report on the Parliamentary Committee of CPEC of the ways in which CPEC can benefit Pakistan, number two on the list stated that it could be a 'counter weight to India by countering Indian pressure with the support of China".[47]

As Pakistan began to boost its nuclear power programme, it demanded an agreement similar to the India-US civilian nuclear agreement signed in 2008, which lifted the sanctions against New Delhi and permitted nuclear trade.[48] In 2015, this demand was once again raised during the seventh round of the US-Pakistan Security, Strategic Stability and Non-proliferation (SSS&NP) working group. However, it gained no traction. Some analysts in this regard have debated that the nuclear cooperation which led to the construction of C-3 and C-4 units in Pakistan, were developed in response to the US-India civil nuclear agreement of 2008.[49]

The last decade has witnessed significant progress in Pakistan's nuclear power programme. Partnership with China burgeoned as Hualong One reactors are being planned for Pakistan's nuclear programme. The construction for Chashma Nuclear Power Plant Unit 3 or C3 began in 2011 and was connected to the grid in 2016. The following year, in 2017, Chashma Nuclear Power Plant Unit 4 went critical.[50] In 2013, the Planning Commission also announced intentions to build 2 more reactors near the Karachi unit 1, namely KANUPP 2 and 3.

Presently, Pakistan has six operable commercial nuclear power reactors which has a combined capacity of 2332 MWe. It contributes 7 per cent to the country's total energy mix.[51] Currently, Pakistan's civil nuclear cooperation is supported only by China, though it does get support from the IAEA to ensure safety of its reactors. In 2018, the IAEA initiated a 4-year programme through which it would coordinate with Pakistan's key nuclear energy institutions in making operations safe and more reliable.[52] Pakistani authorities have expressed their interest in increasing nuclear power production over 6 fold from 1430 MW to 8800 MW in the next decade.[53]

Challenges and Concerns Regarding Pakistan's Civil Nuclear Programme

Amidst the expansion process, several concerns regarding Pakistan's nuclear programme have been raised. Although the size and capacity of Pakistan's nuclear programme is small, the apprehensions surrounding it are serious. Several of these pertinent concerns are:

Concerns of Nuclear Safety and Security

All commercial reactors in Pakistan work within the IAEA safeguards and most international nuclear monitors too have given Pakistan's nuclear programme satisfactory reviews. Their nuclear power plants are also said to have additional safety features such as fail-safe control rod drops, highly developed filtration systems and double containment structures that are capable of enduring the impact of even an aircraft crash.[54]

However, concerns of nuclear safety still exist considering that Pakistan has witnessed several nuclear-related accidents in the past. In 1989 for example, KANUPP lost almost a third of the heavy water in its reactor due to a spillage which led to the shutting down of the reactor for several months.[55] At the time, it was also speculated that there had been several other spilling accidents which were hushed-up.[56] Again, in 2008 a gas leakage at a heavy water plant near Khushab town killed two people.[57, 58] In 2011 there was a nuclear emergency after heavy water leaked from a feeder pipe to the reactor. Fortunately, no radiation was reported. These incidents coupled with Pakistan's unsafe industrial safety records raise scepticism of nuclear safety and security.

In the nuclear industry, safety is paramount and anything less than top-grade safety arrangements could prove to be dangerous. This is because while the chances of a nuclear accident happening is lower than the chance of accidents taking place in other power-generating technologies, the impact however, could be massive as witnessed in the unfortunate Chernobyl accident in 1986 and the Fukushima accident in 2011. In this regard, Mark Hibbs, a senior associate at the Carnegie Endowment for International Peace states that "If there was a lesson we learned from the Fukushima accident, it's that, if you are going to get into the nuclear business, and if you don't have world-class technology, good logistics, enough personnel, a lot of money and experience managing crisis situations, then you are not going to be able to manage a severe accident."[59]

As the nuclear energy cooperation between China and Pakistan expand, it has been raising concerns with regard to the kind of reactors being manufactured and supplied by China. Chashma I for example, which was built by the Chinese proved to have several problems. It was based on the Chinese indigenous model of Qinshan I, which was mired with faults. In fact, since the Chinese were unable to fix the problem in their reactors nuclear vessel it eventually had to be repaired by American engineers from Westinghouse.[60] In addition, the ACP-1000 reactor projects have not been free of challenges either. A lawsuit was filed against the PAEC and the Pakistan Nuclear Regulatory Authority by activists who claim that the construction of the unit began without a satisfactory environmental impact assessment.[61]

Another concern with regard to nuclear safety is the location at which the nuclear power plants are situated. For example, two nuclear reactors are sited just 40 km from the populous city of Karachi which has over 16,000,000, residents.[62] Such a densely populated region is usually an unfavourable spot for siting nuclear power plants. The US Nuclear Regulatory Commission guidelines recommend reactors to be constructed in a place with a population less than 500 people per square mile within a 20-mile radius.[63] In comparison, the area around the Karachi power plant has over 6,450 people per square mile. An accident in these nuclear facilities thus could have a devastating effect as civilian evacuation could be very challenging. To make matters worse Karachi is also situated around major tectonic fault lines. This makes it vulnerable not only to earthquakes but also to tsunamis.[64] This is especially alarming considering that traditional studies of tectonic fault lines may be outdated, as was in the case of Fukushima. Scientific research by Britain's National Oceanography Centre and Canada's Pacific Geoscience Centre, which came out in 2013 states that what was considered to be the largest earthquake in the Makram area could be much bigger than what the PAEC has anticipated. The study claims that the region could be susceptible to earthquake of a magnitude as large as 9.2.[65] Not only would a nuclear accident result in a huge casualty but would also crumble the economy since Karachi also hosts a large number of industries in and around the city. Since it is Pakistan's main port, it contributes to about 42 per cent of the national GDP.[66]

The PAEC authorities have acknowledged the chances of a catastrophic nuclear accident taking place and have an emergency plan prepared. However, according to a press briefing given by the project manager of the new reactors, the plan extends only for people living out to 15 km from the site. In this regard, the magnitude of a nuclear accident is difficult to predict and the question of whether a 15 km evacuation plan would suffice remains.[67] It is no relief that Pakistan has a poor record in effective disaster management. The state machinery's response as evidenced during the 2010 floods has been poor which has created space for militant organisations to take part in relief operations, with the objective of gaining people's support.[68]

In addition to nuclear safety which is a common global concern, nuclear security is another pressing concern in the case of Pakistan, especially considering the instability in the country. While safety assurances were given by Yukiya Amano, the former Director-General of the IAEA, during his visit to Pakistan in 2018 who stated that the new Kanupp II and III plants are "very heavily protected",[69] concerns of nuclear security still persist. This is because the overall security situation of a country is an important factor when it comes to maintaining critical infrastructure since they could prove to be a potential target for attacks by terrorists or other violent groups. In the case of Pakistan, it is known to be a hub for militant organisations. Not only has the government lost control of several provinces to the Taliban and other terror organisations, but the security situation has also deteriorated so much that the sales of armoured cars and bulletproof glasses in apartments have increased in Pakistan.[70] The 2020 Global Terrorism Index which measures the impact of terrorism on countries, ranks Pakistan in the 7th position out of 135 countries, just after Yemen.[71]

In this regard considering the level of violence and instability in the country, nuclear power plants may become a target for attacks, not only in an attempt to steal fissile material in order to make dangerous explosives or blackmail the authorities, but also because it would make a symbolic statement considering its economic and national importance. This is not unlikely considering that terrorists have attacked heavily guarded establishments in the past. For example, in 2011 terrorists attacked PNS Mehran the headquarters of the Pakistan Navy's Air Arm, killing five people and setting several aircraft on fire.[72] In 2014 another attack took place at Karachi's international airport killing 18 people.[73] In the same year, Al-Qaeda militants attempted to hijack a Pakistani navy vessel too.[74] A military takeover could also be a possibility, considering the power the Pakistani military yields. Since the military already has control over the nuclear weapons facilities and the close relation between Pakistan's civil and military nuclear infrastructures this may be possible. The unreliability of the Pakistani military was proven in the 2011 PNS attack and the 2014 naval hijack attempt where it appears that Al-Qaeda was able to infiltrate the Pakistani military.[75]

Concerns of Nuclear Proliferation

One of the primary concerns regarding Pakistan's civil nuclear programme is whether it is acting as a smokescreen for the expansion of its nuclear weaponisation programme. These concerns stem from Pakistan's history of proliferation as it has been linked to surreptitiously providing nuclear weapons technology to several countries through Pakistani scientist Abdul Qadeer Khan's network. Pakistani investigators have admitted to AQ Khan's assistance to Iran's nuclear weaponisation program in the 1980s, although they claim that this network functioned independently "for personal financial gains "and had no links to the Pakistani state or had any sort of official linkages.[76] These claims however have not been fully accepted by the international community and there are reasons to believe that the Pakistani state had abetted AQ Khan's proliferation activities. In addition, Pakistani sources have claimed that AQ Khan's nuclear cooperation with Iran emerged from what was supposed to be a benign sharing of nuclear technology for peaceful purposes.[77] There also have been alleged reports of a possible joint nuclear weapons program between Pakistan and Saudi Arabia in the 1990s.[78]

Second, the line between a civil nuclear programme and a nuclear weapons programme is very thin. For example, with uranium, if enriched to low levels it can act as fuel to power nuclear reactors which can help in generating electricity. However, if uranium is purified in centrifuges for a long enough time to make them highly enriched, it becomes fuel for a bomb.[79] In this regard, considering that Pakistan's civil and military nuclear facilities are closely linked and both programmes are shrouded in secrecy, this leaves a lot of space for speculation.[80] Recently, there have also been reports of Pakistan's attempt at expanding the infrastructure of its nuclear weapons programme. A report by the Institute for Science and International Security reveals that they have has been tracing a construction of a large-scale enrichment plant in Pakistan. Although it was stated that the enrichment plant was being constructed to make low-enriched uranium for nuclear power reactors, there are reasons to speculate if their nuclear programme could work as a convenient camouflage. The report further speculates if a large gas centrifuge plant was actually being constructed there perhaps for military purposes.[81] However, the opaque nature of Pakistan's nuclear programme makes it difficult to ascertain this.

Violation of International Norms

The Pakistan-China energy nexus has also been perceived by the international community as a challenge to the existing non-proliferation systems, specifically the Nuclear Suppliers Group. The NSG regulates nuclear trade among countries to ensure any non-proliferation activities. The NSG rules mandate that the recipient country should be a signatory to NPT and that all its nuclear-related activities should be within the full scope of safeguards, if it wants to buy nuclear technology from any of its member states. Despite Pakistan being a non-signatory to the NPT, China has been engaging in nuclear commerce with Pakistan, despite being a member of the NSG since 2004. This nuclear cooperation has been objected to by several countries. However, China and Pakistan have argued that the new reactors being sold are an extension of the agreement signed between the two countries in 1986, way before China's entry to the NSG. This has been perceived by many scholars as China and

Pakistan's attempt at flouting rules and trying to establish their own conventions. The nexus between Pakistan and China are further believed to be dangerous, taking in consideration the history of proliferation between the two countries.

Conclusion

Pakistan's drive to bolster its nuclear power capacity raises serious questions regarding the safety and security of its nuclear power programme. The expansion of nuclear power to meet its goal of 8800 MWe of nuclear power by 2030 for example may strain the oversight capacity of regulators and may result in compromising the safety of the plants. In this regard, while nuclear power certainly offers several benefits to Pakistan, considering the unstable situation in the country, the economic and security trade-off's must be assessed, especially while planning a major boost in the civil nuclear programme.

Considering the increasing interest in developing renewable power in the country and acknowledging the availability of resources, the scope for developing renewable power in Pakistan is immense. In this regard, a diverse energy basket may help Pakistan in achieving energy security. A small but safe and effective nuclear programme may thus add value to the country's energy policies. By helping in developing the energy security of Pakistan, nuclear power, by extension could also help in promoting the economic development of the country. Economic development in this regard could go a long way in gainfully employing its citizens and providing more stability in the country by reducing the vacuums that has led to increasing violence in Pakistan.

It is difficult to ascertain if the proliferation concerns pitched against Pakistan hold any merit. This is because Pakistan's nuclear industry is shrouded in secrecy and deliberate ambiguity. Thus, there is no definite way of saying if these concerns are serious or not. The lack of transparency in this regard not only raises several safety concerns internally but also leads to a trust deficit vis-à-vis other countries relations with Pakistan. If Pakistan wants to move beyond its nuclear pariah status and gain credibility, it would require to be more transparent in its activities.

Increased transparency and communication can thus go a long way in gaining international confidence.

There are several challenges that restrict the growth and development of Pakistan's civil nuclear programme. One of these challenges is the lack of engagement with the global nuclear industry. In this regard, Pakistan has been seeking an agreement similar to the Indo-US deal of 2008. However, to earn such a concession it is important for Pakistan to prove its creditability. With its aggressive nuclear posturing and continued support to terrorist organisations within and outside of the country, such a concession may in fact prove to be dangerous, as it may embolden Pakistan to go against global security norms without being held accountable. As long as Pakistan remains a country of concern from the nuclear security and proliferation point of view,the granting of an exemption to NSG rules appears to be a distant prospect.

II: Tracing the Development of Bangladesh's Civil Nuclear Power Programme

Bangladesh is all set to launch its civil nuclear programme, with its first reactor scheduled to go critical by 2023. The country, home to 160 million people has placed its expectations on nuclear power to generate about 9 per cent of its electricity by the next decade which could help in meeting its rising energy demands and boost its economy while also reducing Co_2 emissions.[82] However, setting up a nuclear power programme is a complicated and long-drawn task which comes with several challenges. In this regard, this section will evaluate the current status of Bangladesh's civil nuclear programme and attempt to analyse the gaps in it and assess its future trajectory.

Understanding the Rationale for Developing a Civil Nuclear Programme

Since the 1960s, Bangladesh has undertaken numerous feasibility studies to assess the scope of developing a nuclear power programme. Several factors have led the authorities to consider nuclear power in their energy basket. Some of these key factors are as follows:

Energy Crisis

Bangladesh faces an energy deficit, with about 10 per cent of its population having no access to electricity,[83] either from the grid or from local installations. Those who rely on the grid keep experiencing frequent power cuts. Although Bangladesh has come a long way with regard to increasing its power supply since it gained independence in 1971, a considerable demand for electricity still remains unmet. With the growing population, increasing urbanisation and rapid industrialisation in the country, the per capita energy consumption in Bangladesh has increased almost two times over to 222.22 kg (oil equivalent).[84] The energy supply however has been unable to meet the rising demands. In 2013 for example, Bangladesh faced a peak electricity demand of 8349 MW. However, the maximum production of electricity only reached about 6675 MW.[85]

Figure 2: Energy Mix of Bangladesh until August 2018

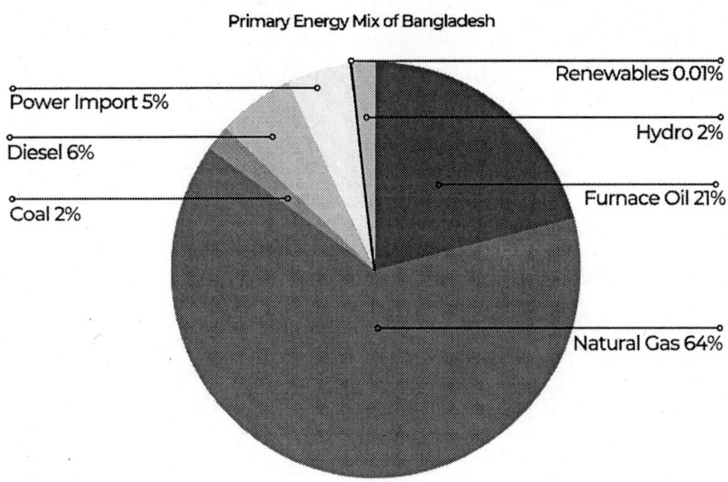

Source: N.K. Das, J. Chakrabartty, et al, "Present energy scenario and future energy mix of Bangladesh."

As evident in the pie chart above, Bangladesh depends heavily on fossil fuels to generate electricity with natural gas contributing to about 64 per cent of the country's electricity generation. However, the increasing use of natural gas has led to the dwindling of domestic reserves. Taking into account that Bangladesh uses about 57 per cent of the country's natural gas production, it is estimated that Bangladesh's reserve of natural gas will be depleted in the coming decade.[86] Due to the dwindling gas production in Bangladesh, the country has resorted to importing gas. This may lead to problems as well, as it is estimated that by 2030 Bangladesh will have over 90 per cent dependency on imported sources of energy.[87]

While presently the amount of coal used to generate electricity isn't significant, it is expected to rise as the authorities have been laying emphasis on coal exploration programs around the country. In addition, there have been plans to establish a coal-based mega-power project. This project seeks to generate 19,200 MW by the year 2030.[88] A boost in the coal energy sector would only worsen the problem of climate change further, to which Bangladesh is already highly susceptible. It is estimated that one in every 7 people in Bangladesh will be displaced by the year 2050 owing to the disastrous effects of climate change.[89]

Although renewable sources of energy have a lot of potentials to develop in Bangladesh, their expansion has been limited. Among the renewables, hydropower is relatively more developed contributing to about 2 per cent of the total electricity mix. However, it has the potential to further develop considering that Dhaka has currently only tapped into just 50 per cent of its hydropower capacity.[90] The contribution of other renewable sources of energy however is miniscule, since they haven't been adequately harnessed owing to political, economic,geographical and technological limitations. For example: despite having the potential to develop solar power in Bangladesh, there have been several impediments to do so. This includes the requirement for a substantial amount of land for the deployment of large-scale solar PV modules. However, considering that Bangladesh is one of the world's most densely populated country, the availability of huge space is a challenge.

Similarly, wind energy is assessed to have scope for development too, however, research on offshore wind speed, etc. have not yet been studied adequately in Bangladesh yet.

With the problem of energy crisis worsening, Bangladesh has been looking for alternate options to develop a sustainable energy policy to alleviate the rising demand for energy demands. Nuclear Power in this regard emerged as one of the key energy options, considering the numerous benefits it offers.

To Fuel Economic Development

As it is widely known, energy security is a key factor to boost a country's economy. Especially in a country like Bangladesh whose economy depends on industries such as ready-made garments, agriculture, industries and manufacturing sectors, keeping the power on has been critical for the county's economic development.[91] As Bangladesh has been working to elevate its status to a middle-income country by 2021 and a developed country by 2041, it has been continually looking at ways to achieve energy security. Towards this end, Rooppur Nuclear Power Plant Project Brochure states "the availability of energy in a secured and affordable manner is the critical input parameters for materializing the country's vision 2021 and vision 2041 through socioeconomic development of all societies, improving quality of life of the population, proper urbanization and industrialisation. The indigenous resources of primary energy would be inadequate to meet the entire incremental demand on a sustainable and long-term perspective."[92] In this regard, considering Bangladesh's energy situation along with the experiences of other countries in their energy policies, the government of Bangladesh decided to pursue a nuclear energy programme to achieve these goals.

Assessing the Development of Nuclear Power and Tracing its Progress

The history and development of Bangladesh's nuclear power project can be studied under three phases based on the progress they've made:

Phase one: Pre-Project Planning

The inception of Bangladesh's civil nuclear programme can be traced back to the 1960s, when it was still East Pakistan. A proposal to build a nuclear power plant was raised in 1961 and since then several feasibility studies were undertaken, all of which concluded that it was a practicable option for Bangladesh.[93] The Pakistani government gave formal approval for this project and the Rooppur site in the Pabna district was selected. Shortly after Bangladesh gained independence, Bangabandhu Sheikh Mujibur Rahman, the father of the nation, decided to set up a nuclear power plant at Rooppur. Towards this end, the Bangladesh Atomic Energy Commission (BAEC) was established in 1973. Other feasibility studies were undertaken to find out if nuclear power was a viable option to meet the energy demands of the country. These studies too concluded in favour of developing a nuclear power project.

In 1986 BAEC started operating a 3 MW TRIGA-Mark-II research reactor. This was utilised to develop research and development manpower training in the field of nuclear power.[94] With energy demands increase, the government in 1999 expressed strong interest in building a power plant at Rooppur. In the following year, the Bangladesh Nuclear Power Action Plan (BANPAP)was approved by the government and in 2001 it adopted the Nuclear Power Action Plan. In 2007 BAEC proposed plans to build two 500 MWe reactors by 2015. Countries like China, Russia and South Korea expressed their interest in engaging in nuclear commerce with Bangladesh and offered technical and financial help to take the project ahead.

Phase Two: Decision Making

The second phase marks a period where important decisions regarding the nature of the civil nuclear programme was decided. This includes the invitation for bids, consideration of proposals, signing of nuclear cooperation agreements etc.

Bangladesh-Russia Nuclear Cooperation

In 2009 the government of Bangladesh accepted a proposal by Russia to build a 1000 MWe AES-92 nuclear plant at Rooppur. Bymid-2009, a bilateral nuclear agreement was signed by both countries. It was decided that the nuclear power plant will include two units, namely Rooppur Unit-1 and Rooppur Unit-2. These reactors will be designed to have a capacity of 1.2 GW each.[95] It was also established that the project will be carried out by the BAEC under the guidance of the Science and Technology Ministry of the government of Bangladesh. The nuclear development project picked pace and in 2012 a nuclear energy bill was introduced in the parliament. This bill chartered the establishment of the Bangladesh Atomic Energy Regulatory Authority. The parliament was informed that the expansion of nuclear power was being considered, envisaging 5000 MWe of nuclear power capacity by 2030. In 2013, funding and financing decisions were finalised and the Bangladesh government signed an intergovernmental agreement for a $500 million Russian loan. This loan was taken to support engineering surveys and training of the workforce among other requirements. The repayment period for this loan was agreed to 12 years with an additional 5 years grace period. In 2013, The Prime Minister of Bangladesh announced plans to construct a second nuclear power plant on an inland river island. For this purpose, the BAEC invited the Japan Atomic Energy Agency in 2014 to study the possibility of building a 2000 MWe power plant. China's Dongfang Electric Corporation (DEC) too conveyed its interest in constructing the second power plant.

India-Bangladesh-Russia Tripartite Nuclear Cooperation

India began to play an important role in developing Bangladesh's civil nuclear programme after signing the 2014 *'Strategic Vision for Strengthening Cooperation in Peaceful Uses of Atomic Energy'* with Russia. Under this deal, it was agreed that the "two sides will explore opportunities for sourcing materials, equipment and services from Indian industry for the construction of the Russian-designed nuclear power plants in third countries".[96] Since India is not a member of the NSG, this arrangement with Russia provided it with a platform to exhibit its capacity as a potential nuclear exporter. Towards this end in 2017, Sekhar Basu the chairman of the Atomic Energy Commission announced India's decision to collaborate with Russia to build the Rooppur nuclear power plant in Bangladesh, during the 61st general conference of the IAEA.[97] In 2017 India committed concessional financing of $1.016 billion to Bangladesh under a line of credit worth $4.5 billion. Kanwal Sibal, the former foreign secretary in this regard stated "...Indian lines of credit create market openings for Indian companies. India is very well placed to provide such services as Russia is already building similar power plants for India at Koodankulam ... A joint venture between Russia, Bangladesh and India reduces costs for Russia and Bangladesh and provides commercial opportunities for Indian companies..."[98] In 2018 an MoU was signed by India's Department of Atomic Energy, Bangladesh's Ministry of Science and Technology and Russia's Rosatom for the implementation of Rooppur nuclear power plant. As per the agreement, Indian companies would be involved in the construction of non-critical infrastructure and installation work, in addition to supplying materials and equipment's.[99] The Hindustan Construction Company also entered into a joint venture with the Bangladesh-based MAX Group for this purpose. In addition, India has also been helping in the training of Bangladeshi nuclear scientists at the Kudankulam Nuclear Power Plant in Tamil Nadu, which too was built with Russian assistance. During Prime Minister Sheikh Hasina's visit to India, she signed three agreements, which included an agreement for the exchange of technical information in the regulation of nuclear safety and radiation protection. Another agreement between the BAEC and India's Global Centre for Nuclear Energy Partnership (GCNEP), appointing GCNEP as the consultant for the construction and operation of the Rooppur project was signed. On March 2021, Harsh Vardhan Shringla, the Foreign Secretary of India announced that Indian companies will also be helping Bangladesh in the development of transmission lines for the Rooppur Nuclear

Power Plant in Bangladesh as part of its credit line. These transmission lines are valued at over US$ 1 billion.[100]

Phase Three: Construction and Laying the Groundwork for Operations

This period marks the preparations undertaken to get the reactors online. This includes the construction of the plant, training of personnel, etc. This period began in 2016 when the site work was 80% completed and a site license was issued by the Atomic Energy Regulatory Authority. In the following year, in November 2017 construction of the first unit began followed by the construction of the second unit in 2018 which is expected to go online by 2024. More agreements were signed with Russia in this period. For example, in 2017 Bangladesh signed a Spent Fuel Agreement with Russia. Soon after, in 2019 a nationwide policy on radioactive waste management was adopted by the cabinet. As it is a turn-key project, Rosatom will manage the power plant for the first years before handing it over to the BAEC. Meanwhile, BAEC has undertaken the task of training its manpower. By 2019 over 500 Bangladeshi's interned at Russia's Novovoronezh II nuclear power plant, and another 1000 Bangladeshi's are expected to intern there by 2022.

Phase Four: Operations

This phase is set to begin in the next few years when the reactors go online. This period will mark the testing, commissioning and operations of the two nuclear reactors. The first reactor is set to get operational in 2023 and the second one by 2024.

Assessing the Critical Aspects for Nuclear Newcomers and Bangladesh's Progress in this Regard

Starting a civil nuclear project is a colossal task which requires in-depth planning and creative problem-solving techniques for critical issues. These include aspects such as ensuring nuclear safety, radioactive waste management, training a new generation of the workforce among others. The following section assesses these factors and analyses the potential challenges BAEC may face in this regard.

Nuclear Safety

Nuclear safety is a key concern that requires a comprehensive plan and infallible mechanisms. Several institutions and mechanisms have been set up to ensure nuclear safety in Bangladesh. For example, the BAEC has established Nuclear Safety and Radiation Control Division (NSRC). This regulatory branch is responsible for matters regarding nuclear safety such as the careful use of radiation equipment's, nuclear waste management, etc. The nuclear safety and radiation control division has been working in close cooperation with the IAEA, which provides guidance on matters regarding radiation control. Bangladesh is also a signatory to several conventions and safeguards agreements.[101]

However, concerns regarding nuclear safety have been voiced considering that Bangladesh is susceptible to natural calamities such as floods, earthquakes, cyclones and tsunami's. In fact, it has witnessed over 200 natural disasters from 1980 to 2008.[102] Flooding specifically could pose a serious challenge considering the 2020 floods which affected over 4 million people in Bangladesh. One of the areas that was massively affected was the Pabna district, the same place where the Rooppur nuclear power plant is sited. In addition to floods, earthquakes also pose a serious challenge considering that Bangladesh lies near 3 active fault lines. The impact of an earthquake could be intensified considering that the plant is situated in a very densely populated area.

In response to these concerns, Prime Minister Sheikh Hasina has assured that the plant maintains a high level of safety and stated that Bangladesh is working with Russia and India to provide human resource training to their employees in these matters. Naiyyum Choudhury, the Chairman of the Bangladesh Atomic Energy Regulatory Authority has also confirmed that these concerns were acknowledged and addressed before receiving the licenses.[103] In addition, project officials have assured that a seismic monitoring station has already been set up and that there is constant monitoring of seismic activities.[104] A passive core flooding system too is built for evading any sort of disaster caused due to flooding. However, despite several safety mechanisms having been adopted, there still isn't a comprehensive law to deal with matters of nuclear risks and possible liabilities.[105]

Nuclear Waste Management

Nuclear waste management is a serious issue in the nuclear industry requiring a highly safe system to store and dispose of it. To manage nuclear waste, Bangladesh signed a "spent fuel sent back" agreement with Russia in 2017.[106] As per the agreement, Bangladesh will store the nuclear waste for a limited period of time, after which the waste will be sent back to Russia. According to the Science Secretary, this provision was made considering that Bangladesh is a densely populated country, while Russia has large free spaces to treat and store nuclear waste.[107] The Bangladesh cabinet has also approved the "National Policy on Radioactive Waste and Spent Nuclear Fuel Management-2019". As per this policy, the government will be creating a 'Radioactive Waste Management Company' (RWMC). The RWMC will come under the BAEC and will be responsible for managing radioactive waste material in the country not only from nuclear reactors but also from, the medical sector, industrial radiography practices, livestock research etc.[108] However, a long-term strategy to deal with nuclear waste doesn't appear to be formulated yet.

Public Acceptance

Public acceptance is a key factor in implementing the civil nuclear programme, especially in a democratic country. Understanding the importance of communicating with the public and creating awareness of its nuclear program, the government of Bangladesh along with Russia has undertaken several steps to increase public acceptance of nuclear power. These public diplomacy initiatives include seminars and exhibitions to educate the citizens on the subject of nuclear power. Press statements regarding policy decisions are also released. The government has also opened a "Public Counselling Office" and a "Public Awareness

Program." There also exist provisions for Bangladeshi students to study nuclear engineering in Russia. Rosatom in this regard organises visits to the Novovoronezh Nuclear Power Plant and invites young Bangladeshi's to attend events such as Forsage 2017 International Forum for Young Power Engineers and Industrialists.[109]

Nuclear Security

Critical infrastructure like a nuclear power plant is vulnerable to attacks by violent organisations in order to make a statement or to steal fissile materials. Towards this end, Bangladesh has set up a security system which includes a composite response force led by the Bangladeshi Army which is responsible for the physical security of the nuclear infrastructure. In addition, the Bangladeshi authorities have signed a protocol with ROSATOM to form a Physical Protection System (PPS) for the nuclear power plant.[110] Speaking on matters of nuclear safety, Prime Minister Sheikh Hasina mentioned that a unit of law enforcement suchas police, defence personnel, etc. have been formed to ensure the security of the nuclear units.[111] The BAEC has also established a Nuclear Safeguards and Security Division to supervise matters regarding the accounting, control and security systems of nuclear materials.[112]

Legislative Framework

BAER Act-2012 is the wide-ranging legal framework that was established to regulate nuclear energy in Bangladesh. It supplanted the *'Nuclear Safety and Radiation Control (NSRC) Act-1993'*. Its primary function is the safe operations of the Rooppur nuclear power plant in addition to any other nuclear plants that will be set up in. Its scope ranges across all nuclear issues from non-proliferation to environmental protection; from emergency preparedness to the transport of nuclear materials; from nuclear liability to decommissioning of power plants. In addition to the BAER, other ministries also hold responsibility towards certain nuclear-related matters. For example, the Ministry of Environment, Forest and Climate Change is responsible for public safety in case harmful radiation is leaked from nuclear facilities.[113] There have also been plans to form an independent regulatory body. For matters of overall nuclear safety, the government emulates international legal safety mechanisms to meet international standards.[114]

Development of Human Resources

Nuclear Power is a highly technical and specialised field which requires qualified and trained personnel for the multi-level functioning of a nuclear power plant. It requires trained manpower for various roles such as regulators, engineers etc. However, Bangladesh does not have enough skilled personnel in this field. Thus the authorities have been focusing on upgrading the skill of their manpower before the reactors go online. For this reason, BAEC has been organising workshops, symposiums and seminars.[115] BAEC has also established a training institute in the field of nuclear science which currently conducts fundamental courses on nuclear technology for young professionals.[116] Several universities in Bangladesh too have started courses on nuclear technology such as the Bangladesh University of Engineering and Technology. In addition, agreements have been signed with other countries, which is helpful in providing training support to experienced players. This includes countries such as India, the United States, Belarus, Russia and Japan.[117]

Conclusion

Bangladesh stands at a crossroads of a major transition from an underdeveloped economy to a rapidly developing one. Energy security is one of the primary factors that will facilitate this transition. Nuclear power in this regard will have an important role to play in managing the rising energy crisis in the country.

The overall future of nuclear power in Bangladesh so far appears to be optimistic. The BAEC is on track with most of the groundwork and it appears likely to meet its timelines. Despite the covid-19 pandemic which stalled the progress of several developmental projects such as the Padma Bridge and the Dhaka metro-rail in Bangladesh, the Rooppur project however remains unaffected and is currently on schedule.[118] However, developing a civil nuclear project is a complex and enormous commitment, which requires a very comprehensive plan of action. In this regard, authorities will also need to be alert since there is a possibility of myriad problems emerging at each stage.

Concerns of nuclear safety are already beginning to stir in Bangladesh especially after the Rooppur pillow scam which exposed several authorities embezzling funds. This has raised serious questions about the nature of the project.[119] As the case of South Korea's nuclear industry has proven, recklessness and venality by the authorities are sufficient to shut down even a well-established nuclear power programme. In this regard, a more transparent nuclear programme with mechanisms to ensure credibility is imperative. Several other objections have also been put forth by concerned citizens and activists that require more clarity and communication from the authorities. This includes apprehensions regarding the decreasing flow of water in the Padma River.[120] This could pose a serious challenge to the nuclear power project since nuclear plants require a huge amount of water for cooling, the lack of which could lead to a nuclear catastrophe. Considering the importance of grid reliance, there have also been speculations that the current grid capacity is inadequate to introduce two new 12 MWe nuclear units. In addition, BAEC will also have to ensure that the development of legal and regulatory infrastructure matches the pace of the construction of the plant. This is important to ensure the safe functioning of nuclear power plants. Considering the frangible nature of the nuclear industry, there must be no scope for laxity or negligence. The future of nuclear power in Bangladesh is thus likely to depend on the way the authorities ensure safety and manage the challenges that come their way.

Notes

1. Afghanistan, Bangladesh, Bhutan, Maldives, Nepal, Pakistan, Sri Lanka and India.
2. Shobhit Seth, "South Asian Countries: The New Face of Emerging Economies", *Investopedia*, March 17, 2020, at https://www.investopedia.com/articles/investing/022316/south-asia-new-face-emerging-economies.asp, accessed on January 10, 2021.

3. Lei Lei Song, "How South Asia can continue as world's fastest growing subregion—Lei Lei Song", *Adb.org,* August 2, 2019, at https://www.adb.org/news/op-ed/how-south-asia-can-continue-world-s-fastest-growing-subregion-lei-lei-song, accessed on January 31, 2022.
4. Omar Yusuf, "Pakistan Streamlines its National Nuclear Power Programme with IAEA Support", *IAEA.org,* February 13, 2020, at https://www.iaea.org/newscenter/news/pakistan-streamlines-its-national-nuclear-power-programme-with-iaea-support, accessed on January 10, 2021.
5. "Nuclear Power in Bangladesh", *World-Nuclear.org,* at https://www.worldnuclear.org/informationlibrary/country-profiles/countries-a-f/bangladesh.aspx. https://www.world-nuclear.org/information-library/country-profiles/countries-a-f/bangladesh.aspx, accessed on March 3, 2021.
6. Mohammed Shawkat Akbar, "Rooppur Nuclear Power Plant Project Brochure", September 2017, *Bangladesh Atomic Energy Commission,* at https://rooppurnpp.portal.gov.bd/sites/default/files/files/rooppurnpp.portal.gov.bd/page/323ceed5_dcaf_40b7_9518_bf407d9b928f/A%20Dream%20Comes%20True%20September%20%202017.pdf, accessed on March 1, 2021.
7. Manpreet Sethi, "Energy Cooperation Under CPEC: Light at the End of the Tunnel?", *Pentagon Yearbook, South Asia Defense and Strategic Perspective,* 2009 (New Delhi: Pentagon Press), p. 114.
8. "Country Profile: Pakistan", *Hydropower.org,* at https://www.hydropower.org/country-profiles/pakistan, accessed on February 28, 2021.
9. "Thermal has largest share in Pakistan's energy mix", *The Express Tribune,* June 12, 2020, at https://tribune.com.pk/story/2240789/thermal-largest-share-pakistans-energy-mix, accessed on March 30, 2021.
10. Zia Mian and Abdul H. Nayyar "Pakistan and the Energy Challenge", *sgs.princeton.edu,* at https://sgs.princeton.edu/sites/default/files/2020-01/mian-nayyar-2009.pdf, accessed on February 2, 2021.
11. "Attack on power lines in Balochistan causes nationwide blackout", *The Express Tribune,* January 24, 2015, at https://tribune.com.pk/story/827139/parts-of-punjab-sindh-balochistan-left-without-power-after-guddu-transmission-line-trips, accessed on March 7, 2021.
12. Maha Rehman, "The curious case of Pakistan's natural gas crisis", *The Dawn,* January 21, 2019, at https://herald.dawn.com/news/1398784, accessed on March 30, 2021.
13. Najma Minhas, "Pakistan Energy Mix: Overview of Gas Sector (Upstream)", *Global Village Space,* January 3, 2020, at https://www.globalvillagespace.com/pakistan-energy-mix-overview-of-gas-sector-upstream/, accessed on March 3, 2020.
14. n. 8.
15. n. 10.
16. "Kalabagh Dam Conflict in Pakistan", *Climate-diplomacy.org,* at https://climate-diplomacy.org/case-studies/kalabagh-dam-conflict-pakistan, accessed on February 25, 2021.

17. Pakistan Economic Survey 2018-19, *Ministry of Finance, Government of Pakistan,* at http://www.finance.gov.pk/survey_1819.html, accessed on April 18, 2021.
18. "Expanding Renewable Energy in Pakistan's Electricity Mix", *Worldbank.org,* at https://www.worldbank.org/en/news/feature/2020/11/09/a-renewable-energy-future-for-pakistans-power-system, accessed on March 29, 2021.
19. Zofeen T Ebrahim, "World's largest solar park to light up Pakistan's future", *The Dawn,* September 8, 2015, at https://www.dawn.com/news/1205484, accessed on April 18, 2021.
20. Jack Unwin, "What does Pakistan's energy mix look like and what is its future?", *Power-technology.com,* September 27, 2019, at https://www.power-technology.com/features/pakistan-energy-mix/, accessed on March 28, 2021.
21. "Pakistan to Ease Power Shortages with Eight New Wind Farms", *T&D World,* October 2, 2020, at https://www.tdworld.com/renewables/article/21143577/pakistan-to-ease-power-shortages-with-eight-new-wind-arms#:~:text=When%20fully%20operational%20at%20the,no%20access%20to%20electricity%20supply, accessed on April 18, 2021.
22. Umair Younas, B. Khan, et al., "Pakistan geothermal renewable energy potential for electric power generation: A survey", *Renewable and Sustainable Energy Reviews,* v. 63. 2016, pp. 398-413.
23. n. 13.
24. Zofeen T Ebrahim, "Why is Pakistan still pursuing coal?", *China Dialogue,* at https://chinadialogue.net/en/energy/11388-why-is-pakistan-still-pursuing-coal/, July 19, 2019, accessed on March 31, 2021.
25. "Pakistan Ranks Fifth Among Countries Vulnerable to Climate Change, Suffered Economic Loss of $ 3.8 Billion", *News18.com,* December 5, 2019, at https://www.news18.com/news/world/pakistan-on-number-5-among-countries-vulnerable-to-climate-change-suffered-economic-loss-of-3-8-billion-2412415.html, accessed on March 26, 2021.
26. n.7, p. 113.
27. n. 10.
28. Asma Khalid, "China-Pakistan Nuclear Energy Cooperation: History and Key Debates", *South Asian Voices,* February 12, 2020, at https://southasianvoices.org/china-pakistan-nuclear-energy-cooperation/, accessed on January 31, 2021.
29. Muhammad Irfan, Zhen-Yu Zhao, et al., "Assessing the energy dynamics of Pakistan: Prospects of biomass energy", *Energy Reports,* V. 6. 2020, pp. 80-93.
30. n. 7, p. 114.
31. Shalini Chawla, *Nuclear Pakistan* (New Delhi: KW Publishers, 2012), pp. 2-3.
32. Ibid., p. 3.
33. n. 31, p. 4.
34. "Pakistani Nuclear Program", *Atomicheritage.org,* at https://www.atomicheritage.org/history/pakistani-nuclear-program, accessed on February 25, 2021.
35. n. 31, p. 9.

36. "A Brief History of Pakistan's Nuclear Program, *Fas.org*, at https://fas.org/nuke/guide/pakistan/nuke/, accessed on February 27, 2021.
37. n. 28.
38. n. 10.
39. n. 10.
40. "Chashma Nuclear Power Plant 2, Pakistan", *World Nuclear Association,* at https://www.world-nuclear.org/reactor/default.aspx/CHASNUPP-2, accessed on February 27, 2021.
41. "Nuclear Power in Pakistan", *World Nuclear Association,* at https://www.world-nuclear.org/information-library/country-profiles/countries-o-s/pakistan.aspx#:~:text=Pakistan%20has%20a%20small%20nuclear,fuel%20cycle%2C%20using%20indigenous%20uranium, accessed on February 28, 2021.
42. Atika Rehman and Beth Walkerhow, "CPEC Projects Will Increase Pakistan's Reliance On Coal – And Emissions," *Science.Thewire,* October 10, 2020, at https://Science.Thewire.In/Environment/Cpec-China-Pakistan-Military-Environment-Coal/, accessed on February 24, 2021.
43. n.7, p. 113.
44. Ibid.
45. Shi Zhiqin and Lu Yang, "The Benefits and Risks of the China-Pakistan Economic Corridor", *Carnnegie-Tsinghua Centre for Global Policy,* December 21, 2016, at https://carnegietsinghua.org/2016/12/21/benefits-and-risks-of-china-pakistan-economic-corridor-pub-66507, accessed on March 1, 2021.
46. Simi Thambi, "The Energy Dynamics of CPEC in China-Pakistan Relations", *Niti.gov.in,* June 20, 2017, at https://www.niti.gov.in/niti/writereaddata/files/document_publication/The%20Energy%20Dynamics%20of%20CPEC%20in%20China-Pakistan%20Relations.pdf, accessed on March 2, 2021.
47. n.7, p. 113.
48. Saira Bano, "Pakistan: Lessons from the India-US Nuclear Deal", *The Diplomat,* June 22, 2015, at https://thediplomat.com/2015/06/pakistan-lessons-from-the-india-us-nuclear-deal/, accessed on February 25, 2021.
49. "Why China struck N-deal with Pak 4 days after Indo-US deal", *The Hindustan Times*, June 29, 2010, at https://www.hindustantimes.com/india/why-china-struck-n-deal-with-pak-4-days-after-indo-us-deal/story-iE7Gh5dEe1lxBJ7VNnFWsM.html, accessed on February 25, 2021.
50. Ibid.
51. "Nuclear Power in Pakistan", *World Nuclear Association,* at https://www.world-nuclear.org/information-library/country-profiles/countries-o-s/pakistan.aspx#:~:text=Pakistan%20has%20a%20small%20nuclear,fuel%20cycle%2C%20using%20indigenous%20uranium, accessed on April 18, 2021.
52. Rabia Javed, "Nuclear energy of Pakistan", *The Nation*, at https://nation.com.pk/28-May-2020/nuclear-energy-of-pakistan. May 28, 2020, accessed on February 27, 2021.
53. n. 2.

54. Ibid.
55. n. 10.
56. n. 10.
57. Farhan Bokhari, "Nuke Plant Accident Kills 2 In Pakistan", *CBSNews.com.* April 8, 2008, at https://www.cbsnews.com/news/nuke-plant-accident-kills-2-in-pakistan/, accessed on March 2, 2021.
58. The nuclear facilities at Khushab are not subjected to IAEA safeguards unlike those at Karachi and Chashma, since it operates its fleet of military reactors there.
59. Tim Craig, "Outcry and fear as Pakistan builds new nuclear reactors in dangerous Karachi", *Washington Post.* March 5, 2015, at https://www.washingtonpost.com/world/asia_pacific/outcry-and-fear-as-pakistan-builds-new-nuclear-reactors-in-dangerous-karachi/2015/03/05/425e8e70-bc59-11e4-9dfb-03366e719af8_story.html, accessed on January 20, 2021.
60. Rina Saeed Khan, "Underpowered and unsafe, Pakistan's nuclear reactors are just big boys' toys," *The Guardian,* April 28, 2011, at https://www.theguardian.com/environment/2011/apr/28/unregulated-unsafe-pakistan-nuclear-reactors, accessed on March 1, 2021.
61. Tahir Siddiqui, "SHC stops PAEC from starting work on N-plants", *The Dawn,*October 17, 2004, at https://www.dawn.com/news/1138514, accessed on February 26, 2021.
62. Karachi, Pakistan Metro Area Population 1950-2020, *Macrotrends.net,* at https://www.macrotrends.net/cities/22044/karachi/population, accessed on February 25, 2021.
63. Pervez Hoodbhoy, Zia Mian And A. H. Nayyar ,"The Nuclear Shadow over Karachi", *Newsweek,* March 17, 2014, at https://www.newsweekpakistan.com/the-nuclear-shadow-over-karachi/, accessed on March 20, 2021.
64. Qasim A Moini,"Karachi nuclear power plants heavily protected: IAEA chief", *The Dawn,* March 15, 2018, at https://www.dawn.com/news/1395361/karachi-nuclear-power-plants-heavily-protected-iaea-chief, accessed on April 2, 2021.
65. Ibid.
66. "Tsunami could 'wipe out' Karachi", *The Express Tribune,* September 10, 2014, at https://tribune.com.pk/story/760436/tsunami-could-wipe-out-karachi, accessed on March 22, 2021.
67. n. 64.
68. In Pakistan, Militants Use Flood Aid To Seek Support, *NPR.org,* August 23, 2010, at https://www.npr.org/templates/story/story.php?storyId=129379169, accessed on March 8, 2021.
69. n. 64.
70. "Pakistan: Armored Car Sales Booming", CNN, YouTube, July 21, 2016, at https://www.youtube.com/watch?v=JFvjA_JwHTI, accessed on March 2, 2021.
71. "Global Terrorism Index 2020: Measuring The Impact Of Terrorism", Institute for Economics and Peace, November 2020, at https://visionofhumanity.org/wp-content/uploads/2020/11/GTI-2020-web-1.pdf, accessed on January 29, 2021.

72. "Terrorists attack Navy airbase in Karachi, destroy three aircraft", *The Dawn,* May 22, 2011, at https://www.dawn.com/news/630878/terrorists-attack-navy-airbase-in-karachi-destroy-three-aircraft, accessed on January 29, 2021.
73. Tim Craig, "At least 18 Pakistanis killed by assailants who stormed Karachi airport", *The Washington Post,* June 9, 2014, at https://www.washingtonpost.com/world/asia_pacific/pakistan-airport-attack-kills-5/2014/06/08/9fbbbe2a-ef46-11e3-914c-1fbd0614e2d4_story.html?tid=usw_passupdatepg, accessed on March 1, 2021.
74. Syed Raza Hassan, Katharine Houreld, "In attack by al Qaeda, lines blur between Pakistan's military, militants", Reuters, October 1, 2014, at https://www.reuters.com/article/us-pakistan-militants-attacks-insight-idUSKCN0HP2MM20141001,accessed on March 3, 2021.
75. Ankit Panda, "Al Qaeda's Worrying Ability to Infiltrate the Pakistani Military", *The Diplomat,* September 18, 2014, at https://thediplomat.com/2014/09/al-qaedas-worrying-ability-to-infiltrate-the-pakistani-military/, accessed on January 22, 2021.
76. John Lancaster and Kamran Khan, "Pakistanis Say Nuclear Scientists Aided Iran", *The Washington Post,* January 24, 2004, at https://www.washingtonpost.com/archive/politics/2004/01/24/pakistanis-say-nuclear-scientists-aided-iran/d895f104-8657-4152-955b-c80560bce200/, accessed on January 29, 2021.
77. Ibid.
78. Silvia De Michelis, "Saudi Arabia's Nuclear Program", *Waging Peace.org,* October 1, 2019, https://www.wagingpeace.org/saudi-arabia-history/, accessed on March 2, 2021.
79. By William J. Broad, "The Thin Line Between Civilian and Military Nuclear Programs", *The New York Times,* December 5, 2007, at https://www.nytimes.com/2007/12/05/world/middleeast/05weapons.html, accessed on January 18, 2021.
80. David Albright, Sarah Burkhard, and Frank Pabian, "Pakistan's Growing Uranium Enrichment Program", Institute for Science and International Security, May 30, 2018, at https://isis-online.org/uploads/isis-reports/documents/Kahuta_Update_30May2018_Final_with_time-lapse.pdf, accessed on February 18, 2021.
81. Ibid.
82. Laura Gil, "Construction Progresses on Bangladesh's First Nuclear Power Plant", *IAEA.org,* January 31, 2019, at https://www.iaea.org/newscenter/news/construction-progresses-on-bangladeshs-first-nuclear-power-plant, accessed on March 3, 2021.
83. "Booming Energy Sector of Bangladesh: 90 Percent Have Access To The Electricity", *BDnewsnet,* July 12, 2018, at https://bdnewsnet.com/bangladesh/economy/booming-energy-sector-of-bangladesh-90-percent-have-access-to-the-elctrecity/, accessed on February 28, 2021.
84. Asif Reza Chowdhury, Raihan Ul Islam Shezan and M.A.R. Sarkar, "The Prospects of Nuclear Power in the Bangladesh, *Bangladesh Economic Association*, at https://bea-bd.org/site/images/pdf/041.pdf, accessed on March 1, 2021.
85. Ibid.
86. N.K. Das, J. Chakrabartty, Mrinmoy Dey, et al., "Present energy scenario and future energy mix of Bangladesh", *Energy Strategy Reviews,* v. 32, 2020.

87. Badrul Imam, "The burden of imported energy", *The Daily Star,* December 13, 2018, at https://www.thedailystar.net/opinion/perspective/the-burden-imported-energy-1504033, accessed on April 4, 2021.
88. n. 86.
89. "Climate Displacement in Bangladesh", *Environmental Justice Foundation,* at https://ejfoundation.org/reports/climate-displacement-in-bangladesh#:~:text=Bangladesh%20is%20exceptionally%20vulnerable%20to%20climate%20change.&text=It%20has%20been%20estimated%20that,of%20sea%20level%20rise%20alone, accessed on March 3, 2021.
90. "Bangladesh: An economic behemoth in the making", *Andritz,* at https://www.andritz.com/hydro-en/hydronews/hydro-news-asia/bangladesh, accessed on April 4, 2021.
91. Anand Kumar, "Bangladesh's Quest for Nuclear Energy", *IDSA,* October 17, 2007, at https://idsa.in/idsastrategiccomments/BangladeshsQuestforNuclearEnergy_AKumar_171007, accessed on March 2, 2021.
92. Shakeel Ahmed Ibne Mahmood, "Air Pollution Kills 195,000 Bangladeshis Each Year", *PAtimes.org,* at https://patimes.org/air-pollution-kills-195000-bangladeshis-each-year/, accessed on March 2, 2021.
93. M.M. Haque, M.S. Islam and M.A. Zulquarnain, "Challenges and Opportunities to Introduce the First Nuclear Power Plant in Bangladesh", *IAEA.org,* at https://www-pub.iaea.org/MTCD/Publications/PDF/P1500_CD_Web/htm/pdf/topic2/2S01_M.M.%20Haque.pdf, accessed on March 1, 2021.
94. Ibid.
95. "Rooppur Nuclear Power Plant, Ishwardi",*Power Technology.com,*at https://www.power-technology.com/projects/rooppur-nuclear-power-plant-ishwardi/, accessed on March 3, 2021.
96. "Strategic Vision for Strengthening Cooperation in Peaceful Uses of Atomic Energy Between the Republic of India and the Russian Federation", *Ministry of External Affairs,* Government of India, at https://mea.gov.in/bilateral-documents.htm?dtl/24487/Strategic_, accessed on April 5, 2021.
97. "India, Russia to collaborate on Bangladesh nuclear plant, New Delhi's maiden atomic project abroad", *Firstpost,* September 20, 2017, at https://www.firstpost.com/world/india-russia-to-collaborate-on-bangladesh-nuclear-plant-new-delhis-maiden-atomic-project-abroad-4063881.html, accessed on April 4, 2021.
98. Elizabeth Roche. "Indian firms to boost Bangla power infra", *Livemint,* April 2, 2021, at https://www.livemint.com/companies/news/bangladesh-nuclear-power-project-l-t-others-awarded-construction-contract-11617271512562.html, accessed on April 5, 2021.
99. "Russia and India sign action plan on new projects", *World Nuclear News,* October 5, 2018, at https://www.world-nuclear-news.org/Articles/Russia-and-India-sign-action-plan-on-new-projects, accessed on April 5, 2021.
100. "India's Credit Line For Bangladesh Covers Nuclear Projects, Rooppur Nuclear Power Plant: Foreign Secretary", *NDTV.com,* March 28, 2021, at https://www.

ndtv.com/india-news/indias-credit-line-for-bangladesh-covers-nuclear-projects-rooppur-nuclear-power-plant-foreign-secretary-2400332, accessed on April 5, 2021.

101. n. 93.
102. "Information on Disaster Risk Reduction of the Member Countries", *ADRC. Asia,* at https://www.adrc.asia/nationinformation.php?NationCode=50&Lang=en&NationNum=13#:~:text=Bangladesh%20suffers%20from%20floods%2C%20cyclones,136%2C000%2C%203%2C363%20and%20190%20respectively, accessed on March 4, 2021.
103. n. 84.
104. Rafiqul Islam, "Water shortages pose risks to Bangladesh's first nuclear plant", *The Third Pole,* at https://www.thethirdpole.net/en/energy/water-shortages-pose-risks-to-bangladeshs-first-nuclear-plant/, accessed on March 4, 2021.
105. Md. Ershadul Karim and Ridoan Karim, "Future of Nuclear Energy in Bangladesh, *The Daily Star,* May 16, 2017, at https://www.thedailystar.net/law-our-rights/rights-advocacy/future-nuclear-energy-bangladesh-1405837, accessed on March 4, 2021.
106. "Bangladesh signs uranium supply deal with Russia", *Newsonair.com,* August 6, 2019, at http://www.newsonair.com/News?title=Bangladesh-signs-uranium-supply-deal-with-Russia&id=369741#:~:text=Bangladesh%20today%20signed%20a%20deal,Nuclear%20Power%20Plant%20(RNPP).&text=The%20two%20countries%20have%20also,Nuclear%20Power%20Plant%20(RNPP), accessed on March 4, 2021.
107. "Bangladesh Govt approves Nuclear Waste Management Policy", *NuclearAsia.com,* October 23, 2019, at https://www.nuclearasia.com/news/bangladesh-govt-approves-nuclear-waste-management-policy/3204/, accessed on March 4, 2021.
108. Ibid.
109. Andrey Shevlyakov, "Changing perceptions on nuclear energy", *The Daily Star,* December 25, 2017, at https://www.thedailystar.net/opinion/perspective/changing-perceptions-nuclear-energy-1509760, accessed on March 4, 2021.
110. Brigadier General Akhter Shahid, "Bangladesh's Experience in Nuclear Energy", Panel Discussion on Sustainable Use of Nuclear and other Radioactive Materials, *VCDNP.org,* at https://vcdnp.org/wp-content/uploads/2019/04/VCDNP-Panel-Talk-21-Mar.pdf, accessed on March 23, 2021. PPT.
111. "Necessary safety measures taken for nuclear power plant, says Hasina", *Bdnews24.com.* July 14, 2018, at https://bdnews24.com/bangladesh/2018/07/14/necessary-safety-measures-taken-for-nuclear-power-plant-says-prime-minister, accessed on March 5, 2021.
112. n. 93.
113. Md. Shafiqul Islam, Shafiqul Islam Faisal, Sadia Khan, "Development and strengthening of the nuclear and radiation safety infrastructure for nuclear power program of Bangladesh", *Nuclear Engineering and Technology,* November 19, 2020, at https://reader.elsevier.com/reader/sd/pii/S1738573320309359?token=5419FCBC1295B5B11110FAF23CF4EEF154766117A9E5CA99B5813649907BF4BB25F7507DD56869A5488B3B0C41DD8695, accessed on March 4, 2021.
114. n. 93.

115. Ibid.
116. Md. Kabir Hossain, "Human Resources Development for Rooppur Nuclear Power Programme in Bangladesh," *International Conference on Human Resource Development for Nuclear Power Programmes: Building and Sustaining Capacity*, May 12-16, 2014, at https://www-pub.iaea.org/iaeameetings/cn215p/Tuesday/IAPs/Morning/Hossain.pdf, accessed on March 6, 2021.
117. n. 111.
118. Reazul Bashar, "Rooppur nuclear power plant on 'fast track' despite pandemic", *BDnews24.com.* at https://bdnews24.com/economy/2020/07/12/rooppur-nuclear-power-plant-on-fast-track-despite-pandemic, July 12, 2020, accessed on April 5, 2021.
119. "16 officials suspended in Rooppur Power Plant pillow scam", *Dhaka Tribun,* October 15, 2019, at https://www.dhakatribune.com/bangladesh/court/2019/10/15/16-officials-suspended-in-rooppur-power-plant-pillow-scam, accessed on February 26, 2021.
120. n. 82.

7. India's Nuclear Energy Programme: Status, Challenges and Future Trajectory

Introduction

India's civil nuclear programme is marked with distinct contradictions. While India has finally achieved international support, it is domestic factors that pose challenges to the development of its programme; On one hand, the nuclear power sector receives reasonably strong political support across party lines, recognizing the importance of nuclear power in ensuring energy security and bringing down CO_2 emission levels in the country. However, on the other hand, the expansion of nuclear power in India has been slow, with nuclear energy contributing to less than 3 per cent of the electricity generated.[1] The slow growth can be attributed to several challenges that have been bedevilling the progress of the nuclear power sector such as long delays in project materialisation, shortages in financing and public opposition among others.

To understand these contradictions, the chapter analyses the status of India's civil nuclear programme while assessing the various challenges dampening the development of India's nuclear power programme. To do so, the chapter is divided into three parts. I analyses the rationale behind India's decision to develop nuclear power and traces the history and development of India's civil nuclear programme. II discusses the various challenges afflicting the nuclear programme and III analyses the changing scenario in the Indian nuclear sector and tries to assess its future trajectory.

I: Drivers for the Development of a Civil Nuclear Programme

India began to develop its civil nuclear programme in the 1940s and has since received strong political support, regardless of the party in power. There are several factors that led to the employment and continued support of nuclear power in India's energy strategy. The key factors are:

Electricity Demand owing to Economic Growth Imperative

In 1947, as India emerged as an independent country after being colonised for almost 2 centuries, its economy was in a state of shambles. From contributing to about 23 per cent of the global GDP in 1820, the growth of the Indian economy was less than 1 per cent from 1900-1947.[2] Naturally, the primary focus of the leaders then was to develop the economy of the country. As economic development is closely linked to energy security, the focus was to develop and boost energy production. At the time when development policies were being formulated, Homi Bhabha a nuclear physicist, who later became the founding director of the atomic energy programme in India, urged for the need for a nuclear power programme. The abstract of a paper he coauthored alongside M. Dayal read:

> "It is said sometimes that we are living on the threshold of a nuclear revolution similar to the industrial and agricultural revolutions through which various countries of the world passed earlier. However, it is not always realised how important the nuclear revolution is for India. Indeed it may be said that the large scale industrialisation of the country and the raising of the standard of living of our people to a level comparable with that of the industrially advanced countries can be carried through only if there is a large scale utilisation of nuclear energy."[3]

Dr Bhabha who was a close acquaintance of the then Indian Prime Minister Jawaharlal Nehru was able to convince him of the importance to develop a potentially limitless source of energy that could promote the development of the country. Thus, under the leadership of Homi Bhaba, the Atomic Energy Commission was established in 1948. Over the years, the energy demands in the country witnessed a sharp rise,[4] and thus the need to boost nuclear power was further realised. Electricity generation developed significantly in the coming years, however, nuclear power played a miniscule role in this growth.

Presently, the need to expand nuclear power is being recognised more, as energy demands in the country are expected to witness a sharp increase. The International Energy Agency (IAEA) predicted in 2021 that energy demands in India will increase more than any other country in the coming two decades.[5] It is estimated that electricity consumption in India will increase at a rate of 4 per cent per year over 2050.[6] In this regard, it is imperative, that the next wave of electricity demand is met by clean sources of energy with a smaller carbon footprint. It is in this context that nuclear power has been gaining prominence.

Currently, India's energy mix is also not economically prudent for several reasons. First, India has been importing a large amount of energy resources to meet the electricity demands. This has led India to become the world's second-largest importer of coal and the fourth-largest importer of liquefied natural gas.[7] Bulk imports of fuel has a huge impact on government revenue as it is extremely expensive. In this regard, increasing the share of nuclear energy in electricity production could help in facilitating lesser dependency on energy imports and saving the country's revenue. In addition, fossil fuels are the major sources of electricity generation in India,[8] the burning of which is one of the biggest sources of air pollution in the country. Apart from the obvious impact on public health, air pollution also has a huge economic impact as it leads to loss of output and increases healthcare costs. A study published in the popular scientific journal, The *Lancet,* estimated that in 2019 alone, disabilities and deaths caused because of air pollution cost India a loss worth 1.36 per cent of its GDP,[9] while another study claimed that air pollution caused due to burning of fossil fuels costs India $150 billion every year.[10] In this regard, considering that nuclear power has virtually no carbon footprint and has a high capacity factor making it more economical, the government of India has been focusing on increasing the share of nuclear power in electricity generation.

Diversification of Electricity Sources to Minimise Vulnerability

As depicted in the pie chart below, fossil fuels dominate India's energy basket with coal contributing to 73 per cent of the total electricity generated, natural gas contributing 5 per cent and oil 0.5 per cent. [11]

Sources of Electricity Generation in India (2018)

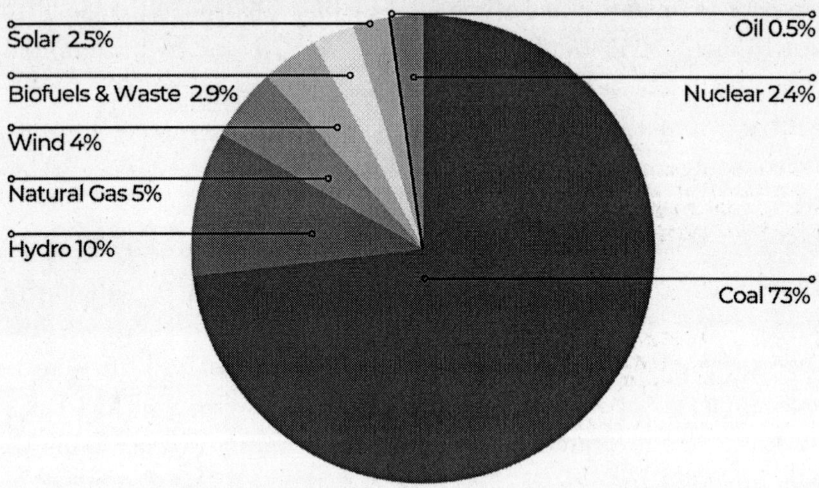

Source: World Nuclear Org.

The share of fossil fuels is expected to further rise, as energy demands are expected to see a sharp increase in the coming years. In this regard, a special report titled "The India Energy Outlook 2021 Report" published by the International Energy Agency estimates that the demand for natural gas will more than triple and the demand for coal will rise from the current 590 million tonnes to 772 million tonnes by the year 2040.[12] Evidently, fossil fuels are projected to play a significant role in electricity generation in India in the foreseeable future. The extensive use of fossil fuels however has a dire effect on public health as a study revealed that India faces the highest number of premature deaths in the world because of the emissions from the burning of fossil fuels.[13] In addition to public health concerns, the challenge is also emerging to be of increasing eco-scarcity of fossil fuel resources and economic sustainability as well. Furthermore, the dependence on imported fossil fuel resources is also not strategically prudent as it makes India vulnerable to price volatility and potential disruptions of power supply.[14]

Acknowledging these challenges, Indian policymakers have been shifting their focus to clean and renewables forms of energy. However, despite the several benefits of renewable power, it alone cannot achieve energy security, considering the many challenges saddling the renewable power sector. For example, it faces the problem of intermittency. In the context of India, solar power does not contribute much in the evenings, which is the time of peak demand in most places in the country.[15] There is also related problems of integration costs and lack of storage technology. Renewables also have location-specific potential in addition to being dependent on seasonality. Some of these sources are land or water-intensive as well.

In comparison, nuclear power offers several benefits that could make up for the limitations of renewable sources of power. For example, nuclear energy is not as land intensive as solar power. As a case in point, the recently inaugurated solar park in Madhya Pradesh is spread over 1590 hectares of land and is expected to produce 750 MWe of energy. In comparison, Kakrapar Atomic Power Station (KAPS) occupies only 959 hectares of land and accommodates 2 operational 220 MWe units, a 700 MWe unit and has another reactor in the pipeline.[16] In addition, not only does nuclear power have an extremely low carbon footprint, but it also has a higher capacity factor than most other forms of electricity-generating technologies. Thus, a mixed energy basket is a prudent solution for India, where the shortcomings of one source of power is made up by the other. Nuclear energy thus can play a significant role in the energy mix by minimising vulnerabilities and can go a long way in enhancing energy independence and steering the country into a sustainable course of development.

Environmental Compulsions for Sustainable Generation of Electricity

As the second most populated country and one of the fastest emerging economies in the world, India has immense energy demands. Unfortunately, as discussed earlier, most of these energy demands are being met by fossil fuels which has led India to become the third largest emitter of CO_2 in the world. India's contribution to energy-related CO_2 emissions is in fact expected to increase from 6.7 to 10.6 per cent soon.[17] Owing to the disastrous effects of climate change due to the extensive burning of fossil fuels, the goal which initially focused on meeting these energy demands has over the years transformed into achieving the demands but in a sustainable manner. To achieve sustainable development and decarbonisation goals, it is imperative to replace fossil fuels with cleaner sources of energy. Nuclear energy gains prominence here as it has virtually no carbon footprints. Speaking of ways to decarbonise energy consumption, Dr Anil Kakodkar, the former Chairman of the Atomic Energy Commission stated that India would require a 30-fold increase in renewable power and a 30-fold increase in nuclear energy in addition to doubling thermal power.[18] In addition, nuclear energy can play an important role to achieve the targets India set under the Paris Agreement of reducing CO_2 emission intensity by 33-35 per cent by the year 2030.[19] In this regard, KN Vyas, Secretary, Department of Atomic Energy (DAE), stated that nuclear energy is an "undeniable" option to fight global warming.[20]

History and Development of India's Civil Nuclear Programme

The vision of the post-independence leadership in India focused on the development of the country. Prime Minister Nehru in this regard reiterated the role of science and technology in nation-building, what he famously referred to as the "temples of modern India". Although, nuclear power for defense purposes is said to be an option Nehru was considering, his emphasis primarily was on developing nuclear technology to supplement conventional energy sources that could power the progress of the country. He articulated the importance of developing nuclear power during the 1948 Constituent Assembly debates on the prospective role of nuclear power, where he referred to it as the new industrial age, which if India does not embrace would remain a "back-ward country".[21] Nehru's decision as discussed in the previous section was influenced by Dr Homi Bhabha, a physicist who was pursuing his education in Cambridge University, and who strongly believed that India needed electricity generated by nuclear power to develop and achieve a standard of living akin to western countries. It was in this context, that India's civil nuclear programme was set up, the development of which can be assessed in the following phases:

Phase One: Inception and Planning (1940s and 1950s)

Under the leadership of Dr Homi Bhabha, India's nuclear power programme steadily developed. Soon after India gained independence, Bhabha was tasked with setting up of the Atomic Energy Commission (AEC), which was established in 1948. The AEC which came directly under the oversight of the Prime Minister was considered a strategic priority. In the following years, the focus lay on the training of the workforce and setting up new institutions such as the Department of Atomic Energy (DAE) which was formed in 1954. India took the assistance of the United States, through the 1953 Atoms for Peace Programme, under which several Indian engineers and technicians were trained abroad.[22] Countries like Canada and France too offered technical cooperation to India.

The Three-Stage Programme

Bhabha had stated before the nuclear bombings in Japan, that "when nuclear energy has been successfully applied for power production in say, a couple of decades from now, India will not have to look abroad for its experts but will find them ready at hand".[23] This has been the endeavour of India's nuclear programme till date. This pursuit for self-sufficiency began when Bhabha conceived a three-stage nuclear programme for India. The programme was envisaged, taking into consideration the dearth of uranium resources in India, which works as a fuel in nuclear reactors. Alternatively, it focused on tapping on the country's vast thorium resources instead, which could work as fuel if immersed in an external supply of neutrons. The three-stage programme was designed as a closed fuel cycle which can feed into each other, so that the spent fuel produced in the first stage, could be reprocessed and used in the second stage to produce power. In the final stage,a sustainable nuclear fuel cycle could be achieved by using thorium.[24] Research and development to technologically and commercially prove this design thus began.

Phase Two: Construction and Development (1960s and 1970s)

The 1960s saw rapid progress in the development of India's civil nuclear programme. In 1963 India signed a peaceful nuclear cooperation agreement with the United States, through which India was supplied with two light-water reactors at Tarapur which gained commercial operation in 1969. The US also provided India with enriched uranium to fuel these plants. It was the first of its kind in Asia and initially generated 210 MW of electricity.[25] Soon after, in 1971, India set up its first pressurized heavy water reactors with Canadian collaboration in Rajasthan- the RAPS-1 and RAPS-2.

Phase Three: Restrictions and Embargoes (1970s-90s)

In 1970 the Treaty on the Non-Proliferation of Nuclear Weapons (NPT) came into force. The treaty articulated three objectives for itself – to allow exploitation of peaceful use of nuclear technology by all under safeguards; to promote non-proliferation by stopping non-nuclear weapon states from developing nuclear weapons and to encourage disarmament by encouraging nuclear weapons states (NWS) to eliminate their nuclear arsenals. However, India did not sign this treaty as it considered it to be unfair and discriminatory in the creation of categories of nuclear and non-nuclear states with different obligations and privileges. In 1974, India successfully conducted its first peaceful nuclear experiment at Pokharan. Outraged by the test, Western countries such as the US and Canada expressed their displeasure by withdrawing their support from India.

Strict restrictions and embargoes were placed on India, which stalled the development of its civil nuclear programme. The US stopped supplying fuel for the boiling water reactors at Tarapur.[26] However, while Western countries withdrew their support, India managed to engineer Chinese help. In addition, the erstwhile Soviet Union came forward and extended its support to India, by signing a bilateral nuclear cooperation agreement. Under this agreement, the Soviet Union agreed to supply heavy water for RAPS 1 and 2, which was previously supplied by Canada.[27]

Aftermath of the 1974 Test

Technology denials and isolation from international nuclear commerce slowed down the pace of development in the nuclear sector. Procurement of equipment and shortage of uranium became major challenges at the time. Speaking of the scale of the embargoes enforced, Anil Kakodkar the former chairman of the AEC narrated an incident where decontamination of MAPS had to be undertaken. The process required a conventional household fitting as an alternate component. However, the stringency of the embargoes were such that an Indian manufacturer who had ties with a US company, was not allowed to even sell a regular household fitting to any nuclear establishments in India![28]

In addition, several other problems surfaced. For example, RAPS-1, of the Rajasthan Atomic Power Station developed problems in its end shield- a vital structural component in the reactor that disrupted reliable operations. As the challenge was a complicated one, there were frequent discussions if the reactor should be permanently shut down. However, it was decided that such an action would dampen the credibility of the nuclear programme at that point.[29] In addition, challenges extended from the grid frequency which needed improvement to the NPCIL facing serious financial troubles. There also was a serious shortage of natural uranium. Several new locations in India were identified for mining and milling uranium, but they encountered challenges over unsuitability of the local geology for in-situ leaching or the growing opposition from local residents.[30] The shortage of uranium, led to the reactors being forced to operate at a lower capacity factor. Dr Kakodkar in this regard narrated how the dearth of uranium led to officials using even scrap uranium lying around in Nuclear Fuel Complex including scraps in the ventilation ducts, which were scrubbed and recovered to make fuel."[31]

Phase Four: Indigenisation and Self-Reliance (1970s onwards)

The embargoes reinstated the need for self-reliance and paved the way for further indigenisation of India's nuclear power programme. Although several delays were caused and the pace of the programme was slowed, the restriction spurred indigenous growth of nuclear technology, as India began to develop alternatives to the denied components and technical expertise. For example, several 220 MWe, and subsequently 540 MWe reactors were indigenously constructed; RAPS-2 commenced operation in 1981 and the Fast Breeder Test Reactor (FBTR) went critical in 1985, by using indigenously developed plutonium-uranium mixed carbide fuel. India thus has been able to demonstrate its capability in the nuclear sector, by being the only developing country to accomplish the ability to design, construct, operate and maintain nuclear power plants while also showing its mettle in manufacturing nuclear equipment's and fuel.[32]

As the programme developed, the Nuclear Power Corporation of India Ltd, (NPCIL) was set up in 1986 for the operation and maintenance of nuclear power projects and the development of new ones. After the unfortunate nuclear disaster in Chernobyl in 1986, a committee was set up to study safety mechanisms in the context of the accident. Several additional measures were undertaken to strengthen the safety mechanisms of the nuclear reactors. After detailed research, it was declared that pressurised heavy water reactor (PHWR) was a safer alternative than the other reactors.[33] India thus indigenously developed PHWR without any external assistance.[34]

1998 Nuclear Tests

India conducted a series of nuclear tests in 1998. This was followed by more sanctions that included a ban on military goods, the sale of certain types of technology and even restrictions on US banks lending to the Indian government. Loans that the World Bank had agreed to lend India for an electric power grid, small hydroelectric generators, and road construction too were stalled.[35] Even China expressed its unwillingness to supply more fuel to India. This began to hamper the infrastructure development of the country, as India found itself isolated from external support.

Countries like Russia however, found a way to go around the international legal commitments and helped India to develop the Kudankulam 1 and 2 project by using an agreement signed during the Soviet era, stating that it could be grandfathered. France too expressed interest in furthering nuclear cooperation with India, but made it clear that to do so, getting the US on board was a pre-requisite, as they were bound by the restrictions of the NSG.[36]

Phase 5: New Prospects in the New Millennium (2000 onwards)

India had set a goal to achieve 10,000 MWe of nuclear power by the year 2000. However, there were several impediments that challenged the pursuit of meeting this target. Prominent among them was the unavailability of uranium. Thus, India had to explore ways to circumvent NSG guidelines to procure more uranium supplies. In addition, there was a need for increased foreign collaboration and access to international technology to boost the nuclear programme. However, despite being unable to meet the targets, India's nuclear power programme had made some significant strides. The embargoes had inadvertently led to more self-sufficiency and indigenisation of its nuclear programme. Nuclear power plants too recorded impressive performances. In addition, India was also successful in developing and testing mixed oxide fuel (MOX), a new kind of fuel assembly which could partially replace enriched uranium.

Inclusion in International Nuclear Commerce

A few years into the new millennium, avenues to re-engage in international nuclear commerce opened up for India. This policy shift was enabled by several factors. Primarily, India had proven itself as a responsible nuclear state as it adhered to a self-mortarium on conducting nuclear tests and observed the principles of the NPT despite being a non-signatory to it. India's vast market opportunity was also recognised by the West. Furthermore, as debates on sustainable development began to gain traction around the world, India's growing energy requirements and the importance to meet them in a sustainable manner were acknowledged by the US.[37]

In addition, other important geopolitical developments of the time also favoured America's engagement with India. Notable among these developments was the revelation of Pakistan's irresponsible behaviour vis-à-vis AQ Khans proliferation network which led to America's disassociation with Pakistan. In addition, the rise of China featured as an important development that warranted the attention of the West.[38] All these factors cumulatively created a favourable condition for US engagement with India. This led to a strategic dialogue between Jaswant Singh, the then Indian Minister of Foreign Affairs and Strobe Talbott, the US Deputy Secretary. The US spokesperson described this engagement as "a global partnership (with India) which encourages India's emergence as a positive force on the world scene."[39] Thus, after being excluded from international nuclear commerce for 34 years, India began to discuss its inclusion in global nuclear commerce.

Indo-US 123 Agreement

After a long period of negotiations, primarily between India and the US, the 123 agreement or the US-India Civil Nuclear Agreement was signed in 2008. The major contours of the agreement were the lifting of sanctions on India, the creation of an India-specific waiver by the Nuclear Suppliers Group,the signing of an additional protocol with the IAEA by India and the amendment of the US Nuclear Non-proliferation Act by the US government. On its part, India also committed to a unilateral moratorium on nuclear testing, separation of its civilian and military nuclear facilities and placement of some civil nuclear facilities under IAEA safeguards.

Soon after, India signed nuclear cooperation agreements with 10 other countries. Unsurprisingly, India's nuclear programme began to develop at a faster pace. The nuclear reactors whose capacity factor had reduced to below 60 per cent at the beginning of the millennium began to rapidly increase. Currently, the capacity factor is close to 80 per cent.

Internal Challenges (2011 onwards)

Just when India overcame external impediments, new internal challenges materialized. The 2011 Fukushima disaster prompted a new crisis of confidence in nuclear power. The Indian nuclear establishment was quick to call for a safety review of its facilities and went to identify areas which could be further strengthened. These were classified into short, medium and long-term safety upgrades. Currently, the short and medium-term safety measures have been completed and implementation of the long-term upgrades are underway.[40] India's Kudankulam power plant is in fact the first nuclear plant in the world to have implemented post-Fukushima safety enhancement features. The safety measures also enabled the plant to be able to weather higher seismic activities and is even said to be able to endure an aircraft crash.[41]

Despite these measures, public sentiment was against the nuclear programme. Different groups that were objecting against the civil nuclear programme, coalesced to conduct protests. As a result, the pace of development of the nuclear programme, once again slowed down. The unit at Kudankulam which was close to completion was forced to stop. Similarly, the preliminary work going on at Jaitapur was also stalled. In response to widespread protests, the Indian President alongside Srijan Pal, Kalam's Officer-on-Special-Duty and Advisor for Technology and Policy published a commentary in a popular Indian newspaper elucidating the need for nuclear energy and assuring the public of the safety of nuclear technology as well as its facilities.[42]

The Civil Liability for Nuclear Damage Act

The Civil Liability for Nuclear Damage Act, 2010 (CLINDA) was passed by both houses of the Indian parliament, as a prerequisite to actuate the Indo-US nuclear agreement. The act was formulated in case of a nuclear accident to compensate victims while placing liability on nuclear suppliers. It faced disapproval and resistance from the opposition party which believed that some clauses of the act were unconstitutional. Incidentally, while India was debating the liability law, the Supreme Court verdict on the Bhopal gas tragedy came out. An accident that took place in 1984 in the Indian city of Bhopal, where a gas leak in a US company lead to the death of about 20,000 people, it was a sensitive issue in India. As critics stated that the compensation for the victims of the Bhopal gas tragedy was inadequate, the discussion on the nuclear liability act was also tainted by this development.

After the controversy surrounding the CLINDA and the protests after Fukushima, the nuclear industry in India suffered a period of remission as investors appeared to be uncertain. The Indian government took several measures to get back the momentum. Notable among these was the signing of the Convention on Supplementary Compensation for Nuclear Damage (CSC) and the setting up of an insurance pool to promote confidence among the suppliers. In the case of nuclear liability issues, India's modus is to come up with solutions on a case-to-case basis. In 2016, India signed a bilateral agreement with Japan to import nuclear reactors and technology. India quickly integrated itself to the global nuclear chain and currently has nuclear cooperation agreements with 14 countries.[43]

Presently, India has 23 operable reactors contributing 2.8 per cent to the total energy mix of and has 8 more reactors under construction.[44] While, these numbers are below those envisaged by the DAE, with an ambition to produce 20 GW of nuclear power by 2020, state support to the nuclear sector continues to be strong. India has set new, ambitious goals with a target to increase the share of nuclear power in electricity generation to 9 per cent by the year 2032 and 25 per cent by the year 2050.[45] In May 2021, Électricité de France (EDF) filed an offer to supply engineering equipment's to build 6, three-generation EPR reactors in Jaitapur. At completion, this will be the world's biggest nuclear power plant.[46] Research on nuclear technology has also been developing steadily, as the following generations of nuclear scientists continue to remain committed to Bhabha's vision of accomplishing a three-stage cycle.

II: Assessing the Challenges in India's Civil Nuclear Programme

Despite coming a long way, the nuclear industry in India continues to be saddled by challenges. Some of the major challenges be devilling the Indian nuclear industry are:

Public Mistrust in Nuclear Power and Anti-nuclear Protests

India has witnessed several anti-nuclear protests over the years that have extended from hunger strikes to demonstrations. These protests have emerged from multiple reasons ranging from land acquisition and rehabilitation to concerns of environmental degradation; from indictments of corruption to concerns of the effect of nuclear power generation on marine life. After the 2011 nuclear disaster in Japan, concerns about nuclear safety once again surfaced, especially among the residents of the Idinthakarai village in Tamilnadu which had been hit by a tsunami in 2004 and has a nuclear power plant in the region. More recently, in 2019 a cyber-attack on the Kudankulam nuclear power plant raised concerns regarding the security of the plant.[47]

In addition, the nuclear power programme has been mired with other challenges. For example, the development of nuclear power plants in India has been slow in the past few years and have taken several more years than their original deadlines to be completed.[48] Projects have also gone significantly over budget. These factors have exacerbated the anti-nuclear movement in India, who claim that the risks are not worth the underwhelming output. The protests have further delayed the completion of projects. For example, the start-up of two Russian VVERs were stopped and the commissioning date for two Areva EPRs were postponed by over a year due to public opposition.[49] Objections even led to the shifting of Westinghouse's first planned project from Gujarat to Andhra Pradesh. In the case of the Kudankulam nuclear power plant, commissioning work was halted for nine months due to local protests.[50]

The DAE has historically been shrouded in secrecy, cosseted by the Atomic Energy Acts of 1948 and 1963 and the Official Secrets Act of 1923. In addition, the government's engagement with the public has been limited in the past. The resulting lack of transparency and communication has led to creating vacuums of scepticism and paranoia of nuclear power by the local populace.

However, in the recent past, the Indian government has recognised that the declining credibility of nuclear institutions in India and the rising protests need to be addressed. Accordingly, for example, the website of the Atomic Energy Regulatory Board (AERB) in addition to publishing information regarding nuclear power in the country also provides a platform for citizens to express any grievances. It also provides information with regard to accessing the RTI (Right to information) section on nuclear power. The website also brings out annual reports, bulletins and press releases on issues related to radiological safety, regulatory decisions, effluent discharges and other sensitive issues.[51] The AERB also participates in science and technology fares and conducts exhibitions to expand public outreach. However, a lot more can be done in this regard. For example, as discussed earlier the French energy group EDF is working with India to build the world's biggest nuclear power plant in the country. At completion, the nuclear facility is projected to provide 10 GW of electricity (which is estimated to be able to power around 70 million households) and create about 25,000 jobs during the construction phase, and around 2,700 jobs permanently.[52] In this regard, communicating the benefits of nuclear power with the citizens could go a long way in promoting nuclear power in the country.

Project Delays and Non-fulfilment of Targets

Poor performance by the reactors is another major problem plaguing India's nuclear programme. While units such as the ones at the Kaiga power plant have a capacity factor of about 90 per cent, and other plants have crossed 100 per cent, the newer reactors,however, have been facing challenges in their performances.[53] The KKNPP for example which began operations in 2013 has the worst performance record in India's nuclear fleet. In 2018, unit 1 remained idle for 6 months due to maintenance issues.[54] The annual World Nuclear Industry Status Report (WNISR), released in September 2019, revealed that Unit 1 at KKNP had a load factor of just 54 per cent in 2018 and Unit 2 of 35.2 per cent[55] This has created challenges for TANGEDCO-Tamil Nadu's electricity distribution company. A TANGEDCO official in this regard stated that they were not able to set any schedule based on the supply from KKNP as "it is as good as not being there."[56] In February 2020, the first unit of KKNP had come to a standstill due to a technical snag. The second unit too was, inactive, as it had not resumed operations since it was halted in December 2019. This resulted in a shortage of 1000 MW of power for TANGEDCO.[57]

Poovulagin Nanbargal, a volunteer group based in Tamil Nadu which works on environmental issues, collected details about the reactor through the RTI act. The details revealed that Unit 1 tripped more than 40 times since its commission in 2013. Unit 2, likewise tripped 19 times since March 2016.[58] Poovulagin Nanbargal in this regard claims that it takes several months to resume operations after each power outage.

In addition, the nuclear power programme in India has been encumbered with project delays and cost overruns. For example, over 39,000 crore rupees is being invested for the construction of the third and fourth units at KKNP, costing two times more than the construction of the first and second units.[59] One of the major reasons for the cost overrun is the delays faced by the projects. The Prototype Fast Breeder Reactor (PFBTR) project for example which was sanctioned in 2003 was authorised at a cost of 3,492 crore rupees and was expected to meet completion within 7 years. However, the project faced major time overruns, which led to price overruns as well, as the government revised the price estimate to 5,677 crore in 2012.[60]

Similarly, the KKNP project witnessed major delays, having taken over 28 years to develop, since it was originally planned in 1988. The major reasons for the delays were the dissolution of the Soviet Union and public opposition. Delays are also witnessed in other stages of development such as in purchases. For example, delays in 100 out of 131 high-value purchase orders that were audited by CAG, ranged from one day to almost 3 years![61] A study conducted by Govind Ranmale and B.E.

Narkhede, that assessed the causes of delays in Indian nuclear power plants, attributed the problem to factors such as dearth in planning, unavailability of materials, issues of quality assurance and stakeholder management, public protests and delays in payment among the others.[62] The economic status of a country could be a factor too, as it is generally known that developing countries have longer gestation periods. However, the Indian nuclear establishment has been fairly successful in overcoming the traditional challenges in the recent past. For example, the construction of Tarapur Atomic Power Plant (TAPP) 3 and 4 was not only constructed well in time but also had lower costs than what was originally allocated for the project.[63] In addition, nuclear institutions too have been coming up with creative problem-solving techniques. For example, to avoid land acquisition problems, new reactors are being built in old nuclear parks instead of setting up new ones.

III: Assessing the Future Trajectory of India's Civil Nuclear Programme

Slow Growth

In 2018, Kaiga 1 an indigenously developed PHWR, in the Indian state of Karnataka set a new world record for operating incessantly for 962 days from May 13, 2016, until December 31, 2018.[64] At the time, the plant load factor was over 99 per cent.[65] Similarly, India's Rajasthan 3 and 5 reactors operated for 777 and 765 days respectively.[66] Despite achieving such significant milestones, the overall developmental trajectory of India's nuclear power programme has been underwhelming, marked by delays and slow growth. With a civil nuclear programme having been set up over 6 decades ago, nuclear power contributes to less than 3 per cent of India's current electricity generation, having an installed capacity of 6,885 MWe.[67] This figure is much lesser than 8,000 MW of nuclear power capacity that Homi Bhabha had envisioned for the year 1980, back in 1954.[68] While the international sanctions on India which lasted for about 3 decades, were one of the key factors responsible for the slow growth, a major expansion in the programme was expected after the 2008 India-US nuclear deal. However, several other factors continue to limit the growth of the programme such as anti-nuclear protests and delays in the development of the second stage of the nuclear fuel programme among others.[69]

The near-term growth rate of the nuclear power sector in the country appears to be slow, as the targets have not been met. For example, India set a goal of generating 20,000 MW of electricity through nuclear power by the year 2020. However, the nuclear capacity in 2020 was only around 6780 MW.[70] In 2011 again, India set a target of achieving up to 14,600 MWe by the year 2032. However, the chances of missing the new targets also seem likely as the new projects set up to achieve these goals are way behind schedule.[71] In this regard, it would be pragmatic for ambitions to be tempered with reality.

The government however, is committed to developing the country's nuclear power programme. The Department of Atomic Energy is aiming to increase the nuclear power generation capacity over 3 folds in the coming decade.[72] Several steps have been taken to achieve this goal, for example, in 2017 over 1 lakh crore rupees was approved for the setting up of nuclear power plants. Scheduled to be completed by the year 2031, they are expected to have a combined capacity of 7000 MW.[73] In 2020, Jitendra Singh, Minister of State for the DAE stated that to augment nuclear power production, nine new reactors are targeted to achieve completion by 2024-25, in addition to 12 other reactors which gained government approval in 2017.[74] Other sites too have gained 'in principle' approval from the government as well, for setting up of more reactors in the future.[75] In this regard, the DAE stated that the nuclear power capacity of India will increase from the current capacity of 6780 MW to 22,480 MW by the year 2031.[76] To intensify near-term growth, several uranium mining operations too have been initiated such as the Rohil Uranium Project in Rajasthan, Kanchankayi Uranium Project in Karnataka, Jajawal Uranium Project in Chhattisgarh and Chitrial Uranium Project in Telangana among the others.

Strides in Nuclear Research and Development

The Indian nuclear industry has made significant strides in the field of nuclear research and development. In 2012, Siegfried Hecker, a former director of the Los Alamos National Laboratory in the US, stated in an issue of *Physics Today* that "*India has the most technically ambitious and innovative nuclear energy program in the world... The extent and functionality of its nuclear experimental facilities are matched only by those in Russia and are far ahead of what is left in the US.*"[77] Most notable among India's scientific endeavours in nuclear technology is the development of the three-stage cycle. The reactor system is designed in a way that it can utilise the vast thorium resources in the country. To materialise this process, India today is a world leader in thorium research and has published double the number of research papers than its competitors between the years 2002 to 2006.[78] The United Kingdom too, has been collaborating with India to take the research forward. Five research proposals of £2 million is being funded by the UK's Engineering and Physical Sciences Research Council and by India's Department of Atomic Energy.[79]

India's nuclear power programme was formulated to be a closed fuel cycle, that could be achieved in three successive stages. In the first stage, natural uranium is used as fuel in pressurised heavy water reactors. The by-product of it, plutonium-239 will then be used to make mixed oxide (MOX) fuels for fast breeder reactors (FBR) in the second stage. India has successfully completed the first stage of the nuclear fuel program and the second stage is very close to achieving success. For this purpose, India has been operating a fast breeder test reactor (FBTR) since 1985 to develop a future breeder reactor for the second stage. India currently is at the verge of launching a prototype fast breeder reactor (PFBR). Located in Tamilnadu, it has a capacity of 500 MW. The completion of the PFBR has been delayed over the years, but is expected to finally get commercialised in October 2022. Tracing the development of the rector, an official stated during the Rajya Sabha question and answers session that "All construction activities (have been) completed and integrated commissioning of all systems (are) in progress."[80] The standing committee in this regard has said, "Even though it would have taken almost two decades [of work on PFBR] when commissioning takes place, this is a pioneering initiative of which India can be justifiably proud (sic). It will transform our nuclear energy programme".[81] Plans are also in progress to build 5 more fast breeder reactors of a combined capacity of 2.5 GW. Research on the final stage, to develop thorium-based reactors too are also in full swing and are expected to be successful in the next few decades. Once proven technologically, this would be a major breakthrough in the field of nuclear power generation, as it does not only minimise nuclear waste but is also more proliferation resistant. The pace at which India develops its three-stage cycle will be a major determinant of the future of nuclear power in the country. This would help India attain energy independence as experts estimate that through this process, India will be able to produce about 500 GWe of power for at least four hundred years using the economically extractable thorium reserves in the country.[82] This could also help in launching India as a leading exporter of alternate nuclear technology.

India has also been exploring the prospects of nuclear fusion technology. It is one of the 7 countries funding the International Thermonuclear Experimental Reactor (ITER) project in France.[83] The ITER project is working on building the worlds largest nuclear fusion reactor, which can generate ten times more energy than what it has been supplied. Larsen and Toubro, an Indian construction engineering company, has also developed a component for this project.

Nuclear Exports and Services

As India has successfully developed nuclear power know-how, it is now moving beyond just domestic development of nuclear power. Apart from extending training and capacity-building assistance to other countries, it is now poised to export nuclear technology as well. However, since India is not a member of the NSG, exporting nuclear technology becomes complicated for the country. It has thus reached an agreement with Russia, allowing it to circumvent around this problem. In 2015 India signed a 'Strategic Vision for Strengthening

Cooperation in Peaceful Uses of Atomic Energy' with Russia. Under this agreement the "two sides will explore opportunities for sourcing materials, equipment and services from Indian industries for the construction of the Russian-designed nuclear power plants in third countries".[84] In extension, India signed a tripartite agreement with Russia and Bangladesh in 2018 to develop the Rooppur Nuclear Power Plant project in Bangladesh. India's contribution to the Rooppur project will be through the construction of non-critical infrastructure, capacity building and installation work, in addition to supplying materials and equipment.[85] India's Hindustan Construction Company has engaged in a joint venture with the Bangladesh-based MAX Group as well. In addition, India has extended its training services to Bangladeshi scientists at its Kudankulam nuclear plant, which too was built with Russian assistance. Bangladesh President Sheikh Hasina signed three agreements to further nuclear cooperation with India during her visit to the country. In addition, Bangladesh's Atomic Energy Commission (BAEC) and India's Global Centre for Nuclear Energy Partnership (GCNEP) also took the cooperation ahead, with the appointment of GCNEP as the consultant for the construction and operation of the Rooppur project.[86] Earlier this year on March 2021, it was announced that Indian companies will be assisting Bangladesh in developing transmission lines for the Rooppur plant, which are estimated to be valued at more than US$ 1 billion.[87] This provides India an opportunity to prove its mettle as a nuclear exporter. Establishing itself in the nuclear exports market won't just advance its domestic "Make in India" initiative but would also help in the promotion of nuclear power as a foreign policy tool.

Conclusion

Several pressing issues beg the need for boosting nuclear power production in India. First, India is expected to soon overtake the European Union and become the world's third-largest consumer of energy. Second, India is presently the third largest emitter of CO_2 in the world. In addition, energy imports are mounting and industrial growth is being challenged by power crises. These factors, compel India to boost a sustainable and clean source of power, to spur economic growth, increase the standard of living of its people and alleviate the climate change crisis. In this regard, a mixed energy basket with a significant role for nuclear power could go a long way in powering the growth of the country and minimising many of the challenges facing Indian society.

India's future as a potential nuclear exporter looks promising. With a long history of research and development in the field of nuclear technology, India appears to be ready to cash on its technical prowess. Currently, the nuclear exports market is dominated by Russia and China, both of which have been tainted with allegations of corruption and political manipulation. In this regard, with India's history of benign foreign policies, India could emerge as a favourable country to engage in nuclear exports with. Nuclear exports, would not only be economically beneficial for India but could also be a strategic foreign policy tool.

However, to export nuclear technology, it is important for India to develop its own domestic programme. There is thus a need for a comprehensive energy strategy, with a clear roadmap and thorough implementation. If price overruns and prolonged delays of projects continue to plague the nuclear programme, the Indian nuclear industry will be at risk of collapse. A more proactive and robust approach is needed to move out of the slump. Thus, the future of India's energy security and its nuclear power sector depends on how India responds to the many challenges it faces.

Most pertinent among these challenges that require immediate attention is that of public opposition. Increased political support and boosting finances won't be sufficient, if the mood of the nation is anti-nuclear. Public support is paramount for the survival and success of a nuclear power project in a democratic country. Gaining credibility could go a long way in consolidating public support. There is also a need for an energised public communication strategy which can generate a better understanding of nuclear power for its citizens. Especially in area's selected to host nuclear projects, it is vital to proactively engage with the local population and communicate the various benefits it offers and address any concerns or grievances of the people. It would be unfortunate if after winning international acceptance, India loses domestic support.

Notes

1. M Ramesh, "Why nuclear when India has an 'ocean' of energy", *The Hindu,* June 13, 2019, at https://www.thehindu.com/business/Industry/why-nuclear-when-india-has-an-ocean-of-energy/article28230036.ece, accessed on April 15, 2021.
2. Shashi Tharoor, *Pax Indica: India and the World of the 21st Century* (Gurugram: Penguin Books, 2013), p. 8.
3. N. Sharma and B. Banerjee, *Nuclear Power in India* (New Delhi: Rupa, 2008), pp. 20-21.
4. Shebonti Ray Dadwal, *Rethinking Energy Security in India Hardcover* (New Delhi: KW Publishers, 2008), p. 110.
5. "India energy demand set to grow fastest in the world; to overtake European Union", *The New Indian Express,* February 9, 2021, at https://www.newindianexpress.com/business/2021/feb/09/india-energy-demand-set-to-grow-fastest-in-the-world-to-overtake-european-union-2261738.html, accessed on May 22, 2021.
6. "India's oil and gas import to double by 2050: BP Energy Outlook", *Financial Express,* September 15, 2021, at https://www.financialexpress.com/economy/indias-oil-and-gas-import-to-double-by-2050-bp-energy-outlook/2083387/, accessed on May 2, 2021.
7. M. Rajshekhar, "India Is One of the Last Big Markets for Fossil Fuels – and It Is Cashing In", *The Wire*, July 7, 2021, at https://science.thewire.in/environment/india-fossil-fuels-demand-greenhouse-gas-emissions/, accessed on May 12, 2021.
8. "Nuclear Power in India," *World-nuclear.org.* at https://world-nuclear.org/information-library/country-profiles/countries-g-n/india.aspx, accessed on May 15, 2021.
9. Disha Shetty, "Air Pollution Cost India $36.8 Billion In 2019", *Forbes,* at https://www.forbes.com/sites/dishashetty/2020/12/22/air-pollution-cost-india-368-billion-in-2019/?sh=1d9d38335c70, December 22, 2021, accessed on May 25, 2021.
10. "Air pollution from fossil fuels costs India $150 bn annually, 5% of GDP", *Business-standard.com,* February 12, 2020, at https://www.business-standard.com/article/pti-stories/air-pollution-from-fossil-fuels-costs-india-usd-150-billion-annually-report-120021201569_1.html, accessed on June 16, 2021.
11. n. 8.
12. "India Energy Outlook 2021", *International Energy Agency*, at https://iea.blob.core.windows.net/assets/1de6d91e-e23f-4e02-b1fb-51fdd6283b22/India_Energy_Outlook_2021.pdf, accessed on May 20, 2021.
13. Chetan Bhattacharji, "Nearly 5 Deaths Per Minute In India Due To Fossil Fuels Burning: Report", NDTV, February 9, 2021, at https://www.ndtv.com/india-news/

nearly-5-deaths-per-minute-in-india-due-to-fossil-fuels-burning-report-2366493, accessed on July 20, 2021.

14. Manpreet Sethi, "Future of Nuclear Power in Asia", *CLAWS Summer Journal,* 2012. p. 152.
15. Rahul Tongia, "Why Renewable Energy is Harder in India than in Other Countries Wednesday", *Brookings Institute,* May 21, 2014, at https://www.brookings.edu/blog/planetpolicy/2014/05/21/why-renewable-energy-is-harder-in-india-than-in-other-countries/, accessed on July 18, 2021.
16. Manpreet Sethi, "Kakrapar: Why Nuclear Power for Electricity Generation?", *Institute of Peace and Conflict Studies,* July 27, 2021, at http://www.ipcs.org/comm_select.php?articleNo=5709, accessed on May 1, 2021.
17. "Nuclear energy as enabler in India's sustainable development goals", CNBCTV18, December 13, 2020, at https://www.cnbctv18.com/energy/nuclear-energy-as-enabler-in-indias-sustainable-development-goals-7717081.htm, accessed on July 17, 2021.
18. *Pib.gov.in,* May 12, 2020, at https://pib.gov.in/PressReleasePage.aspx?PRID=1623194, accessed on July 18, 2021.
19. n. 17.
20. Myths linked to nuclear energy should be busted: MoS Jitendra Singh," *Financial Express,* October 19, 2013, at https://www.financialexpress.com/industry/myths-linked-to-nuclear-energy-should-be-busted-mos-jitendra-singh/1740042/, accessed on May 3, 2021.
21. Laveena Lee, "The Indian Nuclear Energy Programme: the Quest for Independence", in *Nuclear Energy Development in Asia: Problems and Prospects* (New York: Palgrave Macmillan, 2011), p. 69.
22. n. 21, p. 71.
23. H.N. Sethna. "India's Atomic Energy Programme: Past and Future", IAEA Bulletin, v. 21, n. 5.
24. Niharika Tagotra, "India's Ambitious Nuclear Power Plan – And What's Getting in Its Way", *The Diplomat,* September 9, 2020, at https://thediplomat.com/2020/09/indias-ambitious-nuclear-power-plan-and-whats-getting-in-its-way/, accessed on May 3, 2021.
25. "Plants Under Operation, Nuclear Power Corporation of India Limited", *web.archive.org,* archived on January 26, 2011, at https://web.archive.org/web/20101217155859/http://npcil.nic.in/main/ProjectOperationDisplay.aspx?ReactorID=73&Page=2, accessed on May 8, 2021.
26. Anil Kakodkar and Suresh Gangotra, *Fire and Fury: Transforming India's Strategic Identity* (New Delhi: Rupa Publications, 2019), p. 75.
27. Pulkit Mohan and Pallav Agarwal, "India's civil nuclear agreements: A new dimension in India's global diplomacy", *Orfonline.org,* October 4, 2019, at https://www.orfonline.org/research/india-civil-nuclear-agreements-new-dimension-india-global-diplomacy/, accessed on May 28, 2021.
28. Ibid., pp. 88-89.

29. n. 26, p. 33.
30. n. 26, pp. 60-64.
31. n. 26, pp. 60-64.
32. Shebonti Ray Dadwal, "India's Energy Security Policy: A Case for Nuclear Power", *Strategic Analysis,* v. 23, n. 8, November 1999, at https://ciaotest.cc.columbia.edu/olj/sa/sa_99das03.html#note12, accessed on May 14, 2021.
33. n. 26, p. 37.
34. A. Gopalakrishnan, "Evolution of the Indian Nuclear Power Program", Annu. Rev. *Energy Environ.* 2002., at https://www.belfercenter.org/sites/default/files/legacy/files/Evolution%20of%20the%20Indian%20Nuclear%20Power%20Program.pdf, accessed on May 18, 2021, p. 378.
35. n. 26.
36. n. 26, p. 97.
37. For more on this see: Manpreet Sethi, "15 years of Indo-US nuclear deal: Benefits transcend nuclear", *Sunday Guardian Live*, July 4, 2020, at https://www.sundayguardianlive.com/opinion/15-years-indo-us-nuclear-deal-benefits-transcend-nuclear.
38. Manpreet Sethi, "15 years of Indo-US nuclear deal: Benefits transcend nuclear", *Sunday Guardian Live*, July 4, 2020, at https://www.sundayguardianlive.com/opinion/15-years-indo-us-nuclear-deal-benefits-transcend-nuclear, accessed on May 3, 2021.
39. Ibid.
40. Atomic Energy Regulation Board home page, *AERB.gov.in,* at https://www.aerb.gov.in/images/PDF/Annual_Bulletin/2018.pdf. p. 21, accessed on May 29, 2021.
41. "Kudankulam plant safest in the world, says Russian official", *The Hindu,* September 20, 2016, at https://www.thehindu.com/news/national/Kudankulam-plant-safest-in-the-world-says-Russian-official/article14544107.ece, accessed on May 29, 2021.
42. A.P.J Abdul Kalam and Srijan Pal Singh, "Nuclear power is our gateway to a prosperous future", *The Hindu,* November 6, 2011, at https://www.thehindu.com/opinion/op-ed/nuclear-power-is-our-gateway-to-a-prosperous-future/article2601471.ece, accessed on June 9, 2021.
43. n. 27.
44. n. 8.
45. n. 23.
46. "India closer to building the worlds largest nuclear plant: French firm", *Livemint,* April 24, 2021, at https://www.livemint.com/news/india/india-closer-to-building-world-s-biggest-nuclear-plant-french-firm-11619242815330.html, accessed on June 7, 2021.
47. Aathira Konikkara , "There's no transparency: SP Udayakumar on the cyber attack on Kudankulam Nuclear Power Plant", *The Caravan,* November 15, 2019, at https://caravanmagazine.in/security/no-transparency-udayakumar-kudankulam-nuclear-plant, accessed on May 29, 2021.

48. "India's nuclear solution to global warming is generating huge domestic protests", *publicintergrity.org,* December 15, 2015, at https://publicintegrity.org/national-security/indias-nuclear-solution-to-global-warming-is-generating-huge-domestic-protests/, accessed on May 29, 2021.
49. Dan Yurman, "Protests delay India's nuclear renaissance", *Ans.org,* November 17, 2011, at https://www.ans.org/news/article-860/protests-delay-indias-nuclear-renaissance/, accessed on May 29, 2021.
50. "Indian government takes steps to get nuclear back on track" , *World Nuclear News,* February 11, 2019, at https://www.world-nuclear-news.org/Articles/Indian-government-takes-steps-to-get-nuclear-back, accessed on May 29, 2021.
51. Atomic Energy Regulation Board home page, *AERB.gov.in,* at https://www.aerb.gov.in/images/PDF/Annual_Bulletin/2018.pdf. p. 21, accessed on May 29, 2021.
52. "India closer to building the worlds largest nuclear plant: French firm", *Livemint,* April 24, 2021, at https://www.livemint.com/news/india/india-closer-to-building-world-s-biggest-nuclear-plant-french-firm-11619242815330.html, accessed on June 7, 2021.
53. B Sivakumar, "Both Kudankulam units shut, 1,000 MW Shortfall for Tamilnadu", *Times of India,* February 14, 2020, at http://timesofindia.indiatimes.com/articleshow/74125162.cms?utm_source=contentofinterest&utm_medium=text&utm_campaign=cppst, accessed on May 29, 2021.
54. "Kudankulam reactor synchronised with grid", *The Hindu,* May 19, 2019, at https://www.thehindu.com/news/national/tamil-nadu/kudankulam-reactor-synchronised-with-grid/article27175281.ece, accessed on May 29, 2021.
55. "Global report on nuclear energy flays Kudankulam units' performance", *The New Indian Express,* at https://www.newindianexpress.com/states/tamil-nadu/2019/sep/25/global-report-on-nuclear-energy-flays-kudankulam-units-performance-2038664.html, September 15, 2019, accessed on May 28, 2021.
56. "Why the TN electricity distributor is in conflict with Kudankulam nuclear power plant", *The news minute,* August 28, 2019, at https://www.thenewsminute.com/article/why-tn-electricity-distributor-conflict-kudankulam-nuclear-power-plant-107983, accessed on May 26, 2021.
57. n. 57.
58. n. 60.
59. n. 60.
60. "India's First Prototype Fast Breeder Reactor Has a New Deadline. Should We Trust It?", *The Wire,* August 20, 2021, at https://science.thewire.in/the-sciences/prototype-fast-breeder-reactor-dae-bhavini-npcil-liquid-sodium-coolant-purchase-orders/, accessed on May 25, 2021.
61. Ibid.
62. Govind Ranmale and B.E. Narkhede, "Delays in Indian Nuclear Power Plant", *Researchgate,* January 2015, at https://www.researchgate.net/publication/300702662_Delays_in_Indian_Nuclear_Power_Plant, accessed on June 2, 2021.

63. Manpreet Sethi, "The Nuclear Energy Imperative: Addressing Energy Poverty, Energy Security and Climate Change in India", *India Infrastructure Report 2010.*
64. The record was beaten by Canada's Darlington Unit 1 in February 2021.
65. "Indian-Designed Nuclear Reactor Breaks Record for Continuous Operation", *powermag.com,* February 1, 2019, at https://www.powermag.com/indian-designed-nuclear-reactor-breaks-record-for-continuous-operation/, accessed on May 30, 2021.
66. Ibid.
67. n. 8.
68. Prerna Gupta, M.V. Ramana, "A Decade After the Nuclear Deal", *The India Forum*, May 26, 2019, at https://www.theindiaforum.in/article/decade-after-nuclear-deal, accessed on July 17, 2021.
69. Indian government takes steps to get nuclear back on track, *World nuclear news.* Org, February 11, 2011, at https://www.world-nuclear-news.org/Articles/Indian-government-takes-steps-to-get-nuclear-back, accessed on June 8, 2021.
70. "Nuclear power capacity to treble by 2031: Govt", *The Tribune*, February 15, 2021, at https://www.tribuneindia.com/news/nation/nuclear-power-capacity-to-treble-by-2031-govt-212513, accessed on June 3, 2021.
71. Govind Ranmale and B.E. Narkhede, "Delays in Indian Nuclear Power Plant", *Researchgate*, January 2015, at https://www.researchgate.net/publication/300702662_Delays_in_Indian_Nuclear_Power_Plant, accessed on June 2, 2021.
72. Mohana Basu, "Govt sets target to increase nuclear power generation capacity by over 3 times in 10 years", *The Print,* March 4, 2020, at https://theprint.in/india/govt-sets-target-to-increase-nuclear-power-generation-capacity-by-over-3-times-in-10-years/375366/, accessed on June 1, 2021.
73. "Myths linked to nuclear energy should be busted: MoS Jitendra Singh", *Financial Express*, October 19, 2019, at https://www.financialexpress.com/industry/myths-linked-to-nuclear-energy-should-be-busted-mos-jitendra-singh/1740042/, accessed on June 1, 2021.
74. Ibid.
75. n. 73.
76. "Nuclear power capacity to treble by 2031: Govt", *The Tribune*, February 15, 2021, at https://www.tribuneindia.com/news/nation/nuclear-power-capacity-to-treble-by-2031-govt-212513, accessed on June 3, 2021.
77. S Raghotham, "What Got Made in India Before Modi, How it Was Done", *Indiadefensenews,* December 22, 2019, at http://www.indiandefensenews.in/2019/12/what-got-made-in-india-before-modi-how.html, accessed on June 12, 2021.
78. Srikumar Banerjee, Thorium Utilisation for Sustainable Supply of Nuclear Energy, *Virginia Tech,* September 2010, accessed on June 2, 2021.
79. A future energy giant? India's thorium-based nuclear plans", *Physics.org*, October 1, 2010, at https://phys.org/news/2010-10-future-energy-giant-india-thorium-based.html, accessed on June 2, 2021.

80. n. 60.
81. Ibid.
82. T.S. Subramanian, "A debate over breeder reactors", *Frontline,* December 1998, *v.15, N.25*, accessed on June 2, 2021.
83. Karan Kamble, "Not On The Money – India's Fusion Energy Ambitions May Be Hampered By Understaffing At The World's Largest Fusion Reactor", *swarajyamag.com,* August 28, 2020, at https://swarajyamag.com/science/not-on-the-money-indias-fusion-energy-ambitions-may-be-hampered-by-understaffing-at-iter, accessed on June 3, 2021.
84. "Strategic Vision for Strengthening Cooperation in Peaceful Uses of Atomic Energy Between the Republic of India and the Russian Federation", *Ministry of External Affairs,* Government of India, at https://mea.gov.in/bilateral-documents.htm?dtl/24487/Strategic_, accessed on April 5, 2021.
85. "Russia and India sign action plan on new projects", *World Nuclear News.* October 5, 2018, at https://www.world-nuclear-news.org/Articles/Russia-and-India-sign-action-plan-on-new-projects, accessed on April 5, 2021.
86. "India's Credit Line For Bangladesh Covers Nuclear Projects, Rooppur Nuclear Power Plant: Foreign Secretary", *NDTV.com,* March 28, 2021, at https://www.ndtv.com/india-news/indias-credit-line-for-bangladesh-covers-nuclear-projects-rooppur-nuclear-power-plant-foreign-secretary-2400332, accessed on April 5, 2021.
87. Ibid.

8. Future of Nuclear Power in Asia: An Assessment

Introduction

Nuclear energy has undoubtedly witnessed a redux in the Asian continent as it has emerged as a prime tool to bolster economic growth while ensuring a low-carbon energy future. Considering the pace of development of nuclear programmes in Asia, it appears that a nuclear renaissance is imminent. The nuclear sector has gained prominence from the realisation that while renewable sources of power are extremely important to attain sustainable development, they however are not a panacea for all energy woes. In addition, the drivers that have led to the development of nuclear power in the continent are diverse ranging from economic and environmental factors to geostrategic and sociological ones. Apart from boosting nuclear power production, Asia is also emerging as a leader in the field of nuclear research and development, with several countries having dedicated institutions focused on developing nuclear technology. Asian countries have also been focusing on exporting their nuclear technology widely.

This conclusive chapter, summarises the course of the development of nuclear power in Asia and analyses the various factors that have influenced its trajectory. In doing so it also attempts to assess the future of nuclear power in the continent and identifies the factors that may accelerate or limit its growth.

Mapping the Trajectory of Nuclear Power in Asia

The 2011 Fukushima accident evidently had a substantial impact on the global civil nuclear industry, where diverging approaches were taken by countries around the world. Interestingly, while the reaction in Western countries was to scale down nuclear power generation, countries in the Asian continent, on the other hand, focused on ramping up the safety standards of their reactors and boosted nuclear power production. This trend can be largely linked to the economic realities of Asian countries which are at different stages of development. They are grappling with the challenges of growing populations, rising electricity demands and limitations of indigenous energy resources. As discussed in the previous chapters, countries took stock of lessons in the Fukushima context and enhanced their safety protocols accordingly. In addition, The International Atomic Energy Agency (IAEA) undertook over 1000 initiatives to boost nuclear safety and enhance cooperation among countries.[1] With a focus on reactor safety, countries in Asia chose to continue to develop their nuclear power programmes.

The following graph in this regard depicts the trajectory of nuclear power generation in Asian countries from 2010 to 2020.

Figure 1: Nuclear Power Generation in Asian Countries from 2010-20

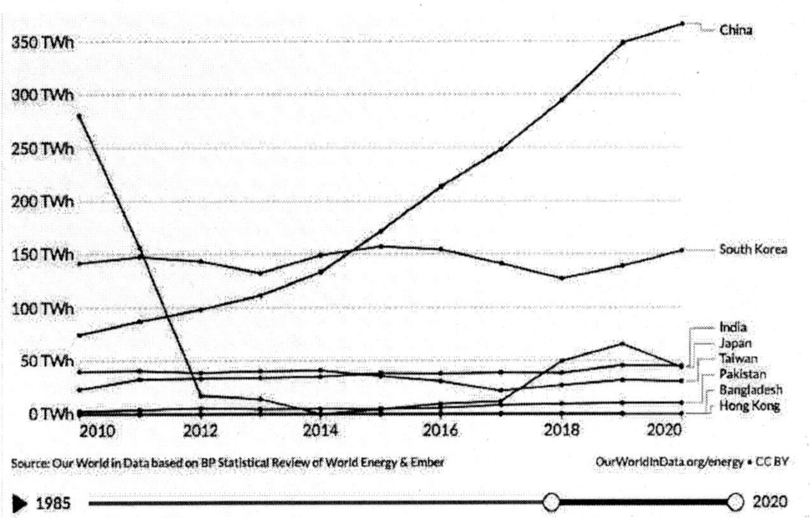

As illustrated in the graph above, after a dip of varying degrees post-2011, the share of nuclear power generation in Asian countries appears to be increasing again. China leads the chart with 295 TWh worth of nuclear energy generated (in 2018). It witnessed a 400% increase in nuclear power generation between December 2010-20 having built 36 new units.[2] These numbers are expected to rise as the Chinese government has set a target to increase nuclear generation capacity to 70 gigawatts by the year 2025.[3] With a continued commitment to nuclear power, China is projected to soon take over the United States and have the highest nuclear power capacity by 2030.[4] Nuclear power has also been touted to be an important tool in meeting China's goal of attaining carbon neutrality by the year 2060.

Likewise, Japan too intends to use nuclear power to achieve net zero greenhouse gas emissions by 2050. However, the pace of nuclear power development in Japan is expected to be slow considering that the government imposed strict regulations after the Fukushima accident and decided to decommission over 20 reactors. While Japan's ambitious nuclear aspirations took a hit after the 3/11 accident, the country continues to employ nuclear power in its energy basket. Currently, 10 out of 33 operable reactors in Japan have resumed operations. Fumio Kishida, the newly elected Prime Minister of Japan has been in favour of restarting nuclear reactors and replacing old ones with small modular reactors.[5] Support for nuclear power is thus secured in Japan at least until the next elections in 2025.

India too has a committed nuclear power programme with ambitious plans in the offing, having declared to boost nuclear energy capacity by three-fold in the next ten years.[6] Currently, India has 23 nuclear reactors producing 6885 MWe of power and has 7 more reactors worth a combined capacity of 5194 MWe under construction.[7] In fact, of the growth projected in nuclear power generation by 2040, 90 per cent of it is estimated to come from China and India.[8] With strong support for nuclear power across party lines, India is likely to witness a major boost in its nuclear power programme.

While South Korea trails behind India with 34 TWh of nuclear power production, its future however appears to be uncertain. Having already shut down 2 reactors, the current South Korean government intends to eventually do away with nuclear power altogether. However, the anti-nuclear wave may not be permanent, considering the increasing pressure on the Korean government to reverse its anti-nuclear policy. The course of South Korea's nuclear programme could thus depend on how the government responds to the demands set forth by its people or depending on the next party that comes to power.

Pakistan too appears committed to developing its nuclear power programme. Speaking of Pakistan's vulnerability to climate change, Pakistani Prime Minister Imran Khan reiterated the importance of generating clean energy during the inauguration of the

Karachi Nuclear Power Plant Unit 2 (K-2).[9] In addition, countries like Bangladesh which is in the process of witnessing a major economic transition is placing their hope on nuclear power too. Bangladesh currently has its first nuclear power plant under construction, which is expected to get operational by 2024 and is planning to set up a second plant as well.[10]

State of Nuclear Power in Rest of Asia

South East Asia

The need for energy independence, now compounded by the worsening effects of the climate change crisis has led to growing interest in nuclear power in South East Asian countries. While there are no operational reactors in the sub-region, several countries have been considering the nuclear option. ASEAN Centre for Energy's pre-feasibility report for establishing nuclear power plants in the region in 2018 reiterated the collective regional interest in this regard.[11] Thailand for example has been considering to develop nuclear energy in their 2036 National Power Development Plan. Similarly, Indonesia has been mulling over the nuclear option for years. Several attempts to start the programme have stalled over time. More recently, discussions on developing nuclear power once again grew traction to make universal access to electricity a reality by 2025. In this regard, the 2015 White Paper on national energy development policy to 2050 included nuclear power generation in their energy mix.

The Philippines too has grappled with the idea of developing nuclear power for decades since it first constructed a nuclear power plant in 1984. However, attempts to promote nuclear power in the country were deterred by several factors such as corruption charges against the utility, the Three Miles Island and Chernobyl nuclear accidents, unsatisfactory safety reports etc over the years. Recently, the interest in nuclear power once again reenkindled in the country with President Duterte ordering a study in 2016 to assess the feasibility of reopening their plant. While discussions continue, strong public opposition has limited its progress. Malaysia, too considered developing a nuclear program, however unsatisfied with the nuclear waste disposal technique, former Prime Minister Dr Mahathir Mohamad decided not to pursue it as he believed that the country did not have the necessary knowledge in the field.[12] Vietnam which had planned to begin the construction of its first nuclear reactor by 2015, shelved the project due to the cost factor among other reasons.[13]

Thus, while the interest in nuclear power is strong in the region, several factors such as high costs, safety and waste disposal concerns have been hindering its growth. This might change in the future as new technologies such as small modular reactors is projected to overcome these conventional challenges.

West Asia

There is a rising interest in developing nuclear power in West Asia as countries in the region have been undergoing rapid development. The interest in the region however is not new and can be traced back to 1994 when the Arab League advocated the need to enhance understanding of nuclear technology. In 2006, the Gulf Cooperation Council (GCC) explored the possibilities of having a joint project in the region and called for setting up a regional nuclear power programme. In the following year, 6 countries led by Saudi Arabia agreed to work with the IAEA to undertake a feasibility study for the same.[14] The interest in developing a nuclear power programme among these countries stemmed from several factors. This includes the growing electricity demands which are expected to increase 30 per cent by 2028.[15] The rising electricity demands could further increase the dependence on fossil fuels in the region which is already high, with fossil fuels contributing to 97 per cent of the electricity generated in the region in 2017.[16] In GCC countries there also exists large demands for desalination which is met by oil and gas. In addition, nuclear power would enable countries in the region that rely heavily on oil revenues to safeguard their oil exports and achieve the security of their supplies. While renewable energy has also gained the attention of the leaders, its foray in the region has been very limited.[17] All of these factors cumulatively boosted the case for nuclear power in West Asia. The interest in nuclear power however took a hit after the Fukushima accident which led to countries like Bahrain, Oman and Kuwait to abandon their projects.[18]

The factors described above however led to the continued interest in nuclear power in other countries in the region, but at a cautious pace. Currently, nuclear power in West Asia has not entirely taken off and only Iran and the UAE have civil nuclear programmes. Bushehr, Iran's first nuclear power plant was launched in 2011 with Russian help and generates about

7.6 TWh of nuclear power, contributing to 2 per cent of the total electricity generated in the country(in 2018).[19] Currently, one other unit is under construction with another in the pipeline.[20] Iran's nuclear programme is however mired in controversy as the country has been speculated to develop nuclear weapons through the garb of its civil nuclear programme.

UAE developed its nuclear programme more recently with its first unit being connected to the grid in 2020. The Barakah nuclear power plant consists of four APR-1400 reactors, of which unit one successfully began operations, unit 2 connected to the grid in 2021, construction of unit 3 was completed[21] and the fourth unit is being constructed. At completion, the four reactors are projected to supply about 25 per cent of UAE's electricity demands reducing up to 21 million tons of CO_2 emissions.[22]

Several other countries are expected to follow suit as countries such as Turkey,Saudi Arabia, Jordan and Egypt are in the process of developing their civil nuclear programme. Turkey, which has attempted to construct a nuclear power plant over 5 times since 1960[23] is finally building the Akkuyu Nuclear Power Plant. Being built with the help of Russia, the VVER-1200 reactor is scheduled to come online in 2023.[24]

In the case of the Kingdom of Saudi Arabia, an ambitious plan of setting up 16 nuclear reactors by 2032 is currently underway. It is anticipated to generate 15 per cent of the electricity requirements in the country. Nuclear production offers several economic benefits to Saudi Arabia, such as meeting the country's energy demands while allowing the oil reserves to be diverted for exports at market prices. Currently, almost one-third of its oil production is utilised for domestic consumption at subsidised prices.[25] In addition, it allows the country to develop alternate sources of electricity generation as the oil reserves are estimated to run out in about 7 decades.[26] Thus,Saudi Arabia engaged in talks with the Trump administration to develop a nuclear power programme. However, as KSA refused to fulfil all of IAEA's requisites, the agreement came to a deadlock and Saudi turned to China for support instead. In 2017 Riyadh and Beijing agreed to cooperate on developing Saudi Arabia's nuclear power programme.

Egypt's plans to build a nuclear power plant which faltered after the Arab Spring[27] is finally taking shape as the country is in the process of constructing its first nuclear power plant. The El Dabaa plant which is also being developed with Russian help is designed to have a total capacity of 4800 Megawatts.

Jordan, which imports more than 98 per cent of its energy requirements and is susceptible to disruption of natural gas supply due to the political instability in the region,[28] is also envisaging a nuclear power programme. In 2015, Jordan was in talks with Russia to build a nuclear power plant with a capacity of 2000 megawatts. Estimated to cost about $10 billion,

Jordan later scrapped this project due to financial constraints. In 2018, it announced the replacement of the project with a small modular reactor instead.[29] Cost appears to be a concern for other West Asian countries such as Bahrain as well which had set plans to develop nuclear power plants by 2017, but were deferred due to high costs.[30]

Countries like Iraq have expressed their interest in building a nuclear power plant to address the looming power shortfall in the country and is currently discussing the scope of cooperation with Russian and South Korean officials.[31] Kuwait too which abandoned its nuclear power aspirations after the Fukushima accident is speculated to have been discussing the scope of developing a civil nuclear power programme with Russia.[32] Other West Asian countries such as Morocco, Tunisia, and Algeria are also considering nuclear options, whereas countries like Israel and Oman have considered it in the past but decided not to pursue it. Syria which was keen on building a VVER-440 reactor in the 1980s, gave up its programme after the Chernobyl nuclear accident. As oil and gas prices plummeted, it once again considered developing nuclear reactors and at the beginning of the century had also built what appeared to be a gas-cooled reactor. Accused of developing nuclear weapons, this facility was destroyed by Israel in 2007.

There however are concerns about Saudi Arabia using its civil nuclear programme to clandestinely develop nuclear weapons as the country has on several occasions indicated its interest in doing so. An example of this is Crown Prince Mohammed Bin Salman's statement where he said that "Saudi Arabia does not want to acquire any nuclear bomb, but without a doubt, if Iran developed a nuclear bomb we will follow suit as soon as possible."[33] Saudi Arabia's close cooperation with China in this regard has further raised concerns of proliferation in the international community.

Central Asia

With copious uranium resources and economies challenged by energy stress, nuclear power has emerged as one of the foremost energy solutions in the Central Asian region now. However, with the regions complicated and delicate history with nuclear power, considering that it has been the testing ground of the Soviet atomic weapons program, civil nuclear power development has not entirely taken off in Central Asia. Currently, only Uzbekistan is in the process of developing a civil nuclear programme. After signing an agreement with Russia in 2017, efforts to construct its first nuclear power plant is underway. The two VVER-1200 reactors are slated to be commissioned in 2028 and 2030,[34] with plans to build more units in the pipeline.[35] As the country depends on fossil fuel to generate over 85% of its electricity,[36] the Uzbek leadership hopes to bring down the carbon footprints of the country by having nuclear power generate 18% of the total electricity generated by the year 2030.[37]

Kazakhstan which has long debated the benefits and challenges of nuclear power, appears to be leaning towards the nuclear option amidst widespread public mistrust in the technology. The country is facing a major energy crisis with President Kassym-Jomart Tokayev, in this regard stating in November 2021 that "we are already feeling the first signs of power shortages in Kazakhstan" and that the country will have to take up on the nuclear option soon.[38] The decision to develop a civil nuclear programme in Kazakhstan is likely to face public backlash, as witnessed in 2019 when Russian President Vladimir Putin proposed to help with nuclear technology. However as the power crisis is worsening in the country, president Tokayev has announced his decision to go ahead with it saying, "Looking into the future, we will have to make an unpopular decision about building a nuclear power plant, but, as they say, the role of a leader is to make unpopular decisions."[39]

The nuclear option also appears to be gaining prominence in other Central Asian countries as the economies are looking for sustainable sources of energy to fuel their development amidst electricity blackouts and skyrocketing energy prices. While no concrete steps have been taken by these countries yet, there appears to be a gradual interest in the technology. Tajikistan for example launched a program to refurbish its Argus-FTI research reactor, which was abandoned after the Chernobyl disaster.[40] Likewise, Turkmenistan and China are exploring cooperation in the clean energy and nuclear power sector.[41]

Nuclear Exports: Will Asia Dominate the Market?

0The nuclear export market which was largely dominated by the US, France and Russia is now witnessing diversification with new players competing for market share. This includes countries such as China, South Korea and potentially India. Thus, along with nuclear power production, countries in the region are also vying to profit off the nuclear energy market. In this regard, the largest nuclear company in China has planned over 30 new reactors through its Belt and Road Initiative by the year 2030.[42] Having reached different stages of talks with countries such as Turkey, Pakistan, the UK, Kenya, Sudan, Argentina and Egypt among others, China is looking to establish itself as a major player in the nuclear exports market.

South Korea likewise, has been looking to expand its nuclear exports portfolio. It successfully won the bid for Barakah nuclear power plant in UAE and more recently in 2021, won a $3.88 million deal to export nuclear technology to Bangladesh.[43] It is also involved in a joint development project with Saudi Arabia to help it deploy a small modular reactor. With about 92 major nuclear power equipment producers in the country, Seoul is looking to promote these companies to incorporate them into the country's global nuclear component supply chain.[44] In addition, South Korea is actively participating in the reactor decommissioning industry as well. The blueprint revealed that the government plans to set up research centres to help in the dismantling and decommissioning of reactors globally.[45]

India too has been keen on exporting its nuclear expertise to other countries. However, since it is a non-signatory to the Nuclear Suppliers Group it cannot engage in direct nuclear trade and thus has found a way to circumvent around the technicalities. Thus partnering with Russia, the two countries have been jointly working in constructing the Rooppur nuclear power plant in Bangladesh. They are likely to continue this arrangement, which helps in reducing costs for Russia and provides opportunities for India to expand its market, in other friendly or neutral countries. Thus, the nuclear exports market is likely to see an overhaul, with major participation from Asian countries.

Factors Influencing the Nuclear Trajectory in Asia

The development of nuclear power has been directly linked to several factors which have cumulatively set the nuclear landscape in the region today. These factors have all interacted with and influenced each other shaping the nuclear policies of countries.

Lack of Indigenous Resources for Electricity Generation

One of the primary factors in this regard is the lack of indigenous energy resources. As the popular French response to the question of why they developed nuclear power goes "no oil, no gas, no coal, no choice,"[46] nuclear energy has emerged as a popular option among countries that lack domestic energy resources. Countries like France and Japan which do not have sufficient domestic energy reserves face challenges of import dependency which is not only expensive but also makes them vulnerable to external, geostrategic variables. Japan for example depends on imported energy resources, which in 2018 reached an unprecedented import ratio of 99.7 per cent for oil, over 97 per cent for LNG and 99.3% for coal.[47] Likewise, countries like South Korea developed nuclear power in response to the oil crisis of the 1970s. Nuclear power thus in such cases provides countries the opportunity to attain energy independence.

Economics

Economic aspects such as the cost of generating nuclear power, subsidies offered by the government etc are vital factors that can determine the decision to promote or rescind a nuclear project. For example in the case of Vietnam, feasibility studies indicated that nuclear power generation would be an expensive pursuit. However, in countries like South Korea, nuclear power production is extremely cost-effective. These economic factors are also close to factors such as political will. In countries like India where there are cheaper forms of electricity producing technologies, the cost factor does not dissuade the course of nuclear development, as it receives strong political support.

Political factors

In fact, political support is one of the major drivers for nuclear power development. In most Asian countries nuclear power developed under strong leadership, with ardent support for the nuclear pursuit. This could be further linked to geopolitical aspirations such as in the case of China, where civil nuclear exports is expanding under the Belt and Road Initiative. This does not only promote China's nuclear industry but also exerts significant influence and control over other countries it engages with.

Public Perception

However, most often than not, political will needs to be backed by political credibility. In the case of the Philippines, it continues to face major public opposition to the prospect of restarting its nuclear power project. The public mistrust in government-controlled nuclear establishments is unsurprising given the history of corruption in the country. Geoffrey Gunn, writer and professor in this regard states "... For over 30 years, until meeting obligations in April 2007, Filipino taxpayers paid 155,000 dollars a day in interest on the plant that never produced a kilowatt of power..."[48]

This is further associated to electoral politics in democratic setups. For example, South Korean citizens grew risk aversive after the huge KEPCO corruption expose. Coupled with concerns of nuclear safety the collective mood of the country was anti-nuclear for a brief period. This led to nuclear energy becoming a major electoral issue in Seoul. Stating anti-nuclear policies as one of his key pledges, Moon Jae-In won the 2017 elections, becoming the President of South Korea. Soon after he took office, President Moon announced his decision to scale down nuclear power generation and eventually phase-out nuclear power in the country. However, as the country began to face major electricity shortages which impacted industries and households alike, there has been increasing pressure on him to revoke this policy.[49] Having been the main source of power in the country for nearly half a century, nuclear power played an important role in boosting South Korea's major economic transition, popularly known as "Miracle on the River Han". As the discussions continue, nuclear energy is contended to be a major issue in the next presidential elections as well.

Elections in this regard is an important factor which determines the efficacy of a country's energy policies, as nuclear policies could keep changing based on the party in power. This tends to be a major disadvantage while looking at the long-standing policies of a country. As a major infrastructure development facet, energy policies need to be set for a longterm, as it takes time to formulate, develop and implement policies. Fluctuations in energy policies thus is likely to result in problems of energy crises in the future. However, the election factor is a complicated one with several underlying political dynamics as nuclear issues may not always be the most pressing concern in a country. Political shifts could also be influenced with other important factors such as economic considerations, environmental policies etc. For example in the next set of elections in the region, handling the COVID-19 pandemic could be an important factor. Thus, the nuclear policies of a country could change depending on the party in power once again.

Environmental concerns

Environmental factors too play a vital role in this regard. For example in cases of countries that are witnessing unabated economic growth like India and China, it usually leads to high Co_2 emissions. Considering that nuclear energy has virtually no carbon footprint, the trade-off between development and environmental sustainability can be minimised. In other cases where a country has to meet the demands of a rapidly expanding population, such as in Bangladesh, nuclear power has emerged as a reliable tool in its energy basket, owing to its incessant nature and high capacity factor.

In this regard, it appears that countries in Asia may have considered one or several of these factors, which cumulatively helped in shaping its nuclear policies.

Conclusion

While the future of nuclear power in Asia appears to be on a positive trajectory now, it cannot be guaranteed to stay this way. As discussed earlier, several factors determine the course of nuclear power in all countries, making their future uncertain. As history has witnessed, several waves of nuclear optimism has dampened each time a nuclear accident took place. The nuclear industry thus is in a state of perpetual tenuousness, where a single accident could unravel the developments made over the years. Likewise, anti-nuclear moods in countries could also change considering the ever-changing variables influencing nuclear policies. This could be in the form of breakthroughs in alternate nuclear technologies, energy vulnerabilities cause by external manipulations, change in power consumption patterns, etc. Thus, while the short-term projections appear to be positive, given the range of factors, the future of nuclear power in Asia cannot be accurately predicted.

However, to develop nuclear power certain key issues and challenges need to be addressed effectively. First, there lies the problem of public mistrust of nuclear power. A concerted approach should thus be taken to translate a highly technical subject like nuclear physics, in simple, layman terms in order to demystify the science behind it. Thus communication from technocrats and policymakers to the stakeholders and citizens can go a long way in quelling the fears surrounding nuclear technology. Effective communication however needs to be back with creditability and accountability.

To boost creditability, there is also the need to boost international cooperation as these partnerships could be helpful in minimising risks of accidents and preventing chances of proliferation. Considering the impact a nuclear accident can have, there is no place for laxity in the nuclear industry. Furthermore, it seems unlikely that the nuclear industry would be able to brave another nuclear disaster. The international cooperation network in this regard needs to constantly determine ways to increase the safety aspects of the reactors, to ensure the expansion of the nuclear industry while minimising the scope for any accidents to occur. Thus, a strong, legal, technical and regulatory partnership is vital in ensuring nuclear safety and security. Focus on R&D on safety and proliferation-resistant reactors in this regard is the need of the hour. In addition, best practices in construction to cut down gestation period and cost overruns needs to be identified and practiced, so as to minimise any shortcomings in nuclear technology and promote nuclear power production.

Several factors warrant the need to maintain safe, nuclear power production. The main factor in this regard is the dangerous levels of dependence on fossil fuels. Currently contributing over 80 per cent of the global energy requirements, fossil fuels pose existential threat to the planet. Transitioning to cleaner sources of power is thus imperative. Nuclear power is already contributing massively on this front having avoided Co_2 emissions worth 74 gigatons in the last 5 decades.[50] Thus, if the world has to achieve the energy revolution that it needs, realistic energy policies need to be set with help from every clean source that it can muster. While renewable sources of energy could play an important role in this transition, it however faces several limitations of their own as discussed in the previous chapters. Thus, until carbon capture and storage become technologically and economically feasible, a mixed energy basket with nuclear power playing a sizeable role is essential.

Notes

1. Nicole Jawerth, "Five Years After Fukushima: Making Nuclear Power Safer", *IAEA.org*, March 10, 2016, at https://www.iaea.org/newscenter/news/five-years-after-fukushima-making-nuclear-power-safer, accessed on October 11, 2021.
2. "Asia's Nuclear Energy Growth", *World Nuclear.org*, at https://world-nuclear.org/information-library/country-profiles/others/asias-nuclear-energy-growth.aspx, accessed on October 11, 2021.
3. Rachel Zhang, "China sets up nuclear safety committee to boost 2060 carbon neutral efforts", *South China Morning Post*, March 25, 2021, at https://www.scmp.com/news/china/politics/article/3126984/china-sets-nuclear-safety-committee-boost-2060-carbon-neutral, accessed on October 11, 2021.
4. Kotaro Fukuoka, " China poised to overtake US in nuclear power by 2030", *Nikkei Asia*, August 31, 2020, at https://asia.nikkei.com/Business/Energy/China-poised-to-overtake-US-in-nuclear-power-by-2030, accessed on October 11, 2021.

5. "Japan's potential new premier supports nuclear power," *Argudmedia.com,* 29 September 2021, at https://www.argusmedia.com/en/news/2258608-japans-potential-new-premier-supports-nuclear-power, accessed on October 7, 2021.
6. Vishwa Mohan, "India to increase nuclear energy capacity three times in next 10 years to reduce its carbon footprints", *Times of India,* September 15, 2021, at https://timesofindia.indiatimes.com/india/india-to-increase-nuclear-energy-capacity-three-times-in-next-10-years-to-reduce-its-carbo footprints/articleshow/86222428.cms?utm_source=contentofinterest&utm_medium=text&utm_campaign=cppst, accessed on October 10, 2021.
7. "Nuclear Power in India", *World-nuclear.org,* at https://world-nuclear.org/information-library/country-profiles/countries-g-n/india.aspx, accessed on October 10, 2021.
8. Melissa Goh, "China and India will lead the world's nuclear power growth, experts say", *CNBC.com,* November 7, 2018, at https://www.cnbc.com/2018/11/08/china-india-will-lead-global-nuclear-power-production-growth-experts.html accessed on October 10, 2021.
9. "Pakistan's newest nuclear plant boosts grid by 1,100MW", *Thenews.com,* May 22, 2021, at https://www.thenews.com.pk/print/838193-pakistan-s-newest-nuclear-plant-boosts-grid-by-1-100mw, accessed on October 9, 2021.
10. "Bangladesh to set up its second nuclear power plant: PM Sheikh Hasina", *newsonair.com,* October 10, 2021, at https://newsonair.com/2021/10/10/bangladesh-to-set-up-its-second-nuclear-power-plant-pm-sheikh-hasina/?__cf_chl_managed_tk__=pmd_HSG0iyGr1CmTl7SYvevRCcxHDVzR.R6loA8VEi5yKf4-1634033442-0-gqNtZGzNAzujcnBszRG9, accessed on October 11, 2021.
11. Pre-Feasibility Study on the Establishment of Nuclear Power Plant in ASEAN", *ASEANenergy.org,* May 2, 2018, at https://aseanenergy.org/pre-feasibility-study-on-the-establishment-of-nuclear-power-plant-in-asean/, accessed on October 10, 2021.
12 Nor Ain Mohamed Radhi, "Malaysia won't use nuclear power, says PM", *New Strait Times,* February 10, 2020, at https://www.nst.com.my/news/government-public-policy/2020/02/564295/malaysia-wont-use-nuclear-power-says-pm, accessed on October 6, 2021.
13. Victor Nian, "Are small modular reactors making their way to Southeast Asia?", *Sustainability Times,* March 20, 2020, at https://www.sustainability-times.com/expert-opinions/are-small-modular-reactors-making-their-way-to-southeast-asia/, accessed on October 8, 2021.
14. "Emerging Nuclear Energy Countries", *world-nuclear.org,*at https://world-nuclear.org/information-library/country-profiles/others/emerging-nuclear-energy-countries.aspx, accessed on November 25, 2021.
15. "Middle East nuclear power to quadruple in ten years", *World Nuclear News,* 6 March 2018, at https://world-nuclear-news.org/Articles/Middle-East-nuclear-power-to-quadruple-in-ten-year, accessed on November 2, 2021.
16. Ibid.

17 Paul Cochrane, "Renewable energy: What does it mean for oil-dominated Middle East?", *Middleeasteye.net,* October 30, 2020, at https://www.middleeasteye.net/news/renewable-energy-oil-middle-east, accessed on November 22, 2021.

18. Anton Khlopkov, Prospects for Nuclear Power in the Middle East After Fukushima And the Arab Spring", *UNIDIR.org*, at https://www.unidir.org/files/publications/pdfs/prospects-for-nuclear-power-in-the-middle-east-after-fukushima-and-the-arabic-spring-402.pdf, accessed on November 20, 2021.

19. Ibid.

20. "Nuclear Power in Iran", *World Nuclear.org*, at https://world-nuclear.org/information-library/country-profiles/countries-g-n/iran.aspx, accessed on November 20, 2021.

21. "Third unit completed at Barakah", *World Nuclear News*, 4 November 2021, at https://world-nuclear-news.org/Articles/Third-unit-completed-at-Barakah, accessed on November 21, 2021.

22. "Barakah Nuclear Energy Plant", *enec.gov.ae*, at https://www.enec.gov.ae/barakah-plant/, accessed on November 20, 2021.

23. Cem İskender Aydın, "Nuclear energy debate in Turkey: Stakeholders, policy alternatives, and governance issues", *Energy Policy*, v. 136, 2020.

24. "Akkuyu 1 construction and components", *World Nuclear News*, December 13, 2021, at https://www.world-nuclear-news.org/Articles/Akkuyu-1-construction-and-components, accessed on December 28, 2021.

25. Mordechai Chaziza, "Saudi Arabia's Nuclear Program and China", mei.edu, August 18, 2020, at https://www.mei.edu/publications/saudi-arabias-nuclear-program-and-china, accessed on November 27, 2021.

26. Ellen R. Wald, "The Middle East Needs Nuclear Power. Here's What America Should Do About It", *Forbes,* July 16, 2019, at https://www.forbes.com/sites/ellenrwald/2019/07/16/the-middle-east-needs-nuclear-power-heres-what-america-should-do-about-it/?sh=60fd24ad1286, accessed on November 27, 2021.

27. Anton Khlopkov, "Prospects for Nuclear Power in the Middle East After Fukushima And the Arab Spring", *UNIDIR.org,* at https://www.unidir.org/files/publications/pdfs/prospects-for-nuclear-power-in-the-middle-east-after-fukushima-and-the-arabic-spring-402.pdf, accessed on November 20, 2021.

28. Ibid.

29. Mohammad Ghazal, "Jordan to replace planned nuclear plant with smaller, cheaper facility", *Jordan Times,* May 26,2018, at https://www.jordantimes.com/news/local/jordan-replace-planned-nuclear-plant-smaller-cheaper-facility, accessed on November 20, 2021.

30. "Bahrain reviews nuclear energy plans as project receives bid", zawya.com, September 17, 2019, at https://www.zawya.com/mena/en/markets/story/Bahrain_reviews_nuclear_energy_plans_as_project_receives_bid-ZAWYA20190917130503/, accessed on November 21, 2021.

31. Khalid Al-Ansary and Anthony Di Paola, "Iraq plans nuclear power plants to tackle electricity shortage", Al-Jazeera, June 8, 2021, at https://www.aljazeera.com/

economy/2021/6/8/iraq-plans-nuclear-power-plants-to-tackle-electricity-shortage, accessed on November 24, 2021.

32. Baset Asaba, "Rosatom in talks to build nuclear plant in Kuwait", Utilities, January 26, 2018, at https://www.utilities-me.com/news/article-5236-rosatom-in-talks-to-build-nuclear-plant-in-kuwait. Accessed on December 1, 2021.
33. Dominic Dudley, "Nuclear Energy Is Becoming A Political Football In The Middle East, But It's Nothing To Do With Iran", *Forbes*, March 21, 2019, at https://www.forbes.com/sites/dominicdudley/2019/03/21/nuclear-energy-political-football-middle-east/?sh=5b860b611862, accessed on November 25, 2021.
34. "IAEA assesses Uzbekistan's nuclear power infrastructure development", *World Nuclear News*, 4 June 2021, at https://world-nuclear-news.org/Articles/IAEA-assesses-Uzbekistan-s-nuclear-power-infrastru, accessed on November 19, 2021.
35. "Uzbekistan adds second plant to nuclear power goal", *World Nuclear News*, 12 July 2019, at https://world-nuclear-news.org/Articles/Uzbek-expands-nuclear-plans, accessed on November 18, 2021.
36. "The most experienced newcomer to nuclear power", *World Nuclear News* , October 3, 2019, at https://world-nuclear-news.org/Articles/The-most-experienced-newcomer-to-nuclear-power, accessed on November 19, 2021.
37. Ibid.
38. Almaz Kumenov, "Kazakhstan looks to nuclear amid crypto-driven energy shortage" Eurasianet.org, November 22, 2021, at https://eurasianet.org/kazakhstan-looks-to-nuclear-amid-crypto-driven-energy-shortage, accessed on December 1, 2021.
39. Ibid.
40. "Russia and Tajikistan to Cooperate in Nuclear", *Rosatom Newsletter*, March 2017, at https://rosatomnewsletter.com/2017/03/07/russia-and-tajikistan-to-cooperate-in-nuclear/, accessed on December 2, 2021.
41. "China, Turkmenistan eye further ties in clean energy like natural gas", *CGTN*, July 13 2021, at https://news.cgtn.com/news/2021-07-13/China-Turkmenistan-eye-further-ties-in-clean-energy-like-natural-gas-11R8wmHG6Y0/index.html, accessed on December 2, 2021.
42. "China could build 30 'Belt and Road' nuclear reactors by 2030: official", Reuters, June 20, 2019, at https://www.reuters.com/article/us-china-nuclearpower/china-could-build-30-belt-and-road-nuclear-reactors-by-2030-official-idUSKCN1TL0HZ, accessed on October 7, 2021.
43. "South Korea to export nuclear reactor technology to Bangladesh", *aa.com*, July 15, 2021, at https://www.aa.com.tr/en/asia-pacific/south-korea-to-export-nuclear-reactor-technology-to-bangladesh/2304967, accessed on December 28, 2021.
44. "South Korea Revamps its Nuclear Energy Export Strategy", *neutronbytes*, September 29, 2019, at https://neutronbytes.com/2019/09/29/south-korea-revamps-its-nuclear-energy-export-strategy/, accessed on December 26, 2021.
45. "South Korea looks to decommissioning", *neimagazine.com*, April 24, 2019, at https://www.neimagazine.com/news/newssouth-korea-looks-to-decommissioning-7168068, accessed on December 29, 2021.

46. Jon Palfreman, "Why the French Like Nuclear Energy", *PBC.org*, at https://www.pbs.org/wgbh/pages/frontline/shows/reaction/readings/french.html, accessed on October 10, 2021.
47. "2019—Understanding the current energy situation in Japan (Part 1)", *METI*, August 13, 2019, at https://www.enecho.meti.go.jp/en/category/special/article/energyissue2019_01.html, accessed on October 10, 2021.
48. Geoffrey Gunn, "Southeast Asia's Looming Nuclear Power Industry", *The Asia Pacific Journal*, February 1, 2008. v. 6. i.2.
49. Jitae Chang, "South Korea Relies on Nuclear Power for 30% of its Energy", *climatescorecard.org*. September 5, 2021, at https://www.climatescorecard.org/2021/09/south-korea-has-a-strong-case-for-the-use-of-nuclear-energy/, accessed on October 9, 2021.
50. Henri Paillere, Jeffrey Donovan, "Nuclear Power 10 Years After Fukushima: The Long Road Back", *IAEA.org*, March 11, 2021, at https://www.iaea.org/newscenter/news/nuclear-power-10-years-after-fukushima-the-long-road-back, accessed on October 9, 2021.

Index